HOW TO POSITION YOURSELF AS THE OBVIOUS EXPERT

In 90 Days Or Less Without Spending A Fortune On Advertising!

Turbocharge Your Consulting Or Coaching Business NOW!

by Elsom Eldridge Jr.
& Mark L. Eldridge

with foreword by Roger C. Parker
and special contributions by
Ed Brown, David Garfinkle, Richard F. Gerson, Steven P. Haas,
Nick Nichols, Susan RoAne, Millie Szerman, Dottie Walters, Patti Wood and
over 150 other Obvious Expert Advisors

MasterMind Publishing, LLC
Heath, Massachusetts
www.mastermindpublishing.com

First in a series – The Obvious Expert® Advisors Publication. The Obvious Expert® is a registered trademark of Mark L. Eldridge
http://www.obvious-expert.com (The Obvious Expert Web Site)
http://www.mastermindpublishing.com (MasterMind Publishing Web Site)

A MasterMind Publishing Book
To order the book, contact your local bookstore or call 321-356-4374
ISBN 0-9720941-6-4 trade paperback

Printed in United States of America

First paperback printing 2004
10 9 8 7 6 5 4 3 2 1

Library of Congress Control Number: 2003100928

Eldridge, Elsom,
     How To Position Yourself As The Obvious Expert / by Elsom Eldridge, Jr., Mark L. Eldridge
              p. cm.
          ISBN 0-9720941-6-4 (pbk.)
          (The Obvious Expert Advisors Series)
          1, Consulting - United States. 2. Marketing I. Eldridge, Mark L. II. Title

ATTENTION SCHOOLS AND CORPORATIONS: Quantity discounts are available on bulk purchases of this book for educational, business, or sales promotional use. Special books or book excerpts can also be created to fit specific needs. Please write to Special Sales Department at 93 Colrain Stage Road, Heath, Massachusetts, 03146 U.S.A. or send email to: info@mastermindpublishing.com

Cover design and inside text design/layout by Michele Bryant • micheleb@aol.com

HOW TO POSITION YOURSELF AS THE OBVIOUS EXPERT

In 90 Days Or Less Without Spending A Fortune On Advertising!

Turbocharge Your Consulting Or Coaching Business NOW!

by Elsom Eldridge Jr. & Mark L. Eldridge

Acknowledgements: Ed Brown, Richard F. Gerson, David Garfinkel, Steven P. Haas, Nick Nichols, Roger C. Parker, Susan RoAne, Millie Szerman, Dottie Walters, Patti Wood, the very special contributions from all of The Obvious Expert Advisors, Executive Editor Linda J. Parker, Editor Diane Sears, Designer Michele Bryant, Dr. Dwight Damon and Peter Schneider, who took time to read this book and make comments, Jean Sutton who provided endless hours of administrative support, Paige Clark, for her design inspiration, and Alice Lanoie for over twenty years of patience, dedication, service and friendship.

In Memory Of The Late

Howard Shenson

The Obvious Expert

1945 – 1991

TABLE OF CONTENTS

FOREWORD

BY
✒ Roger C. Parker ✒

The best way to appreciate the importance and relevance of *How To Position Yourself As The Obvious Expert* is to start each day by reading the headlines in the morning paper.

Each issue contains a fresh harvest of carnage from the world of corporate employment. News from the white collar world keeps getting worse and worse as hard-working employees are sacrificed to greed at the top.

"Work harder for less!" is the order of the day. Corporations no longer reward hard work and loyalty. Loyalty goes in only one direction.

Today, in contrast to only one generation past, you have to go it alone. You simply can't depend on your employer to reward you adequately or to give you even a measure of security. Reward and security now go to those who go out on their own, establish their own brand, and become a recognized expert in their field, which is precisely what Elsom and Mark Eldridge show in this great book.

I was proud to be a "fly on the wall" from the earliest days of this book. When it was first conceived, I applauded it because it was so vitally necessary. Today, it's even more necessary.

How To Position Yourself As The Obvious Expert shows you an alternative to the stress and insecurity of corporate employment. *How To Position Yourself As The Obvious Expert* provides a road map to success, describing detailed tips and techniques you can use to ensure yourself a more satisfying and secure future on your own as a consultant than you can enjoy as an employee of even America's most highly-rated corporations.

The book you're holding in your hand is a cook book of recipes that have contributed to the success of hundreds of others like you. *How To Position Yourself As The Obvious Expert* furnishes you with lessons from the successes of those who have proven their credibility. Read the book, put a check mark by the ideas you plan to try first, and then apply them. Success can be yours. Or, you can accept pay cuts and early retirement packages.

Case Studies I've Observed

Many of my friends have enjoyed great success following the techniques described in this book. Others have tried going it the "employment" way and are either suffocating in their jobs or, following release from servitude, selling cars "till they get on their feet."

- J.W. was the program director of Seattle's classical music station. He was responsible for okaying every piece of music played, plus was on the air daily for four hours himself. He lost his job on a Friday over an insignificant personality issue. Following many of the techniques in this book, he went on to lead the life he always wanted, producing jazz festivals and CD's and hosting two six hour jazz programs a week which are broadcast to hundreds of thousands of listeners in 47 different markets.

- R.L. was director of corporate communications for a leading software publication. The stress was taking an awful toll on his family and his health. He got out, wrote a book and established an international reputation for his firm. His reward? A million dollar home on the shores of Lake Sammamish plus an opportunity to speak and consult on every continent.

- G.M. was the marketing manager of a successful retail store, but didn't have the right last name (i.e. he wasn't the owner's son.) He subsequently left and looked for a marketing niche he could command. He now enjoys great success and total control over his time as a consultant helping high-tech firms market to grammar schools and high schools.

- S.B. was a top-rated USAir pilot. He loved flying. He never injured a passenger or a plane in over twenty years. Luckily, he had a law degree and was able to negotiate early retirement. He's now a professional negotiator, in demand with area lawyers, and sleeps in his own bed every night. . . and, in his second year, is earning the same as he used to.

When You Finally Get It

I feel sad when I think about those who waste valuable years of their lives in unfulfilling jobs, when they could be enjoying great success; Mindy was a perfect example.

Mindy is an intelligent, personable woman. For too many years she was an administrative assistant at one of America's top universities. Mindy's passion was to work in museum marketing. She had the demeanor, training and passion for museum work to be a natural! But, although she faithfully sent out résumés, she spent years with nothing to show for it. No job offers, no acknowledgements. It was as if she was dropping the résumés down a sewer grating. But then she realized, it didn't have to be this way!

After years of coaxing and urging Mindy to publish a monthly one-page "Museum Marketing" newsletter, she finally tried it. All she had to do was print ten copies on her desktop printer. Her marketing plan required just three steps:

1 Position herself as an expert, and send her "Museum Marketing" newletter to the ten museums she wanted to work for!

2 She let them know she was available as a consultant. She took some time to visit and consult with them, working nights and weekends as necessary to fulfill her commitments.

3 She worked to become so valuable to them that they make her an offer she couldn't refuse!

The three-step plan worked for Mindy and a plan like this canl work for you, too. That's what this book is all about! It's all about positioning yourself as an expert in your field and getting clients (and, if desired, employers) to come to you. In this job market, you simply can't expect to get anywhere approaching employers with nothing more than résumés in hand. That's not how it works. And if it works, it's only on a "bare survival" basis.

The key to success, outlined in this book, is to get clients and employers to come to you! Become desirable. Become respected. Become visible. Become a demand item instead of a commodity!

One Last Case Study

Twenty-eight years ago, that's what I did. I was fired from my last job just when my employer was enjoying his period of highest sales and profitability. I was 3,000 miles away from home and the father of a six-month-old son. As described later, I immediately vowed to become a respected authority. I approached the leading trade magazine in my field and offered to write a four-page article each month in exchange for a quarter page ad.

Six months after my discharge, I was making more money and doing what I do best—enjoying my days off and working when I wanted to—typically until three and four in the morning.

If I did it, you can do it too. Say goodbye to the disappearing stock options, deferred raises, sacrificed bonuses and the constant insecurity of: "Who's going to be next to go?"

Let's face it—you'll have an easier job of it than I did. Because, when I did it, I didn't have an Elsom Eldridge or a Mark Eldridge to show me the way. I had to figure it out by myself, and pay the price of learning from my mistakes.

But you don't have to. With *How To Position Yourself As The Obvious Expert* in hand, you're spared the trial and error process that I, and countless others, have had to go through.

PREFACE

BY

✒ Mark L. Eldridge ✒

My father, Elsom Eldridge Jr., has been a consultant and business coach for more than two decades. While his client flow is now consistent and generous, this has not always been the case. Elsom's entry into the world of successful consulting required a few strategic adjustments and re-adjustments.

Elsom is talented, passionate about his business and well educated, but when he first started, he floundered financially and struggled to win clients. He was an expert, but in the beginning, his potential clients just didn't find it obvious.

Initially, to market his business, he had followed the typical approach of creating and mailing a fancy brochure to his potential clients. The slick and glossy marketing piece touted the benefits of hiring him as an educational consultant.

But the brochure wasn't working. Consequently, educational consultant Eldridge wasn't working much either—at least not on consulting projects. In his first quarter, he could not cover his marketing cost of $8,500, which included the beautiful brochure. He could not cover it because his total client revenues for that period were $2,130!

To make up the deficit, he kept his day job teaching at Cal State Fresno (Fresno State University). He also moonlighted as a church organist, played music for weddings and put on a tall black top hat and performed magic shows for children's birthday parties. Meanwhile, it was his struggling consulting business that was in dire need of some magic—like perhaps finding a way to turn one of those white rabbits into a check made payable to "Cash".

Great man, great service, great education. So why he was stuck as an overworked, financially stressed-out consultant/teacher/organist/magician? Why didn't he have more clients? Fortunately, Elsom has far too much intuitive business savvy to struggle for long.

Many people miss the best approach when they are stuck for the right solution, but not Elsom. He did not continue down the same path, sending out more and more brochures, hoping for a different result. Instead, he went in search for a guru on consulting—a master guru. He found his wizard in the late Howard Shenson, professor at the University of Southern California. Shenson, known and respected as the Dean of American Consultants, became Elsom's Obvious Expert.

Howard's insights jump started Elsom's consulting practice, which has remained revved and rolling ever since. Together the two of them partnered many times, promoting consulting seminars nationwide. Elsom not only became one of the top seminar promoters in the country, but one of the top consultants and coaches to consultants in America.

Let's face it, we have all wondered the same things about consulting. We have all faced similar problems and asked the same questions, like why can some people turn away clients, while others beat their heads against the wall trying desperately to attract them? Or why do so many people strive to become a successful consultant and so few succeed? And how can some consultants pull paying clients out of their magic top hats while others only get rabbits? The answers have nothing to do with magic, except that once you learn them, you will probably find them magically simple to execute.

The secrets that Howard taught Elsom, plus Elsom's distinctive expertise and some insights of my own, are clearly explained on the pages of *How To Position Yourself As The Obvious Expert.* Along with this wisdom, every page includes a real world experience from one of over one hundred of today's top professional consultants—each one an Obvious Expert in his or her field.

Beginning in Chapter 1, you will learn eleven different low cost, no cost strategies to effectively gain exposure and to enhance your professional reputation. Over 100,000 consultants in seminars Elsom and I have taught have proven thousands of times over that these strategies work!

This book tells you precisely how to add critical marketing know-how to your personal niche expertise. You can become recognized as The Obvious Expert in your field, with an abundance of clients calling you, eager to pay your fee, because they have no other choice. They have no other choice simply because you have made it evident to them, that to solve their problems, you are the obvious solution.

Charlie "Tremendous" Jones, accomplished speaker and writer, once said, "You will be the same person in five years that you are today except for the people you meet and the books you read." He could not be more correct—it is people and books that change us. For consultants, it is vitally important to associate with the right people—expert consultants.

When I was first running my seminar promotion company and spending $25,000 a week in print advertising, I did not go to other professionals in the business to learn from them. This turned out to be a major error in judgment.

The seminar industry's market was changing. Newspaper advertising stopped being the most effective way to reach prospects. Direct mail became the answer, but I missed it. I was not learning from the experts in my industry and I simply was not aware of the new trends. Participating in professional associations and networking to meet new people and develop opportunities opens many doors. Just as importantly, it can protect you from your own misjudgment.

For many years now, Elsom and I have been working to improve the image of the consulting profession. Consulting is not regulated by a government agency, a watch group or any other established industry standards. That is one of the reasons why Elsom and I, with the help of Howard Shenson, founded an Association for Professional Consultants. If the overall industry was not regulated, at least we could define an identifiable group within the industry that was.

We have put in place a Code of Professional Ethics for consultants who desire to improve our industry and work at the highest standards of professionalism. We have created an organization where consultants in their community, throughout the nation, and around the world can learn from and share with other consulting experts.

Become an Obvious Expert. Meet life changing people. Read life changing books. Make *How To Position Yourself As The Obvious Expert* a priority read. Read it and apply what you learn. Neither you nor your consulting business will be the same in five years, or even in five months, if you do.

You are already a unique person, shaped by the unique collection of experiences of your life. You have an expertise that no one else has. Your expertise creates for you the potential to establish and maintain a profitable niche in today's business market. Your niche may be similar to someone else's, but it remains unique—it is distinctively the 'intellectual property' of your life.

Certainly in my professional career, I have turned to Obvious Experts many times. However, it was as a father, that I experienced my most profound need for an Obvious Expert.

My little son was only six months old when a hemangioma—what you may think of as a raised birthmark—began growing on his upper lip. The problem we initially thought was a cosmetic concern quickly became a medical crisis as the growth became so large my son had difficulty eating. Recommended surgery only put him in more pain and misery, and his mother and I became frantic to find an expert with an answer. One doctor even suggested surgically removing one half of our son's face!

I began a quest to learn as much as possible about hemangiomas. During my search, one doctor's name came up over and over again. One particular medical research book, which I recall paying $159 to buy, mentioned his name so many times, that I became convinced he was The Obvious Expert on hemangiomas.

We soon learned that parents around the world brought their children to be treated by this doctor. Who to turn to was evident. We had only one choice if we wanted to put our son in the hands of The Obvious Expert. Moreover, because we had found The Obvious Expert on hemangiomas, our son is a healthy, happy and handsome child today.

Adversity is an incredible teacher, isn't it? Until the experience with my son, I never realized that even though we are the most knowledgeable society in history, we individually really know very little. Time and again each of us needs answers, information and solutions from Obvious Experts.

My father and I are deeply grateful to all of The Obvious Experts who have shaped and contributed to our knowledge and our careers. We are especially grateful to those who shared their wisdom in this book. As Charlie "Tremendous" Jones reminds us: people and books change our lives. Let this book and the people behind it, change yours.

Mark L. Eldridge

INTRODUCTION

BY

🖋 Elsom Eldridge, Jr. 🖋

Y^ou are not reading the original introduction I planned for this book—instead you are reading an introduction rewritten by a most unplanned event.

2002, for me, was both catastrophic and extraordinary. The experiences of that year taught me more about being The Obvious Expert than I had ever imagined knowing—in some ways, more than I previously had learned from a lifetime of study. Because of these experiences, my perceptions, my goals and my life changed forever. And if you think about it, this is a pretty radical statement from a man of my age, who typically has faced life's headaches feeling both undaunted and in control. Ironically, it was a headache—literally—that started it all.

Think about it. Do you recall the last time your head hurt? Perhaps it was one of those headaches that develop from the events of your day or maybe it was the kind that creeps up on you because you didn't get your morning coffee or you decided to work through lunch. Either way we usually ignore such headaches, gulp down a couple of painkillers and keep going; we never expect the headache to become life altering.

I woke up with my headache—a complaint unusual for me but no cause for undue concern. As my morning unfolded, the aching behind my eyes escalated; it changed from nagging pain to full-blown throbbing. By midday, I was panicking. My vision was bizarrely distorted and the pain in my skull unrelenting. Fortunately, a family member was nearby to get me medical help. My condition was headed downhill fast.

Admitted to a local hospital through the Emergency Room, I spent the next hours undergoing a barrage of medical tests. Finally the doctor came to my bedside to tell me his findings. A minor stroke, he said and then the young neurologist calmly added that life, as I had known it, was changed forever.

"Your vision is permanently damaged," he explained "and probably your memory has taken a hit as well. Forget a career in consulting. Your only option is to make some serious lifestyle changes and hope for a miracle."

This certainly did not sound minor to me. Like most people, I have faced my share of problems in life. When confronted with obstacles, we all know the choices. One can climb over them, journey around them or occasionally, just blast straight through the middle of them. But this was different. I was being told that I faced a problem that had no solution. To say this felt like the darkest moment of my life doesn't even scratch the surface of the hopelessness I felt.

I had built a career in consulting. I was the consultant's consultant—a recognized expert in my field, author of numerous books, co-founder of the International Guild of Professional Consultants (IGPC) and sought after by others as an expert in the industry. And, as all good consultants know, memory is a consultant's number one product.

Clients pay consultants for expertise that comes from lived experience and learned experience in a chosen field. If a consultant can't draw on his mental database because he can't remember—well, he can't exactly call himself a consultant!

It was several days later, back at my home as I sat curled up on my couch, wrapped in a blanket of self-pity, that a second life altering event occurred. Rex Trailer, one of my long-time colleagues, interrupted my misery to confirm a meeting we had scheduled before my illness. Quickly I filled him in on my situation—I guess I was searching for sympathy, understanding or maybe just an ear. But Rex did not give me sympathy. Instead, he gave me something I needed much, much more. He gave me hope.

Rex's wife, Cindy, had experienced a stroke that threatened to be debilitating. Cindy's stroke however, turned out to be only an obstacle in her path—an obstacle she found a way to go over, around and in some ways, straight through.

Because her stroke had been so much more severe than my own, and I saw how dramatically Cindy had recovered, I knew there were options out there to help me. All I needed was expert help. All I needed was to find an expert with solutions.

I found my Obvious Expert in Dr. Robert Sorge, of Asbury Park, New Jersey. Dr. Sorge took the hope that Rex and Cindy had given me, and added to it his lived experience and learned experience. He gave structure to my hope by giving me a plan. He created a support system for the structure by being there to counsel me. Together Dr. Sorge and I confirmed the good news that my memory remained sharp, accurate and undamaged. He helped me find ways to use microcurrent technology and therapy to improve my vision, and he took my previously careless health habits and chiseled them into a new routine and a new lifestyle.

In perspective, my stroke was a wake-up call. It led me, with the help of an Obvious Expert, to become healthier and wiser than before. It taught me the necessity for more balance in my life—more recreation to offset my workload, more laughter to even out life's low points. Most clearly, my stroke of luck taught me just how important an Obvious Expert can be in a person's life.

Maybe you have been fortunate and none of the headaches in your life have turned into the kind of strokes that come in the form of serious illness, divorce, death of a loved one, lost job or financial devastation. Even if you have only faced headaches, you know about troubled relationships, career setbacks and the pressures of too many bills to be paid or not enough hours in the day.

Wherever you are on your life path, here is my offer to you:

> **Let me be The Obvious Expert of life altering wake-up calls, while you take advantage of what I have lived through and what I have learned.**

My stroke of genius convinced me that each of us can choose the life we wish to live and we can create it by establishing ourselves as The Obvious Expert in our chosen field. Let me give you hope that you can have the career you want, the lifestyle you desire and all of the clients you need to make it happen. Follow the plan explained in this book. Use the book, The Obvious Expert Workshops and the resources of IGPC as the support system for your plan. Make it a life altering plan. And most importantly, put yourself in the position to give back to the world by using what you've lived and what you've learned to offer hope, a plan and a support system to others.

Through this book and through our Professional Consultant Certification programs, my son Mark and I share with you the strategies we have lived, learned, developed and taught. At the beginning of each chapter, I also relate my personal war stories, with the desire that you learn from them and fight fewer such battles yourself.

Inevitably, each of us still faces challenges and sometimes, catastrophic events in life. You can choose to strike out or you can recognize that you have been dealt an opportunity—an extraordinary stroke of luck.

Now is an exciting time in the consulting profession. Opportunity abounds if you are willing to respond to a wake up call. Choose how you wish to live your life, and then use The Obvious Expert to turn yourself into The Obvious Expert.

Elsom Eldridge, Jr.

Who Are The Obvious Expert Advisors?

In 2001, we began a search to identify one hundred of the top minds in consulting—and all of its related fields. We wanted to compile for our readers, a guidebook on consulting, built upon our knowledge and expanded by the hints, observations and wisdom of the obvious experts who are out there today defining the consulting profession through their successes and accomplishments.

The more potential Advisors we contacted and interviewed, the more we realized that we could not begin to narrow it to only one hundred experts. As you read these pages of our best advice (throughout which you will find liberally sprinkled the advice of others) you will notice that each page bears a sidebar. These sidebars are the thoughts and observations that each of our chosen Obvious Expert Advisors selected to share with you. We think you will find these sidebars sometimes profound, sometimes funny and always extremely helpful.

A full directory of *The Obvious Expert Advisors* begins on page 255.

Strategies on Becoming the Obvious Expert™

The solution is really very simple. The fastest way to increase your business as a consultant or coach is to get people to recognize you as the obvious expert in your field. But to achieve this recognition, it is not enough to be an expert, know you are an expert and announce to the world that you are an expert. Recognition comes only when you take the necessary actions to position yourself as the premier obvious expert.

Developing and implementing a structured plan in order to achieve the recognized status of obvious expert is the vital element many consultants and coaches overlook—and later suffer from accordingly. This book gives you a line of attack; an indispensable plan that takes you out of the ranks of the overlooked and underpaid.

Apply the no cost, low cost marketing strategies prescribed and described on the following pages. You can master the techniques that make the difference between succeeding as a top-tier consultant or just sustaining as one of the pack.

Let's face it—anyone can hang a shingle and claim to be a consultant. They can work to attract potential clients with examples of how consulting helps the client. They can make phone call after phone call or send brochure after brochure in their attempts to drum up business. But even if they are the most knowledgeable consultants in the world, potential

Bail Out With A Lifejacket

So many people are being laid off; many others are just tired of the rat race and the long hours in their jobs, and would like to be their own boss.

Several years ago, I was the Director of Human Resources for a large energy company in Denver. These were high-flying times and they had lasted for several years. I could see that a correction was coming and I wanted to be ready to run my own business. I started my human resources consulting practice on the side and I wrote a book about how to do just that.

By the time the industry crashed, I had a few clients and was on my way to a successful practice. I approached the President of the company I was then working for about handling the outplacement for the people we were going to lay off and he gave me a contract. It helped launch my consulting practice, and today I am successful as an HR Consultant and author of more than a dozen books on Human Resources Management.

MARY COOK
MaryCook1@aol.com

clients will not turn to them if these consultants have not used effective plans to properly position themselves and gain recognition as experts.

Clients call on consultants who they believe to be credible, reputable and top-notch in a specific field. They call on obvious experts. These clients know of, and respect an obvious expert and what an expert can do for them, even before they pick up the phone to contact him or her. And obvious experts—unlike average consultants—can be selective in choosing clients rather than scrambling for what business they can get.

Think about it; imagine clients seeking you instead of you courting them. Imagine so many potential clients knocking on your door or ringing your phone that you might refer some of them or subcontract portions of their work to other consultants. Imagine taking only the contracts you find interesting or especially lucrative. Visualize yourself turning the tables and having the luxury of interviewing potential clients to determine whether they are qualified to be working with you instead of it so often being the other way around.

Even as we tell you this, you may already be programming negative thoughts and preparing objections, such as, "How can I gain experience as a consultant if I can't get hired because clients believe I lack experience?" Or, "How can I get clients to give me referrals, if I don't already have clients? How can I go to the next level of clients and clinch top-dollar contracts if I have not worked on top-dollar contracts already? And how can I make people see me as the obvious expert?"

Don't panic, this is a conundrum with a solution. Apply the suggestions, insights and consulting gold found in this book. You will be using confirmed successful marketing techniques that gain you recognition and place your name in strategic, high-visibility locations. You will be showing potential clients, instead of telling them that you are an authority in your field.

When you put the principles of this book to work in your consulting practice, you will find yourself working with clients eager to hear what you have to say—people whose problems you know you can solve and who are willing to pay the fees you always wanted to charge.

For starters, they tend to work very hard at building an image and a reputation. Nothing is more important in the business of consulting and marketing your consulting services than creating an appropriate image and reputation in the marketplace you serve. And to do this well, you must be comfortable in your role as a seller of consulting. Many brilliant consultants fail to financially sustain their business because they fail to take the essential step of using an effective plan to continuously market themselves and build a powerful marketing identity.

Successful consultants always have a passion for their field of expertise. They immerse themselves in their practice with laser focus and they use proven strategies to communicate with their market.

You too must cultivate your own never-ending passion. As a consultant, you owe it to yourself and to your clients to do what you love, love what you do and market yourself in such a way that your clients not only benefit from your expertise, but enjoy the assurance of knowing their problems are in the hands of the obvious expert.

This book contains an eleven-step plan, packed with hundreds of marketing strategies to help you become a recognized expert in your field. Start with the successful consultant's essential: **authorship**, and then watch your business grow.

Publishing a book or a series of reports has become, in recent years, a clear-cut and doable process. Being published is the critical first step you should take to establish yourself as an obvious expert.

A published book with your name as author enhances your business reputation no matter what field you are in or how you have previously approached marketing in the past. Even in this modern world of technical sophistication, simple authorship of

Be On-Purpose

In the mid-1980's I saw leaders frustrated with growing their organization. The roots of their challenge lay in a combination of mediocre business and life planning. At the core of this was lack of an identity anchored by purpose. I field-tested simple ways for lives and businesses to be on-purpose. The results came. Compelled to share what I had learned, I wrote two books. The result, when it comes to being on-purpose, I was the *Obvious Expert*.

The benefits of authorship are many. One is entree to potential clients. Another is exposure to like-minded persons who further sharpen your expertise. The most rewarding benefit is when readers share how your message has positively touched their life or business.

Be On-Purpose!

KEVIN W. MCCARTHY
http://www.on-purpose.com

the printed word continues to distinguish those who lead from those who follow.

Immerse yourself in the process of writing and publishing your wisdom. Then enhance your positive results by applying the other ten suggestions found in these chapters. As you achieve more and more success from following this approach, you will be eager to place all of the strategies in play and to reap their excellent benefits.

Here's a preview of the eleven steps of the plan:

Create A Unique Selling Proposition (USP)

Sometimes called, "the elevator speech," the USP is how you brand yourself and your business. This exercise helps you find the magnetic words to attract interest from potential clients and differentiate yourself from the competition.

Publish Books And Reports

Publish or you shall perish! Once you have your name on a publication, or better yet, several publications, you are considered an obvious authority on your subject. Today, getting published is easier than ever before—with ways that don't cost a fortune or require a lifetime.

Speak On The Lecture Circuit

Speaking, even only in your local community, establishes you as a go-to person in your field and helps you build referrals. Even if you have no previous public speaking experience, this chapter shows you specific strategies to help you stand behind a podium and turn listening audiences into paying accounts.

Teach Seminars And Workshops

Conduct seminars or workshops; they translate into automatic respect for you as the authority on your subject, while adding substantial dollars to your income stream. Follow our advice and

Write Columns In Your Area of Expertise

As an independent book editor as well as a freelance writer, I became an obvious expert by using my innate skills. I wrote sample columns called *"Ask the Book Doctor,"* sent them to statewide writers' organizations, and offered to provide a continuing column for free. I requested only two things in return: The column had to include my contact information, and I kept all rights to my material. As a result of the columns, I reach new clients every month who all perceive me as the obvious expert in editing. A paid advertisement would not have been as convincing.

Because I have kept all my rights, I will later publish a book of my columns, an example of "Do the work once, benefit many times."

BOBBIE CHRISTMAS
http://www.zebraeditor.com

those who attend your seminars will become your disciples, spreading the word about your expertise.

Publish Your Own Newsletter

The title of editor or publisher has always elicited respect and been a proven door opener. Add it to your name by publishing your own print or electronic newsletter—what better way to regularly keep your name and your services in front of your clients and potential clients?

Write Magazine And Journal Articles

Writing articles increases your name recognition while boosting your credibility as a source of expert information. This is true no cost marketing.

Use The Media Effectively

Once you understand how your business is newsworthy, use strategically written and distributed press releases to gain positive publicity. Positive media attention that is perceived as non-biased reporting is far more valuable than any advertising you can ever buy.

Create A Content-Based Website

An interactive, timely and informative website is a strategic key to local, national and worldwide recognition. With the power of the World Wide Web, your potential market expands instantly from 'around the neighborhood' to 'around the globe'.

Actively Participate In Associations

Interacting regularly with your peers is a good way to exchange ideas and stay fresh and current in your field. As an added benefit, leadership participation in industry associations can get your name in front of potential clients, enhance your credibility and pave the way for introductions that facilitate

---

Get Your Name In Print

Last week, I was about to begin my morning workout at my local gym when a man whom I had urged to enroll in my speed-reading class greeted me with an interesting comment. He said, "Darryl, you made it! You're in print."

He told me he had seen my name and my course listed in the brochure from *The Knowledge Shop*, an educational center where I taught. For months, I had gently chided and sometimes more bluntly promoted my speed-reading class with this man. He always had a reason not to enroll. But suddenly I had become the obvious expert because he had seen my name published.

Moral of this story? You become the obvious expert not by reminding people that you are an expert, but by attracting them with your name in print, associated with a quality organization.

DARRYL HOLD
tutorpro@teacher.com

Increase Your Visibility

As an Automotive Business Management Consultant, I have helped a number of independent service businesses improve their bottom line by employing a wide range of activities to boost traffic and increase revenues. One approach I've used successfully here has been a high-quality direct-mail marketing program produced in-house. I combined this with my active participation in networks such as the local Chambers of Commerce, convening selected focus group research studies, and hosting several hundred guests at business after-hours mixers as well as a huge grand opening and open house celebration. The response has been outstanding:

- Revenues significantly exceeding our projections
- Exceptional and sustained local buzz, and
- A growing high-profile presence in the community—all in less than eight months!

This positioning as the obvious expert has successfully brought new clients for both C&M Auto Service, Inc., and New World Auto Shop, my consultancy. We are known widely among our peers as experts in our field.

R. DALE LEIGH
http://www.cmauto.com

---

more business.

Network Effectively

Networking is all about speaking with the right people at the right time and delivering the right message. Do it well and it is mutually beneficial while it boosts your influence within your business community.

Give Back To Your Community And Your Nation

Community or cause-related marketing is one of the most positive and effective marketing methodologies known. It has been successful for Ben and Jerry's, the Grateful Dead and even helped cigarette manufacturers put a more socially palatable spin on their industry. Learn how it works, how you can make it part of your business life and how you can take giving to a higher level. Enhance every aspect of your life as you follow your path to becoming the obvious expert.

> *If you are going to be the obvious expert, you need to have a body of work.*
>
> Doug Hall

Elsom's Story:

High School Dropout to Harvard Degree

WAR STORY #1   *Throughout my life, learning and applying strategies for success has proven to be critical. Many years ago, when I was in high school, I lost interest in my classes. In the 11th grade, I decided I had just had enough. I rebelled, stopped going to school and left home. When I returned home a year later (older and wiser), I started* teaching piano and organ lessons. I also created a musical kindergarten, sold electronic equipment in a retail store and did any work that didn't require a high school diploma. The older I got, the more I realized I loved teaching, and the more I knew the reality was that I must finish my education.

I decided to go back and get a high school diploma, a Bachelor's Degree and eventually Master's Degree—or at least this was my plan. I wanted to study Early Childhood Education and Adult Education. My goal was to learn how teachers could inspire students so that other children wouldn't drop out of school the way I had.

A friend explained to me that it was sometimes possible to use life experience in order to be accepted directly into a Master's program at a university, without a Bachelor's degree or even a high school diploma. That sounded like a great strategy to me.

I applied to the University of Massachusetts; I had heard (my apologies to the Administration of U Mass) that their Admissions Office accepted almost anyone. Maybe so, but they did not accept me! It took the admissions officers only a few short weeks to consider my application and then turn me down cold.

Rejected and dejected. Why should a university accept me, I thought. But I did not give up; I simply changed my approach. As in any successful business proposal, I just needed a win-win proposition.

The next three applications I sent to other universities identified how I could be helpful to them and how they could be helpful to me. I lined up high-profile alumni who gave me stellar references. And then I waited.

Quickly I got feedback; it wasn't rejection, but I wasn't exactly accepted either. Universities were interested, but to get in, I would have to pass the entrance exam. Great! I hadn't taken a test in years and I had never been a good test-taker. I faced two alternatives: take the GRE, the Graduate Record Exam, which involved a half day of test taking, or take the MAT, the Miller

Be THE Authority

A book is an incredible marketing tool. Business cards, brochures and proposals get tossed; books are kept. They position you as *THE* authority, the person noted and quoted by print and electronic media. Want to get past a gatekeeper? Nothing succeeds like a personally autographed book directed to the decision maker. We've created a mini-empire based on *The Complete Guide to Self-Publishing*. We preach what we practice: Self publishing. It provides an affordable sales tool, keeps us in total control and yields huge profits. The passive income stream is unbeatable: a clerk fills orders while we're paid handsomely for consulting.

MARILYN AND TOM ROSS
http://www.SelfPublishingResources.com

Start And Build Your Own Network

When I moved to Washington, D.C., I knew two people. I had no other family, political or business connections. Experts said consultants starved on every corner and that I would fail. But at eleven months I broke even, and at eighteen months I had more work than I could handle!

I had a great run for years and became the recognized expert in positive practical communication strategies for leading faster, easier, better organizational change. How? I networked everywhere. I listened to my intuition and refused job offers that did not fit my purpose, even though I needed the money. I stuck to my integrity, speaking only the truth. I deeply held to positive strategies, such as visualization and affirmations.

LINNE BOURGET
http://www.whatyousayiswhat
youget.com

Analogy Test, which could be taken in about one hour. As you can imagine, I chose the one hour option.

To prepare, I bought a book on the MAT and spent exactly an hour and a half of my life taking a sample test plus a little more time grading it. Then reality hit—hit hard. I had scored 12 out of a possible 100 points on the sample test—this was going to be harder than I anticipated. But, I had already made up my mind that I could get into Graduate School, and I believed I could do the work once I got there. My real challenge, it seemed, was going to be finding a way to pass the entrance exam!

For the next thirty days, I immersed myself in preparations for the test. I bought every book I could find on the MAT, I took every practice test, and I researched every unique strategy I could find. I developed similar tests of my own, waited two days, and then took them. I tried to think like the exam makers. I lived this way for ten to fifteen hours each day of the thirty days. During the time, I developed my own strategies on how to master the MAT.

Four weeks after I officially took the test, my score arrived in the mail. The results were printed on a card, which on one side, listed normative test data for applicants to graduate school programs categorized by their intended field of study. My memory is not 100% on these 1972 statistics, but the results showed more or less that applicants applying to pursue Engineering studies typically averaged in the mid-50's on the test, those applying to pursue studies in Business averaged in the high 40's and candidates headed for a career in Education averaged in the mid 40's. I turned the card over and saw my own score—76.8.

Here's the lesson learned: Anyone can become an expert in something that truly interests him or her and for which there is a driving goal. My effort evolved into my new mission, to become a test-taking expert and strategist; an educational consultant, helping both teachers and students learn and grow from exams instead of tests just meaning anxiety and failure.

Three graduate schools accepted me into their programs; I

chose the Harvard Graduate School of Education. In 1974, I earned a Master's Degree in Education and got a 'real job' working for the Office of the State Superintendent of Public Schools in Montana. Three years later, I began teaching at Cal State Fresno (Fresno State University). I figured I would teach as I built my consulting practice.

My specialty in consulting was helping teachers understand how to prepare exams, so that students could be empowered by education rather than disenchanted. I was passionate about my cause—I had not only my own bad memories of classroom frustrations, but by this point, I was reliving it all over again through my children.

When my son Elsom III, at that time a third-grader, came home perplexed by his grade on his science test, the need for me to help effect change in education became clearer than ever. You see, he had been asked to name three great inventors and had answered the question by listing: Thomas Edison, Eli Whitney and God. Of course, the teacher, much to my son's puzzlement, had marked God as an incorrect answer. My heart sank watching his bewilderment that his right answer was somehow a wrong answer. I knew that there were ways to create better tests, to really help children learn better. And I could get my message to teachers, principals and school districts—if only more clients would give me a chance.

That's when I turned to the obvious expert Howard Shenson with my problem. The first time we met together, I handed him my four-color, sixteen-page brochure with the embossed watermark and varnished cover and said, "I need you to take this brochure and make me successful."

Howard Shenson looked at the brochure and then at me, smiled and said, "I can't do that."

"No, no you don't understand. I have a lot of money invested in this brochure and we need to do something with it," I explained.

He shook his head as he replied, "The problem with the

Spread The Word About You

Three things will help establish you as an expert:

1 Publish, because, publishing speaks of authority, even if it is self-publishing. I initially wrote my book with no expectations that a real publisher would ever pick it up. The cost of self-publishing a 200 to 250 page soft cover book isn't any more than printing a high-quality brochure, but the book has a longer shelf life and, if you've done a good job, it will even be read.

2 Once the book is out, make yourself available to any news reporter and editor you can meet. Let media people know you are available for comment. They will quote a published author much more often than they will quote someone who is not published.

3 Network, network, network… get out and meet people. In the final analysis, most of our consulting work still comes as a result of word of mouth. You never know when the guy you met at a Chamber event will give your business card to a friend who happens to be a CEO of a company that could use your services.

C.B. "CORK" MOTSETT
http://www.bdspec.com

Stretch Farther

Always follow your inner voice that prompts you to do or say something to someone.

When leads are given, follow them until you feel satisfied. Satisfaction may not mean a sale or another person enrolled in your class, but it brings a visible completeness to who you are and how you present yourself. Being complete about who you are imparts to the other person a sense of sureness, security—no question that you know what you are talking about.

Stay true to who you know you are but also be willing to stretch further than you have ever before. Being true to yourself does, at times, mean taking risks even if you don't perceive yourself as a risk taker. Being true to yourself is holding your values, not limiting yourself with old thoughts and beliefs that you have accepted, such as: I can't teach or I can't sell.

You can do what you thought impossible, when you know that what you are talking about is the truth for you. You are already doing it everyday in many subtle ways but don't recognize or acknowledge it for what it is.

CAROL BOCZARSKI
cboczarski@hotmail.com

brochure is that it won't work. You need to do something else."

"But Mr. Shenson, I have a lot of these in my garage. I have invested a great deal of money in them. There must be some way to use this brochure."

"The problem," he said, "is that the brochure, despite how beautiful it is, rarely gets to the people you want to reach. The people you are trying to contact are very busy, so they hire other people to keep you away. They have a gatekeeper that sits at a desk with a receptacle at his feet; the receptacle is usually round, rectangular or square. The uninvited mail is zealously dumped into that receptacle—day after day, over and over again. So it doesn't matter that you repeatedly sent out those wonderful expensive brochures—most of them ended up in the trash."

I must have looked pretty disheartened, because he quickly went on to explain, "What you need to do is this: You need to have the people who might hire you to be their consultant—your potential clients—determine for themselves, on their own, that you are the expert in the field and to then give you a call."

"How in the world do I do that?" I asked, and he leaned back in his chair and started to explain.

The advice I received did not change my skills in Education. It did not make me a different person, nor did it change what I could deliver. There was nothing altered about my qualifications—the only difference it made was the crucial one. I gained essential credibility. I took the first in a series of important steps and I became THE OBVIOUS EXPERT.

The rest, of course, is history.

EE Jr.

A SPECIAL CONTRIBUTION FROM
❧ Susan RoAne ❧

The Mingling Maven

Susan RoAne calls the story of how she became an obvious expert her SAGA. In 1979, San Francisco Unified School District laid off 1200 teachers and both Susan and her husband at the time, were on the lay-off list. As Susan says, "we were out of luck and out of the career that promised 'you will always have something to fall back on'." But Susan saw an opportunity.

Her career successes include being a highly sought public speaker, author of bestselling books, seminar leader and frequent interview subject for the press, including CNN, The BBC, The *Wall Street Journal,* the *New York Times* and many, many more.

W hen I was laid off, my friends called and were frantic but I realized that in order to learn something we must go through a PROCESS, not just offer or be offered a sentence or two of support. So I designed one of the first career change workshops geared for teachers in San Francisco. My workshops received good ink thanks to an article in the San Francisco Examiner by a reporter who was a guest speaker in my 6th-7th-grade class a year earlier.
Over one hundred attendees showed up at each seminar and once we finished our funding, I had a business. Simultaneously, I went on radio to promote and support the concept of career change for this enormous amount of good teachers about to lose jobs. I said 'yes' to something that was very much out of my comfort zone and took that risk. My prior involvement in politics had taught me a lot about garnering support, getting the word out and using good follow-up.

The business editor for the Examiner heard the interview and asked if we could do a San Francisco-based careers series. For

Clients Are Your Business Partners

I always remember that the clients are the real experts. They are my judges and they will lift me up or set me aside. Therefore, credibility and ethics are the keys that I use to open the doors to successful selling and a thriving business.

My clients know when I value them. They also know when I do not. If at any time, I shirk my responsibility to them and provide them with less than my best effort, I will have forfeited my own credibility and ethics and the customers will be forever lost to my competitors.

My own advice to me is this: 'Get up today, tomorrow and every day reminding yourself that your potential and existing customers are really your business partners. You owe your best to every one of them. If you fail to give 100%, Murphy's Law will prevail and the words, *Out of Business* will be your epitaph.'

LINDA PINSON
http://www.business-plan.com

Interviews Will Catapult You

After self-publishing *Look Back and Laugh: Confessions of a Teen in the Thirties* describing my adolescence on the streets of New York during the Depression, I managed to get a lot of publicity in newspapers like the *L.A. Times* and the *N.Y. Times,* and on public radio and TV. These interviews made me an "obvious expert" and enabled me to help would-be writers to follow my example. I've sold hundreds of my books at seminars discussing *Telling and Selling Your Life Story.* Teaching *Writing From The Heart—Recording Your Family History* at a local Senior Center has made me dozens of new friends.

JEAN DESMOND
http://www.jeandesmond.com

three years I worked with him and two other outside consultants, designing one of the first careers series and I wrote a majority of the columns. Frankly, all the career issues we now read about were exactly the same—only the Internet is new.

Doing this gave me the 'street cred' as a career consultant, coach, keynote speaker and writer, plus lots of material I included in subsequent books. I continued to act as a mentor, networking guide, a source whose brain was often picked. In 1999, I formalized my author/coaching/communication consulting business as PICK MY BRAIN Consulting. I have a third wave where I coach would-be authors from start-up to planning their PR as would-be mingling mavens. The networking and brainstorming skills serve me and my clients well. But it is a process built over two decades of writing best selling books, How To Work A Room, The Secrets of Savvy Networking, and What Do I Say Next?, continual quotes as an expert in the print media (From Cooking Light to Cosmo; from Entrepreneur to Wall St. Journal, online zines, radio, TV, newsletters and using my website as a content venue, that is the mix that makes me a Master.)

Being nice to every freelancer, offering to help with their next assignment and recommending other experts has been my mantra and helped me along the way to help others. I always made sure that every time I was interviewed there was shared laughter and connection as people, not just as an expert to interviewer. But my start was doing something to help my colleagues and myself who were ousted from our chosen profession.

I paid a lot of dues and that is how one becomes an Obvious Expert with substance, connections and 'street cred.' I am now recognized and have branded the concept of working a room and networking. I keynote conferences, teach classes and continue to write that which supports my area of expertise. And the shared laughter is even more important now than ever.

For more information on
Strategies for Consulting, visit:
www.obvious-expert.com/strategies

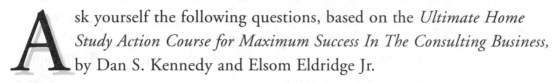

Identifying and Fueling Your Passion

Ask yourself the following questions, based on the *Ultimate Home Study Action Course for Maximum Success In The Consulting Business,* by Dan S. Kennedy and Elsom Eldridge Jr.

#1 How do I really feel about travel? Do I like it? Does work travel create a logistical burden in my personal life, such as too much time away from my family?

#2 How do I really feel about notoriety? Do I want to be famous in my particular field? In my home city? Nationally?

#3 How much money do I need to make? How much money do I want to make?

#4 Do I want extensive interaction with others? Limited? As little as possible?

#5 Do I enjoy wearing business attire? Would I prefer to do business from home while wearing my pajamas?

#6 What is my best work schedule? Do I need or prefer to be free on weekends? Would it be beneficial to work while my children sleep or are at school?

#7 Do I want to work alone? Do I want to work as part of a team? Do I want to subcontract some work to others?

#8 Am I more comfortable working with CEO's of big companies? Small business owners? Younger people? Older people?

#9 Where is my desired focus—teaching and advising? Or developing and implementing?

#10 Do I enjoy my chosen consulting vocation (or intended future consulting vocation) so much that I wake up eager to get started on my work each day? Do I think enthusiastically about it, even during leisure time, even when I am on vacation? When I have the option to read for pleasure, do I read information about my field of expertise, because I have a driving, ardent interest? Do I love what I do?

Your answers to these and similar questions you may formulate on your own, should help shape the way you 'design' (or re-design) your consulting business.

Do not just think about your responses; write them out fully, as if you are submitting them to someone else for review—because in some ways you are. Have a 'meeting' of both the Conscious You and the Subconscious You. Listen to the voice from each side of your psyche. Let the Conscious You make a list of what you need in your life. Next, let the Subconscious You list what you want in your life. Identify all the things that are common to both lists—this is your highest zone of resolution.

The contents of the zone are determined when you prioritize and reconcile your needs and your wants, so that you best satisfy the greatest number of factors from both facets of your life.

When you commit your career, your job satisfaction, your present livelihood and perhaps even the economic future for you and your family to your vocation as a consultant, you need to be certain that you have pledged yourself to a cause about which you are truly passionate.

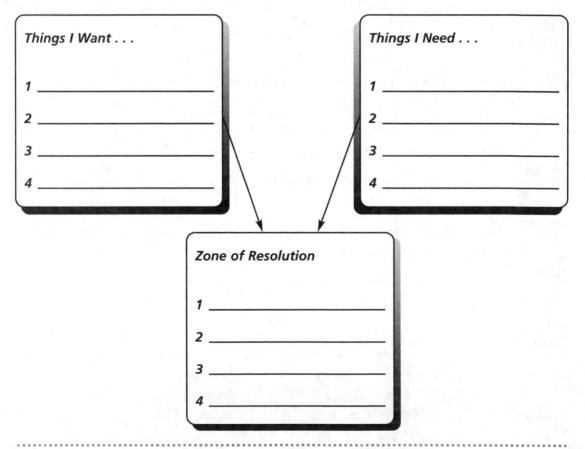

The Editors of Victoria Magazine, in their book, *The Business of Bliss, How To Profit From Doing What You Love,* (©1999, Hearst Books) tell the stories of a group of business people, (in this case, coincidentally all women) each of whom has built her career around her passion. They describe these successful entrepreneurs and consultants in this way:

> **"**
>
> *. . . Women who gathered up their resources, their childhood dreams, their particular talents, their unique vision, and poured them into a business of their very own. What they gained was not a life free of hardship, but one of few regrets and soaring triumphs. A fuller sense of themselves, the world, and their place in it.*
>
> **"**

Following your life's passion as a consultant certainly does not guarantee you freedom from problems, but it does promise you many wonderful benefits, including the freedom to make your own choices and the 'privilege' to either soar or sink because of those choices. And when you think about it, that is a pretty remarkable benefit.

At this point in your life, you many not yet have synchronized your passion and your career to be 100% in harmony. Sometimes it is okay for your current passion to be the plan of working toward your real passion—in fact, such a plan can be highly motivational. And do not assume that your passion always remains the same throughout a lifetime. Circumstances can require or inspire you to change your passion. But whether you currently are fueled by your passion or simply by the pre-passion that leads to your passion, one or the other must be present in order for you to survive and thrive as a consultant.

Before you begin the next chapter, before you start on the path to becoming the obvious expert, examine and reexamine your goals. Make absolutely certain that you are creating a career that fuels your passion and that you are nurturing a passion that will fuel your successful consulting career.

Ask yourself the following three questions, developed by Richard Johnson, President of 21st Century Marketing, and the curriculum developer for the International Guild of Professional Consultants CPMC certification training:

1   **What drove you to get into your business?**

2   **What passion drives you every day to stay in business and keeps you trying to grow your business?**

3 **Complete this sentence: My company is the only company that . . . (or I am the only consultant who. . .).**

B.A.K-Up Your Career for Success

Your goal is to gain recognition as *THE* person who can solve a specific set of problems. The good news is, you do not have to put twenty years of experience under your belt to do this. Simply follow a success formula that contains three ingredients:

"Belief + Action + Knowledge = Success"

You must believe that you are an expert. If you do not believe it, you will not convince anyone else to believe it either.

Believe in yourself, and at the same time:

◆ **Take action to continually build knowledge in your field of expertise**

◆ **Take action to expand your knowledge on the subject of marketing yourself**

◆ **Take action to validate for potential clients the knowledge that makes you indisputably an expert**

If you leave out any one ingredient, the formula does not work. Belief, Action and Knowledge—think of it as the way you 'bak-up' your efforts to ensure ongoing success and become the obvious expert.

CHAPTER 2

Who Are You? Define Your Unique
Selling Proposition

WAR STORY #2 *"Be a generalist, but market yourself as a specialist. Know who you are, and know how you are different from anybody else."*

These words didn't hit home the first time Howard Shenson said them to me. I had to live them before I understood them. I may have known who I was, but my limited client base revealed I was not successfully communicating who I was to my clients or potential clients.

In the early stages of my career, I was marketing myself as an educational consultant. One of my passions was helping both children and adults learn more effectively, more easily and with better comprehension and retention. Ironically, I was so anxious to gain my client's confidence that I always emphasized my Master's Degree from Harvard. I neglected to tell clients that I was a high school dropout.

The truth is, I was afraid. Not graduating from high school, I thought, was my weakness. In reality, the fact that I had not graduated from high school, but had still gone on to receive my Ed.M. from Harvard, was a superlative and distinctive success story.

My clients included people whose children, or they themselves, were being challenged by the routines of the educational system. My atypical educational path enhanced my appeal to them. Most importantly, it helped distinguish me from my competition.

Howard's words took almost a year to really sink in. I had to stop looking at how I wanted to sell myself and start looking at who my clients wanted to buy before I began using my unique

Short, Distinctive And Powerful

In starting my career, I did not know what to call myself. I was trained as a Ph.D. Clinical Psychologist and had completed two internships in that field. However, I wrote my Ph.D. dissertation on sales superstars and learned that I enjoyed working more with salespeople and executives than I did working with people with psychological problems.

I started with a long Unique Selling Proposition and then gradually shortened it over the years. I ended up becoming well known on four different continents as The Sales and Marketing Psychologist. I now encourage all of my clients to try to come up with the shortest, most distinctive and powerful USP possible.

DONALD MOINE
http://www.DrMoine.com

---

educational background to make my point.

I was different from my competitors because I knew firsthand about learning how to learn. I had been there. I had gotten into the minds of the test makers. I had personally experienced the reality that anyone can adjust his courage in the face of tests and dynamically improve his own performance. I knew it because I had done it. I could show other people how to do it too. This was my specialty. Mine alone.

This became the basis of the Unique Selling Proposition that was right for me to use at that time in my career: "Strategies for better learning, higher grades—guaranteed—from the educator who went from high school dropout to Harvard Master's degree."

EE Jr.

Who Do Your Clients Think You Are?

As a consultant, (or other type of business professional) you have a business image. This image is either one you deliberately and carefully orchestrated and put out in the world, or it is simply the one that evolved because your clients (or your *competitors*) labeled you in a certain way.

Obvious expert **Paul Franklin**, of the Franklin Group, says, "You already have an image out there in the community, or with your target market. You want to be in control of what that image is and not just let it happen.

"And it stands to reason that if you have an image, then it is in your best interest to make sure it is the image you want to have.

"You want consciously to 'fix' that image in the brains of your prospects and your clients. You want to create your Unique Selling Proposition, your USP."

Paul explains that your USP:

- Is your best marketing shot.

- Distinguishes and differentiates you from your competition.

- Fills a void, a gap or a vacuum.

"It is," he adds, "short and easy to use. Most importantly, you have to 'live' it; it is not hyperbolic."

> *Writing a USP is more than describing your company, or what type of person you are, or even what type of job you do. Your USP must define the overt benefit and dramatic difference you bring to your client. It must be written greatly . . . Figure out how to articulate it so it is a* mind-stopping *thought.*
>
> Doug Hall

Define Your Unique Offering

To be a successful consultant, you don't necessarily need to be the best or fastest, but you do need to separate yourself from the crowd by being unique. Identifying, developing, and incorporating your USP into everything you do is challenging. But the reward is worth the effort.

Your unique selling proposition, or USP, is a two or three sentence explanation of who you are and what you do. You use it to explain to a potential client the benefit you can bring to them, how their lives will be improved by what you do, and why you are obviously the best choice to provide them this service. The listener should be able to tell from your USP how your business is different from other consulting practices. Your USP should highlight your specialty or specialties. It will not address everything you do, or all of the services you offer. It should serve

Just Brand It!

There is a fair way to even the playing field to your advantage. It's called personal branding. The leading professionals, those whose client bases seem to expand even during down times and who boast high incomes, continually attract clients because they have created a personal brand identity. If you want to turn yourself into a saleable, valued asset—instead of just another face in the crowd—you must build your brand.

Take the multi-billion dollar category of athletic shoes. You have Nike®, the colossus. Hard on its heels you have Reebok®, Adidas®, Fila® and others. What's the difference between them, other than logos and advertising?

Virtually nothing. So why does Nike own the world of shoes?

Brand identity. People buy based on how a brand makes them feel emotionally. They don't buy based on logic. If "Just do it©" strikes a chord with a football player, he's going to grab Nikes.

The same truths apply to any product or service. If you can build a brand identity around your practice—something that instantly creates a reaction in your audience—you will attract clients and maintain your client base, no matter what times are like.

PETER MONTOYA
http://www.petermontoya.com

Differentiate Yourself

With access to such a huge market via the Internet, it's more important than ever to differentiate yourself. Your Unique Selling Proposition comes from within you. Especially when marketing consulting services. Who are you? What makes you unique? How can this be a direct benefit to your clients? Think of yourself as a franchise.

When you think of Subway®, you think sandwich; McDonalds® and you think burgers.

What do you want your prospects and customers to think when your name is mentioned?

Keep it simple. We can't expect prospects to remember too much. They already are overloaded with too much information! Make it easy for them to know what you do and to remember what you do and how it is unique from your competition. This is the power of a good USP!

Ross Huguet
http://www.rosshuguet.com

only to begin a conversation. It should spur the listener to say, "Tell me more!"

Your USP should be so second nature to you that you can tell it to anyone at a moment's notice. You never know when you'll need it—and when you do need it, you never know how much time you'll get to use it before the opportunity slips away.

For this reason, some people call the USP their "elevator speech". Your USP is something you should be able to convey to a stranger during an elevator ride lasting one or two minutes. It should be in non-technical terms that even someone outside your industry can understand. It should be something that makes the person interested in knowing more about your business, and something that encourages questions and dialogue between you.

When someone asks you "What do you do?" you cannot be ambiguous. If you do not have a clear answer you can give quickly and concisely, that person will not be able to determine why and how to do business with you or if they could refer business to you. You will have missed an opportunity to reach that person and that person's network of contacts.

On the other hand, if you go overboard in explaining what you do—rolling out a laundry list of all the different services you offer—the listener will get the idea that you are a jack of all trades and an expert at none.

In reality, you probably do many different things for many different clients, but for the purposes of your USP, or your elevator speech, you must choose to emphasize one specialty or one unique feature of your business.

Create Your USP

Writing your USP is challenging. Many consultants don't take the time to effectively position themselves with a USP, or they haphazardly throw one together because they feel they need to have one.

Paul suggests that you test market your USP with friends and clients. He recommends that you even take three or four of your clients to lunch and get input directly from them about how they perceive your business identity.

State your USP in uncomplicated, effective language expressing the essence of what it is you do. Convey to the listener the heart and soul of your unique skill—the very aspects of your vocation about which you are the most proud and the most passionate. Understanding how your offerings compare with those of your competitors is key to helping distill your ideas about your USP into that simple, pure flow of language that intrigues and engages your potential clients.

Doug Hall, author, speaker and founder of the #1 corporate innovation and research facility in the US, the Eureka! Ranch, outlines what's needed in your USP in his book, *Jumpstart Your Business Brain* (©2001, Brain Brew Books). Doug reminds us that the basic strategy for ensuring success in introducing any product or service is incorporating three factors into your marketing strategy:

1 **Overt benefit**—What's in it for the customer? Marketing professionals know you must focus on benefits of your service instead of features, but Doug says that you must be direct. You can't expect potential clients to read your mind, or read between the lines. You must tell them specifically what they could get by hiring you.

2 **Real reason to believe**—What kind of credibility can you offer? You must explain to potential clients why you are more qualified to work for them than your competitors are. Tell them what makes your credentials so special.

3 **Dramatic difference**—How is your service dramatically unique? The difference between what you offer and what the client could get from others must be substantial.

Everybody Is Selling Something

When you receive a telephone solicitation offering some product or service, are you likely to buy from someone you don't know?

Probably not. The new millennium has spawned a service-based economy in which companies are reaching out to cultivate new customers and striving to retain the ones they already have. Accomplishing this task and remaining competitive in this environment will depend on the quality of your business relationships. If all of your marketing and sales decisions are short term, you'll never derive long-term benefits.

Get to know your customers and strive for more repeat business and referrals. Spend less time chasing money and more time building relationships. Success in business depends on relationships . . . and relationships take time.

JEFF RUBIN
http://www.put-it-in-writing.com

> " *. . . today's consultants have to be able to figure out if they have anything to sell or not and, . . . overtly, specifically be able to state the benefit of what they are going to deliver to the client. That benefit should be dramatically different.*
>
> Doug Hall "

Keep It Simple

When someone asks me what I do, my answer is simple. "I write books."

That statement does two things. First, it tells folks one of the things that I do that's also highly likely to interest them. Folks like to talk to authors. Second, it gives them an opening to make a statement linked to what I do and that's of interest to them. If they pick up on my conversational lead, we're off to a discussion that can easily lead me to volunteer information on my publishing services for folks who want to do a book, on my consulting work, on my speaking, or on my books.

WALLY BOCK
http://www.bockinfo.com

In many cases, your USP can help you find creative ways to market yourself. For instance, your USP could lead to a slogan, which could lead to a mission statement, which could lead to a marketing campaign, and so on.

Federal Express® is a great example of a USP that evolved into an identity. When Federal Express® first started there were already numerous companies that had been around for years in the special delivery business. Wisely, Federal Express® distinguished themselves from the competition by saying that they were the company to use, "When it absolutely, positively must be there overnight."

Know what your business stands for, and then deliver that message in everything you do. Your USP must remain consistent though all your marketing materials. You can't use different USP's on your business cards, letterhead, capability statement, press releases, newsletters, action outline and in your speeches and still expect potential clients to hear your underlying message. Stay focused.

Eventually as your business grows, your USP may evolve. When Federal Express® became the largest overnight shipping provider, and the US moved into a more global economy, FedEx® changed their marketing strategy with their USP/slogan of, *The World On Time*.

A strong, precise USP will act like radar, targeting the right prospects for your offering. There are certain clients you want and, equally important, certain clients you don't want. Far too many consultants engage in shotgun marketing, desperately seeking every client they can get. The problem is, this is not very profitable. Your particular situation, your business strong suits and specialized experience make what you have to offer much more valuable to certain prospects than to others.

Creating your USP requires being aware of your company's—and your competitors'—strengths and weaknesses, and it requires lots of open-minded creativity on your part. Copying someone else's USP will simply put you back in the pack with everyone else. Besides, your business is unique; your USP should be unique also.

For more information on
Adopting a Unique Selling Proposition, visit:

www.obvious-expert.com/usp

Differentiation, Overt Benefit And Reason To Believe From The USP Of An Obvious Expert

. . . Global Networking Specialist Robyn Henderson has never advertised in 10 years.

Robyn has spoken in 10 countries, presents over 150 times each year and all her work comes from referrals, her website and networking . . .

ROBYN HENDERSON
http://www.networkingtowin.com.au

Overt Benefit, Differentiation And Reason To Believe From The USP Of An Obvious Expert

. . . We help Americans and Japanese overcome cultural barriers and develop more effective working relationships . . .

Bilingual team with excellent credentials and experience . . .

Deep expertise in the unique challenges faced by Japanese firms operating in the US . . .

ROCHELLE KOPP
Rochelle@japanintercultural.com

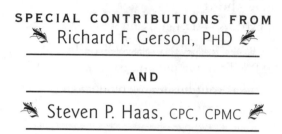

INTERACTIVE WORKSHEET

Developing Your Own Unique Selling Proposition

SPECIAL CONTRIBUTIONS FROM
Richard F. Gerson, PhD

AND

Steven P. Haas, CPC, CPMC

Dr. Richard Gerson is President of Gerson Goodson, Inc. He is an internationally renowned consultant, speaker, author and trainer who works with both Fortune and Inc. 500 companies as well as small businesses. He is the author of sixteen books and more than three hundred articles on the topics of performance improvement, employee and customer retention, sales, leadership development and team building

Steven P. Haas is principal and founder of Enterprise Development, a Minneapolis-based consultancy dedicated to assisting small and emerging businesses in their ongoing development and evolution. He has been part of award-winning teams who have done interactive marketing projects for 3M, Carlson Marketing, Disney and Disney Online. Steve is an advisor to the International Guild of Professional Consultants (IGPC) and dedicates much of his free time as a development specialist with the Service Corps of Retired Executives (SCORE).

Two Approaches to Help You Define Your USP

 Guidelines for USP Development

 Conduct a focus group with key members of your staff in order to gain perspective of your company's unique differences. If you do not have other employees, turn to your peer counselors or trusted advisors.

Contact a select group of regular clients and ask them why they continue to do business with you.

Conduct a strategic analysis of your key competitors in order to isolate your specific strengths and weaknesses.

Compile all information from each of these activities and clearly define the unique qualities of your business.

Now in less than 60 words, write a dynamic statement to demonstrate that your business is truly unique and fills a specific void within the marketplace.

Next turn your USP into a memorable marketing hook that you can use in all of your marketing activities and business communications.

Finally, integrate your USP into all current and future marketing activities and both oral and written presentations.

Sample USP:

At (our company) we view marketing in an entirely different way—we believe that you already have a variety of true marketing assets—
What we really do is help you identify these assets—optimize and leverage them to grow your business exponentially—in three ways instead of just one—

Sample Marketing Hook:

We provide catalyst and strategy to small and emerging businesses bringing them more clients and more profits—more often—

Sample Metaphor:

Do you know how a doctor helps you resolve your health problems?

We do the exact same thing for your business—we go in—assess the situation and work with you to implement prescribed solutions—

Sample Response:

Oh—I get it! Tell me more—

E X E R C I S E

Ask yourself these questions:

1. What business are we (or am I) in? What is it we *really* do?

_____

_____

2. Who are our preferred clients and what is our target market?

_____

_____

3. What are the three most important results our potential clients are looking for?

_____

_____

4. What are the three most important reasons clients should do business with professionals and product/service providers such as ourselves?

_____

_____

5. What are the three reasons clients should do business with us instead of our competitors?

_____

_____

6. What is the main problem our target market is experiencing? (Where's the pain?)

_____

_____

(continues on next page)

7. What is the unique solution that we provide to this problem? (What makes us unique?)

_____

_____

8. What are the techniques that we use to achieve the results that we promise?

_____

_____

9. What is the primary benefit or benefits our clients will receive as a result of doing business with us? (Describe the ultimate results that you provide for your clients.)

_____

_____

10. Now . . . in less than 60 words, write your unique selling proposition and include a memorable marketing hook that can be integrated into all of your marketing efforts.

_____

_____

_____

_____

_____

_____

_____

_____

_____

_____

_____

_____

Note: *a powerful and effective USP will demonstrate that your business is truly unique and fills a specific void within the market.*

A SPECIAL CONTRIBUTION FROM
Paul Franklin, THE FRANKLIN GROUP

Another distinguished Shenson disciple, **Paul Franklin** is a master of direct marketing, seminars and consulting. Among his many accomplishments, Paul considers one of the successes of which he is the most proud is the defining and creating of an effective typology for consulting and the seminar business.

#2 Understanding Your USP

The image you want to project to the target audiences you want to reach is your USP; your uniqueness. It is an important benefit you render to your customers.

A good USP addresses a void, fills a gap or another specific need and does so in the minds of the prospective clients. You must zealously tell your customers how you are different and what void or gap you have filled.

A good USP is simple. It is your best marketing shot. It will stick in the minds of your customers as what you stand for that has value to them.

Rule #1: You must appeal to someone and that someone cannot be everyone.

Rule #2: Your USP has to speak REAL BENEFIT to your customers. It's got to be real.

Rule #3: You must make distinguishing yourself from the competition THE PRIORITY in all of your marketing, public relations and promotional efforts.

Rule #4: Your customers and prospects can't know how you are different unless you continually tell them. *DON'T MAKE THEM GUESS!*

A USP is your defining characteristic. It:

◆ **Sets you apart and ahead of your competition**

◆ **Aggressively stakes out a market position**

◆ **Addresses a void, a gap and/or a specific need**

◆ **Is what people will remember about you and what you want them to remember**

◆ **Is not platitudinous but is as specific and direct as you can make it**

◆ **Is how you pick out of the crowd, the people who want what you have to offer**

Finding Your USP includes:

◆ **Starting with a staff (or peer) brainstorming session.**

◆ **Includes lunch with your best clients or surveys of your best clients.**

To better explain this, here is a working example from Paul's client files:

"I tell consultants to sit down with their staff, or even by themselves. They can come at this from one of two ways:

Think of all the things that your clients have said about you that are good things—what they like about you, or, think of all the things you have heard clients say they don't like about their consultants—other consultants. Next, flip those negatives into positives that you could use to build your Unique Selling Proposition.

Once you have done this, isolate three or four points. Then take two or three of your best clients out to lunch and ask them: which resonates best for you?

Finally, don't stop there. Put it out, but continue to refine it."

Example:

A mechanical engineer in Southern California went through this exact process to develop his USP. We discovered there were things clients did not like about other mechanical engineers. They did not like that mechanical engineers were never on time and never on budget.

Our answer was simple. *"On time and on budget"* became my client's USP.

But after using it for a while, he knew it was not playing out right. It wasn't resonating in his market. So we went back to clients and said: "Is there anything else? What are we missing?"

We learned that there was one more part to the complaint—never right the first time.

The USP became, **"On time and on budget, and right the first time."**

Then we added one more important word: **Guaranteed!**

EXERCISE

Try writing your USP again, this time following Paul Franklin's suggested approach. Compare your results with your earlier attempt.

_____

_____

_____

_____

_____

_____

_____

_____

_____

_____

_____

_____

_____

_____

_____

_____

_____

_____

_____

Publish Your Book or Reports
—Or Else!

CHAPTER 3

WAR STORY #3 During our first work session together, my mentor, obvious expert, Howard Shenson, asked me if I had ever thought about writing a book.

"Sure," I said, "I've thought about it for five years. I'll write it as soon as I get all of the information together."

"Well, there's no such thing as getting ALL of the information," Howard replied. "Even if you don't know it all, you know more about your passion than the average person knows about it," he continued. "And you definitely know things that other people want to know."

The more I sat there thinking about it, the more interesting the concept became. Now, what topic would I choose? What subject did I really know?

I thought immediately of the SAT, the two-part college admissions test, known as the Standard Aptitude Test. This nerve-wrecker measures the math and verbal reasoning skills of the college bound. I had been coaching both teachers and students on strategies for elevating SAT scores.

A wealth of helpful test taking tips were fresh in my thoughts, like the fact that there are seventeen key words a test taker can learn, the prefixes and suffixes of which unlock the meanings of thousands of other English words, and therefore answer other numerous test questions.

Howard gave me an assignment. For the next two weeks, I was to dump all of my knowledge about the SAT onto paper. I should prepare strategies in the math and verbal areas of the SAT and compose some sample tests and annotated answers. Howard said he didn't care whether I ended up with fifty pages, one hundred or two hundred; he just wanted me to dump all of my

Open Doors To Myriad Opportunities

My personal experience with book writing is mind-boggling. Someone once asked me how much I made for my first *Guerrilla Marketing* book. The answer I gave was $10 million.

The book itself only paid me about $35,000 in royalties, but the speaking engagements, spin-off books, newsletters, columns, boot camps, consulting and wide open doors resulted in the remaining $9,965,000.

If any consultant wants to open wide the doors to myriad opportunities, my suggestion is: Write a good book!

JAY CONRAD LEVINSON
http://www.jayconradlevinson.com

knowledge until I had exhausted the topic.

"Wait," I tried to explain, "I'm teaching at the University, I'm the organist at the Episcopal Cathedral and I am scheduled to be the magic act at three children's parties within the next week. I don't have the time to compile sample SAT exams!"

"Do you want to do this or not?" Howard asked, but he did not pause for an answer. "Have you ever immersed yourself in something you believe in?" he asked. "Your consulting business is not going to go anywhere until you position yourself as an expert; until you do that, there is not really a reason for us to meet again."

So I started typing. For the better part of fourteen nights, I pounded away on my IBM® Selectric typewriter. Two weeks later, I walked into Howard's office with 160 typewritten pages in my hand. On his desk waited 250 copies of printed book covers. Each was 11×17 index stock, printed in red, white and blue. The title read, Strategies for Scoring Higher on the SAT by Elsom Eldridge Jr.

I pointed to the bottom of one of the covers, where the words, The National Test Preparation Center, were printed on each cover. "What's that?" I asked.

"That's your publishing company. Elsom Eldridge Jr.'s publishing company," Howard replied.

At a local copy center, Howard and I ran 250 photocopies of my typewritten pages, front and back. He then directed me to a trade press that did perfect binding. We put my pages and the new covers together. We had a book. I was an author with a book in print.

Published author—so what else was different about me? Absolutely nothing.

And there was nothing different about the service and product I could deliver, either. Nor was there anything different about my qualifications. The only difference was that I instantly had greater credibility. I had taken an important step. I was becoming the obvious expert.

With the publication of Strategies for Scoring Higher on the

SAT, *Howard recommended I send out ten copies every day to the same prospects to whom I had unproductively sent brochures. This list of non-responders included school superintendents, principals, teachers, school board members and influential parents.*

"Think of it as your new brochure," Howard said. "And the nice thing about a book," he pointed out, "is that most people never throw books away."

He went on to explain to me that people often are too busy to read every book they receive, and mine would be no exception. In fact, today's statistics show only one of every ten books purchased is ever read. So, the book you write may end up on a shelf in someone's office along side several other unread books. But your name now is up there with those of authors whose books your potential clients have valued enough to purchase. Your work is categorized along side that of other experts.

Along with each of my books, Howard recommended that I send a personalized cover letter somewhat like this:

Elsom Eldridge Jr, Educational Consultant
111 Published Author Parkway
Anytown, Any State USA 12345

January 1, 19XX

John Jones, Principal
Anytown Middle School
#42 Potential Client Boulevard
Anytown, Any State 12345

Dear Principal Jones:

Enclosed is a copy of my latest book, which I believe your students and teachers will find very useful.

Strategies for Scoring Higher on the SAT offers you and your faculty new insights which can be put to immediate use.

Sincerely,

Elsom Eldridge Jr.

Elsom Eldridge Jr.
Educational Consultant

Assess Your Goals First

As I was trying to figure out what I was going to do with the rest of my life and my consulting business, I identified the two things that I liked to do and that I was also good at: writing and speaking. As a writer, I started a two-page newsletter that provided a nugget of useful information on teamwork and a reference to some current project. At the same time, I made a serious effort to get on the speaking circuit of professional conferences in human resources. My conference talks again provided the audience with practical ideas that could be put to use immediately and gave them an opportunity to see me in action. The positive response to the newsletter gave me the confidence to pursue my dream to publish a book.

In 1990, Jossey-Bass published my first book, *Team Players and Teamwork,* and the rest, as they say, is history. The book led to both more speaking engagements and more books. I have since published some different team resources for practitioners. The key to remember is that it all started with a self-assessment that focused on two questions: 1) What do I like to do? and 2) What am I good at? In the end, it meant that I had identified my purpose in life: to communicate practical ideas for successful teamwork.

GLENN PARKER
http://www.glennparker.com

Notice that my letter was not blatantly asking for business. It was simply delivering a free book that would help that person with something at some time in the future. A single-sheet flier describing my consulting services was slipped into the back of each book so that the person reading my letter—or the person who later pulled my book off the shelf for reference—would know what kinds of services I offered and how to find me.

I followed Howard's advice and sent out ten books a day, five days a week. In two weeks, I had my first call from a school that asked whether I could do some training for its teachers on the topic of preparing for the SAT. Then I started getting calls from schools that wanted assistance training teachers to create tests that would help students learn better.

Before I knew it, I had more business than I needed, but I did not stop. I kept sending out books and continuing other forms of marketing myself to get my name out there. And I kept watching my business grow.

This all came from a book I had immersed myself in writing for exactly two weeks. If Howard had allowed me to take a year to write my first book, I would have taken a year—or longer. Look how much business I would have missed. Worse, after a year of failure, I might have lost the dream of ever being a successful consultant.

Publishing that first book, as well as the subsequent ones, changed my life in three ways:

1   Prospects who called had already identified a specific problem they were committed to solve.

2   These prospects already recognized me as the obvious expert, who could help them solve their problem.

3   No one ever again asked me to cut my (now higher) fees in half. Now they said, "Do you have time to help?"

EE Jr.

Create A Buzz

I leverage my exposure by marketing through other people's efforts. It's more than just publicity or word of mouth. It includes creating a certain 'buzz' about my practice. More importantly, it includes multiplying my marketing by offering a complimentary report, article or book that can be reprinted or distributed freely. Especially with the help of the Internet, I can create in a file that can be easily copied and passed around. For example, I wrote a small free tips book that has been downloaded more than 100,000 times. It has brought me more business than any other form of marketing.

MICHEL FORTIN
http://successdoctor.com

Why Haven't You Written a Book Yet?

> " *Writing ranks among the top 10% of professions in terms of prestige.*
>
> Jean Strouse, *Newsweek,* as quoted by Dan Poynter in *The Self-Publishing Manual: How to Write, Print and Sell Your Own Book*
>
> (2001© Para Publishing) "

Has the idea of writing a book always intrigued you, but you don't know where to start? Or you think you don't have time? Or perhaps, it doesn't intrigue you at all, and just sounds like some sort of punishment? Let's get all these thoughts out in the open and move past them, because for starters, writing a book is not optional.

You see, writing a book is not only the best way, it is the indisputably essential way, to establish your credibility in your field of expertise. Using authorship as a marketing strategy brings you an on-going flow of clients who are deliberately and purposefully seeking you.

Here's the best news: You don't have to be a great writer to publish a great business book. Also your book doesn't have to be a Charles Dickens masterpiece to get across what you want to say, nor does the process of writing have to consume all of your time. You can publish an informative, authoritative book in a very short amount of time for a nominal cost. Since you must write a book and get it published, it is good to know that there are some workable strategies for doing it.

Keep in mind that your first book does not have to compete with every book in the bookstores. In fact, initially you are going to be just using it as a marketing tool to build your reputation as the obvious expert. Did you know that today sixty percent of all books are not sold in bookstores? They are distributed through other channels, such as book clubs,

Write About Your Passion

When I wrote *Elder Rage, or Take My Father . . . Please! How To Survive Caring For Aging Parents,* I didn't have a clue about publishing. I had just spent a torturous year care giving for my elderly parents and felt compelled to teach others what I had learned. Since I had never written anything but a postcard, I knew I needed endorsements. I was honored to receive 44: Steve Allen, John Bradshaw, Hugh Downs, Duke University, Dr. Dean Edell, John Gray, Mark Victor Hansen, Johns Hopkins, Regis Philbin, U.S. Senator John D. "Jay" Rockefeller, Dr. Bernie Siegel, Dr. Nancy Snyderman/ ABC News . . .

These celebrities were kind to help me get started, and then the book gained a following. Now I am a national speaker on eldercare awareness and reform. Write about what you know and are passionate about.

JACQUELINE MARCELL
http://www.ElderRage.com

Stick To Your Convictions

Don't be afraid to say what you mean, even if it upsets some people. When I wrote *The Surrendered Wife: A Practical Guide to Finding Intimacy, Passion* and *Peace with a Man*, I knew the title would be misunderstood, but at the same time I felt strongly it was the right title. My publisher wasn't so sure—until we got calls from *Dateline, the Today Show, The View, Time* magazine, *The New York Times* and *People* magazine.

Some people were infuriated by the title. But behind the controversy was a paradigm shift that helped hundreds of thousands of women save and transform their marriages by relinquishing control of their husbands' lives and focusing on their own happiness. The title created incredible interest in the book. Sure, I took a lot of heat, but I also became a *New York Times Best Seller.* Most importantly, women who needed my book got the message because it was everywhere in the media.

Laura Doyle
http://www.surrenderedwife.com

associations, seminars or the Internet. Your goal is to get something in print and use the right distribution channels to get it to your target audience.

You do not have to go through one of the big publishing houses to get in print. You can always go back later and negotiate with top name publishers after you have begun a grassroots effort to share your words with the world. For now, just publish a book to use as your ultimate marketing tool—anything else that happens with your book beyond that is the whipped cream on top of the icing already on your cake. See—the pressure over this 'book writing' task is already beginning to lighten up, isn't it?

Now factor in the next bit of good news—you don't have to know everything in the world about your subject matter to write a good book. You just have to know more than most people know about your subject. You need to know something that other people will want to know and you need to be able to organize what you write in a way that other people can follow. We guarantee that by the time you are finished researching what you need to research in order to write the book, you will be an expert on your subject nonetheless.

Okay, so you may be thinking, 'Even if I can get this written, I can't give away all of that information. If my book teaches others everything I know, then clients won't need me. They won't hire me. And won't I be training my competition?'

These are common misconceptions and they should not be a concern. In the first place, you cannot help everyone in person, one-on-one. Think of your readers and your clients as having the potential to be two different audiences. Many of the clients inspired to turn to you because of your book will realize your expertise can help them. But perhaps they aren't ready to hire you as a consultant; they are candidates for your other informational products. People in positions of authority—those who can afford to hire you—make the best clients. They want to see that you know enough to have written a book, that you have solutions to their problems and then they want to hire you to solve their problems better, faster and more efficiently than they could do themselves.

And when it comes to your competition, look at it this way: you want consumers and potential clients in general to perceive consultants in your field as valuable, helpful and ethical. You want to educate others that consultants in your field are essential to solving problems. You are never harmed professionally when you raise the bar for standards in your industry unless you had planned on never learning more and never advancing in your skills and knowledge yourself.

If you are currently ahead of your competition in the quality of service you provide, and you continue to strengthen and refine your skills, then you are likely to always stay ahead of your competition—and you know what they say about imitation and flattery.

Now about your concerns over not having enough time to write your book; history has proven that time is not always the critical ingredient:

> Robert Louis Stevenson wrote *The Strange Case of Dr. Jekyll and Mr. Hyde* in three days.

> Fyodor Dostoevsky (always on deadline for his books) wrote *The Gambler* in twenty-six days.

> Jack London averaged more than three novels per year, every year for sixteen years.

No computers, no word-processing, no spell check, not even electric typewriters. Enough said?

They'll Say, You Wrote the Book!

"

If you hear a voice within you say 'you cannot paint,' *then by all means paint, and that voice will be silenced.*

Vincent Van Gogh

"

Create Products To Increase Your Visibility

It doesn't take very long as a consultant to realize that it's crucial to your long-term success to produce and market some products with your key ideas. Here are some products you can create for increased reputation, visibility and income.

1 Single Audiotape.
Tape a program and/or several pages of scripted material and then blend the live and scripted pieces together.

2 Topic Summary Card.
Summarize your key points and laminate them on a 3×5 card.

3 Workbook.
Produce a 16 to 96-page workbook covering your key ideas.

4 Audio Album.
Consisting of two to six cassettes, fifteen to thirty minutes per side.

5 Single Video.
Encourage your customers to videotape one of your programs.

6 Book.
This is the best credibility builder! If you can't find a good publisher, consider self-publishing. You can substantially increase your market visibility and generate tens of thousands of dollars of extra revenue every year by simply creating new products and selling them creatively before, during and after every one of your consulting engagements.

TONY ALESSANDRA
http://www.alessandra.com

Get Your Message Out To The Public

I spent 20 years helping people learn how to invest safely without using a broker. But this was on a one-on-one basis. Being a freelance writer and needing to get this information out to the whole population, I wrote a book about it; *Building Your Financial Portfolio on $25 a Month (or Less)*. Almost five years later, and now in its third edition, the book has been read by more than 100,000 people, not including library readers and our seminar attendees. Now I have a best selling book that has won several awards and I am getting my very important message out to the general public. Writing and actively marketing this book has led to doing more than 100 seminars a year around the country as well as overseas. As the old saying goes, the author is the expert.

BOBBIE CHRISTENSEN
ELPBooks@aol.com

Here are some coping strategies to get you started on your book:

Narrow your subject matter. You are not writing an encyclopedia. Don't try to write your knowledge about everything in the world. Pick one piece of one subject that you think you know more about than most people know. "How to" topics especially lend themselves to this type of writing.

Start writing. Sit down at the computer, write longhand on a piece of paper or speak into a tape recorder. Do whatever you feel comfortable doing, but dump out everything you know about your subject matter. It doesn't have to be perfect. It doesn't have to be organized. It just has to be sorted in a way that you can later go back and determine what you have and what to do with it. When you're finished laying it out, you can clean up your writing or have your tape transcribed by someone else and print what you have. Another approach to get started writing is using an outline. Be sure to try the outlining exercise at the end of this chapter.

Hire someone to write for you. If you absolutely feel you cannot write, you are not alone. There are captains of industry who are not good at constructing logical sentence patterns, managing grammar or even just finding the right words. This problem does not have to be a showstopper. You can pay a ghostwriter to create your book. Ghostwriters typically spend hours interviewing you and poring through your notes, workshop agendas, speeches, research and other documentation on your subject matter. They will turn your knowledge and thoughts into a cohesive format ready to publish. When published, the book will bear your name as the author. If you need this kind of support, you may be surprised at how easily this alternative can be put into action.

Write Reports

If you want to get something published quickly, without taking time to write a book, a good alternative is to write a report. A report is an authoritative look at your specialty subject, typically anywhere from twelve to forty-eight pages in length.

Just as with books, reports can be sent to potential clients and other people you meet, who may someday need your services. Reports can be more industry specific than books, focusing in-depth on a particular facet of an issue that might be helpful to a potential client or group.

As with books, people are far less likely to throw away a meaty report on a subject that pertains to their industry—especially if you add a little fancy binding to it, so that they can easily bookshelf the report with their other reference books. If readers glean even one piece of valuable information from your report, they will see you as an expert in your field.

Try this simple and effective way to master authoring both reports and a book. Give yourself deadlines, then write and publish one report each month on a related theme. At the end of a year, you will have twelve published reports. And guess what? Twelve reports just happen to translate into an ideal length for a book. Add your introductory chapter, organize your reports topically and publish them.

The Best Publisher May Be 'Self-Publisher'

Self-publishing is a quick, economical way to achieve authorship. You take your book, or perhaps collections of your newsletters, special reports or seminar content, and go directly to a printer. With the new technology of digital printing you can print small quantities of books, say twenty-five to fifty copies for $5 to $10 each. If you print a larger quantity, like 3,000 books, you could get the price down to less then $2 each—that's less investment than what some consultants have made in fancy brochures.

You can handle all of the marketing and distribution of the product yourself or hire people you choose to do it for you. As a self-publisher, you invest your time and money, but you receive

Take Your Show On The Road

Writing a book gives evidence that you are an expert. Marketing the book is often an overlooked necessity. It pays to take your show on the road. Book signing events are high-impact, low-cost publicity at its best, and media coverage makes a huge difference.

Before one signing event for *A Millennium Primer: Take Charge of Your Life,* four TV and radio hosts interviewed me and the newspaper ran a story with a color photo of the book. There was standing room only that evening! Everyone bought a book, and many stood in line to talk with me afterward. One young woman commented, "My family is waiting for me in the car, but I don't want to leave." Seminars and speaking engagements often follow signing events and further your reputation as an expert.

JO CONDRILL
http://www.goalminds.com

the benefit of having complete control of the process and all of the profits along the way. More importantly, self-publishing can save you valuable time.

Working with a publishing company typically involves the process of submitting query letters to the publisher, awaiting permission to submit your manuscript or sample chapters of your book and then waiting again for the publisher's reply. Actually getting a printed book in your hands takes even longer, with the typical average being eighteen to twenty-four months before the words you have written finally reach the marketplace. Add a few publisher rejections, which force you to start the process all over again, and you can see why many authors turn to self-publishing. The already tedious route becomes even more frustrating if you have time-sensitive material. Self-publishing eliminates the waiting; it is a proactive process.

According to a *Writer's® Digest* poll, sixty percent of all publishing firms do the final editing, twenty-three percent select book titles, twenty percent will not consult the author on the cover design and thirty-seven percent don't involve authors in promoting their own material.

A publishing company may offer only four to six percent royalties, compared with the one hundred percent you get if you self-publish. And your costs can be greatly offset by all those tax advantages you gain through self-publishing and self-promoting.

Dan Poynter, in his book *Writing Nonfiction, Turning Thoughts into Books*, (2000©, Para Publishing) describes the New "Book" Model: technology has finally arrived to enable us to write, produce, sell and promote books faster, easier and cheaper. And with technology you can multipurpose your "book" into downloadable CD and eBook versions. You can bring maximum value out of your work by spinning off audiotapes, videotapes, magazine excerpts, foreign-language editions and more.

Ultimately the choice of publishing company versus self-publishing is a decision that every author has to weigh and

Write It Right

Writing a book is very simple. However, writing a good book that will be read is a difficult, arduous, gut-wrenching process that will push you to the very limits of your being. When you communicate orally, you can twist the truth and make stuff up as you go. But when your words are put to paper, they must be honest and accurate because you will be held accountable for them.

So make a commitment to block the time and to do the work. And whatever you do, don't skimp on the details or on the talent you surround yourself with. In the end, you will have created a body of knowledge that will feed your business for years to come.

ERIC CHESTER
http://GenerationWhy.com

evaluate the best option for his or her product and situation. But do not think that publishing or self-publishing is strictly an either/or choice. Many times the ideal answer is for the author to plan to do both.

Authors Ken Blanchard and Spencer Johnson's remarkably successful book, *The One-Minute Manager*, was self-published first, for use in their workshops. Twenty thousand plus copies and a few revisions later, they sold the book to a publishing house, which took it to the top of the *New York Times* bestseller list.

Self-publish and reap the almost instantaneous benefits of having a book in your hand; then contact publishers (or let the publishers come to you) and reissue your book, publish future books or do both. Just remember, for immediacy and control, you can't beat self-publishing to guarantee that you get your book in your hands, when you want it, the way you want it. And did you know that the idea of self-publishing is not exactly new?

Charles Dickens did not start writing *A Christmas Carol* until October of 1843. He was motivated—not by great creative inspiration—but by his personal need for extra Christmas cash. Dickens finished this great classic by Thanksgiving, in less than six weeks writing time, and then he self-published!

It seems that Dickens wanted the book out in time for Christmas sales, he wanted to control the design of the cover and he wanted to choose the paper stock himself. Publishing houses were just not cooperative. So, despite absence of television ads, mass merchandising bookstore chains in malls, and no appearances on Leno, Oprah or Good Morning America, *A Christmas Carol*, hit the market as a self-published book. It sold over six thousand copies in the first week it was on the racks.

Follow Your Vision

Writing and publishing a book is a great starting point if you want to be considered an expert in your industry—but it is only the beginning. The key is to write a 'good' book that is better in some way than those already written on the subject and then to market it in every way possible.

In 1986, I was advised that it was fruitless to write another business planning book. Sixteen years later, the "fruitless" book, *Anatomy of a Business Plan,* is still on the market in its fifth edition and it has helped more than a million business owners through the process of writing a business plan. Listen to yourself and follow your vision.

LINDA PINSON
http://www.business-plan.com

An Eye-Catching Cover Is Key

Because the cost to produce a book is so high, I decided to test the waters by producing a fifty-page 'sound bite' color-fully illustrated pamphlet titled *Brainwriting! for Sales.* Local bookstores kept it close to the checkout counter as last minute, point of purchase sales.

Buoyed by its success, I embarked upon my second *Brainwriting*, this time a 200-page book. I had hoped that it would be distributed nationally. Thank goodness I found a knowledgeable book agent to guide me through the maze of self-publishing do's and don'ts. The most important part of selling a book to the public is the front and back cover. I worked with three graphic designers before I found the winning illustrations for the front cover. Marketing could not even begin until that process was complete. Hooray! *Brainwriting* is now in its third printing.

IRENE LEVITT
http://Irenelevitt.com

66

Most authors struggle for years to write a book. My first book, Guerrilla Selling, *took 15 months. Now we write them in 12 days. When my co-author Mark Smith and I do a book, we pack ourselves off to a cabin on a lake in Minnesota. We turn the whole place into a writing lab, with a flipchart, two laptops, a printer, Internet hookup, and boxes and boxes of books and research backmatter. We keep each other focused and motivated, and we conquer writer's block by setting a 7,500-word goal for the day. If we make it, we go fishing. Otherwise, we work late. We eat a lot of brain food: fish, nuts, eggs and beer. The writing progresses in intense creative bursts, separated by long, languid days of re-writing and editing, punctuated by brilliant sunsets, fighting bass, and fresh-from-the-lake bluegill. The book unfolds in its own way, like a rose opening in the sun. It feels more like a vacation. We've done three books this way, including* Guerrilla Negotiating, *and all three have been wildly successful, earning hundreds of thousands of dollars in royalties, speaking and consulting fees.*

Orvel Ray Wilson

Book Shepherds

If all this still seems overwhelming and that it would take too much time and effort, then you could always hire a consultant who specializes in book production (otherwise known as a book shepherd) to handle part of or even the whole process for you. Book shepherds use their expertise and contacts to make sure your book project is properly handled from beginning to end.

From consulting on the initial concept, editing, typesetting, design, selecting the right printer, obtaining a distributor if desired, and marketing. They work with authors to efficiently and economically guide them step by step through the production and marketing process. For a free downloadable report on *"How to Quickly and Affordably Get Your Book Published"* visit the website:

www.mastermindpublishing.com/bookshepherd.

Book Work

Once you have the actual printed document that bears your name as the author, (usually piled up in boxes in your garage) it is time to put the book to work. Your book now replaces any brochure you might have used as an initial contact tool. Send your book to people who might need your services, or who might know someone who might need your services, now or in the future.

Instead of asking for business, you now are sending your prospects a cover letter that says you are enclosing the book in case they should find it helpful. You are planting the seeds in their minds that you are the person they should seek when they need help in your area of expertise. Instead of trying to tell them that you are knowledgeable, you are showing them proof and letting them deduce that you are the obvious expert.

Ideally, your book will create immediate activity within your business. As people start connecting your name with your specialty, you will be sought out not only by prospects, but also by the media or by business leaders who have a vested interest in what you do.

Find a Corporate Partner

Our valued friend, Roger Parker got his publishing start in an innovative way: He found a company that had a problem he could solve by writing a book and he offered to do it for a low price. The company had nothing to lose and Roger had

Ask Other Consultants To Contribute

After becoming a professional organizer in 1996 and creating a website and ezine shortly afterward, I was constantly being contacted about how to become an organizer. I've recently completed *Secrets of a Professional Organizer and How-To Become One.* Besides my own knowledge, I solicited other organizers to contribute quotes, tips and articles to be included. This worked out well, especially for areas I wasn't the 'expert' in, and as a result I have fifteen other experts in my book.

Decide what areas/topics you want to include in your book and start collecting everything you can find on your topic, especially your own writings and thoughts. Before you know it, you will have all the information for your chapters. Then it is just a matter of organizing your materials into chapters. Because of my book, I now have many new consulting clients and my value has doubled!

JANET HALL
http://www.overhall.com

Share Your Mission Through A Book

Writing and publishing a book is a great way to take the information you have and share it with the public. My book, *Sipping Tea and Doing Business* has helped to position me as an expert business and marketing consultant. I have been asked to speak on numerous occasions and have received publicity due to writing this book. Through the book and this concept, we have developed a member association and partnered with other organizations to provide services for women in business and aspiring business entrepreneurs. In addition, the book has given us national exposure.

SHERONDE GLOVER
http://www.sippingteaonline.com

everything to gain because writing the book would help him finally get into print.

The company, which manufactured software, had begun selling a new product that not all of its customers were using to its full potential. Roger's book would be a 'how-to' telling them, in basic language, some simple tips for using the software. Roger proposed that the company give away the book as a bonus to customers who registered their software after purchasing it. That way, the company would be able to keep in touch with the customers to sell them upgrades on the software. The company's salespeople could also use the book as a leave-behind when they met with potential clients.

"There is something magical about a book you can hold in your hand," Roger says. "We chose the minimum physical size that had value: 5×7 inches and sixty-eight pages. This size book has substance, it feels good and it had a lot of substantive information."

Today Roger has over thirty books under his belt, including bestseller, *Looking Good in Print; The Streetwise Guide to Relationship Marketing on the Web; Microsoft Publisher 2000: Professional Results; Microsoft Office Windows for Dummies; Roger C. Parker's Guide to Web Content and Design;* and *Desktop Publishing and Design for Dummies.*

Before he broke the ice with the first corporate book, he sent out proposals to publishers and was turned down countless times. No one wanted to take a chance on an unpublished author. Once he wrote that first book, which went out to about 250,000 people, publishers started coming to him. Suddenly he was perceived as the obvious expert.

Sell Your Books and Reports

After your work is published, you can actually turn your books and reports into a revenue-producing venture. You can sell them from your website, through print ads in periodicals or at the back of the room when you are conducting a seminar.

Consultants commonly sell reports even after they write their first, second, third or one-hundredth book. Reports cost very little to produce because you can photocopy them on demand and invest only in exactly the number you want to sell on any given day. Yet, despite their low production cost, you can sell reports for the same price (or more) as you sell your book. People may eagerly pay $50 for a special report, because they are getting the benefit of the information now instead of having to wait for it to appear in book form. A good report puts the reader ahead of their competition.

Reports can also help you bankroll your business, not only through direct sales but through new leads. Frank Candy, President of the American Speakers Bureau and an IGPC faculty member who has written numerous reports, says one in particular led to quite a bit of business.

The Ultimate Guide to Successful Tradeshow Marketing came out in 1995 after a friend asked Frank to conduct a seminar for people who would be setting up booths at a tradeshow. The friend thought if Frank could teach people how to successfully work their shows, the event would be better, the tradeshow booths would get better results and the organization sponsoring the event would be much happier.

The problem came in the scheduling; booth participants couldn't attend a seminar and set up their booths at the same time. So Frank offered to write a report. His friend said, "Great. Can you have it done in three days?"

"I did," Frank says. "The eight-page report has withstood the test of time and has continued to be a staple in the tradeshow industry. This one report has generated well over $100,000 in business for me."

Go Electronic

These days you do not even have to spend the money on paper and publishing to have a book or report on your list of accomplishments. Certain software programs allow you to

Get Endorsements From Booksellers

Publishing my first book, *High Income Consulting,* still an international best seller after 12 years, was easy. Ron Holland, himself a writer of several best sellers, suggested the way to have publishers beat a path to your door. I wrote a one-page synopsis and a brief letter asking the key retailers whether such a book, if I wrote it, would sell. My phone rang off the hook with publishers, alerted by their favorite book buyers, fighting each other for a book that I had yet to write. Eight more books, translations into 13 languages and 10 years of royalties later, I am still grateful to Ron for the best advice I ever acted on.

TOM LAMBERT
www.centreforconsultingexcellence.com

Revenue Streams

Publishing a book is not only a potentially significant money-maker in and of itself, but can dramatically increase your credibility and marketability in your field. The derivative revenue streams are as many as you can imagine. Publishing is also much easier than ever before. It is no longer necessary to hire an expensive agent to write dozens of proposals and schmooze the New York publishing houses. Thanks to the advent of print-on-demand technology, for a few hundred dollars, anyone can have their print-ready book catalogued with the Library of Congress and available for distribution through the largest online channels like Amazon and Barnes & Noble.com. Capturing your specialized knowledge and expertise in print may be the greatest credential-builder and marketing tool you have ever pursued.

DAVID WELLS
http://www.thesimpleway.net

publish in electronic format, so people can download and read your eBook, carry it around on their PDA or, print it and read it anywhere, anytime they choose. Select software that will format your eBook to do what you want it to do, such as include hyperlinks, graphics, searches, forms and other non-text elements.

Publishing an eBook is as easy as creating a website. One unique advantage to an eBook is that it lets you change your mind after you have published. Once you have written your book, you can always update your information anytime you like to include new data or new suggestions and resources. Best of all, you can put an eBook into the hands of your clients and prospects instantly.

A good source for more information about eBook technology and the options available for publishing electronically, is the website **http://e-books.org**. This site describes itself as a non-commercial repository of information related to eBook research and products. The site is designed and maintained by the Kent State University Institute for CyberInformation for FX Palo Alto Laboratory, Inc.

In addition to eBooks, some consultants have had success selling their books in audiocassette tape or audio CD format. There is a special advantage to audio books, because they are so effective for an audience that commutes to work or travels frequently.

Just do it. With all due respect to Nike—just do it! Once you've done it you are the expert. You know the correct answers . . . you know who to call, what to say, where to go, when and why things happen. You are the obvious expert.

Robert Britton

IGPC faculty member, Nick Nichols, says audio books have worked for him. He converts eBooks into audiocassette tapes in his home studio. If you do not have professional equipment, you can go to a recording studio, spend approximately two hundred dollars, and get a professionally made tape that you then convert to an audiocassette. Make multiple tapes in whatever quantity you need at an audio duplication service and you have audiotapes ready to sell, send for self-promotion or both.

"When you meet people, give them an audiocassette of what you've done," Nick says. "An audiocassette has as great an impact as a special report or a book does, because it's you talking and potential clients can listen to the tape in their car or at home; they don't have to physically sit down and read it. This can be an effective way of getting your obvious expert message out to people so that they know you know what you're talking about and that you can help them."

Another strategy used by prolific author and consultant Fred Gleeck, is interviewing someone in his field whose specialty complements his but does not directly compete with it. Fred and an industry peer whose business was similar to his; both recorded telephone interviews of each other. They had tapes made of the interviews, and each of them distributed the tapes.

"When you have another expert interviewing you, it helps you build your obvious expert credibility because that person can ask you very targeted questions and can make comments about you and your work that wouldn't be as credible if you said them yourself," Fred says. "Even if you're just the interviewer, you build obvious expert credibility with people because they associate you with the other expert."

Set a Deadline and Get It Done

It does not matter whether your book is three hundred pages or a thirty-page report. Either way, your clients will perceive it as an authoritative publication—which is how you can make it work for you. Write and publish. You will end up with concrete

Write About It!

If you don't consider yourself an expert on a topic yet, the easiest way to become one is to research, write and publish a book, eBook or workbook. Through the writing process, you will learn a great deal! Of course, it helps to write about what you have a strong interest in.

I did just that. I enjoy learning about "whole life" issues—love, labor and leisure–and used my interest as the basis to write a series of books called *Get Smart!* Now I am able to make profits from the sale of *Get Smart! About Modern Romantic Relationships, Get Smart! About Modern Career Development, Get Smart! About Modern Stress Management,* and half a dozen workbooks/eBooks that I have developed. It's easy once you get started!

What would you like to get smart about and become an expert in?

MICHELLE L. CASTO
http://www.getsmartseries.com

proof of your expertise, written in your own words. You will be delighted with how good this feels.

There is no way any single book can outline everything everyone needs to know about a particular situation, or resolve all of the problems your clients might run into—don't try! Clients recognize that they need to come to an obvious expert for specialized and in-depth service.

Being an author, and having a book or report with your name on it, sets you apart from the competition. After all, who would a potential client rather hire: the consultant who studied all the strategies in his or her field, or the consultant who wrote the books that the other consultant used for study?

> 66 ———————————————————
>
> *In today's world, a consultant who hasn't written a book isn't much a of a consultant. . . A book is the ability to articulate a collection of wisdom.*
>
> Doug Hall 99

Here is one more thought on the topic of writing. Forget the value of a book as a self-promotional tool. Forget how much it adds to your perceived authority and expertise. If you wrote your book and no one ever read it but you, your efforts would still have great value to your consulting business. Why? Because you will never know and understand, you will never have such ownership of knowledge, as you do after you have been through the process of organizing, defining and putting your thoughts into words.

Take a subject that you know infinitely well, believe you know inside and out, and then write about it. When the process is complete, you will be astounded to realize how much more and how much better you came to understand your own area of expertise simply because of the writing process.

Why do teachers direct their students to write essays, why to psychologists direct their patients to write journals? Translating

95% Mental

Writing and getting published is 95% mental, and I don't mean intellectually. The mental aspect I am referring to is determination. Remember this—Planning to write is not writing. Thinking about writing is not writing. Talking about writing is not writing. Researching to write, and outlining to write are not writing. None of this is writing. Writing is writing. Place this little ramble somewhere near where you write. Don't listen to anyone who isn't 100% behind what you are doing. Don't quit on your dream, and I promise anyone who is reading this, you will be published!

ROBERT JOLLES
http://www.Jolles.com

our thoughts, intuitions and intellectual data into organized statements and a language 'code' forces us to deal with the information in both an abstract way and a concrete way. It also forces visual and kinesthetic learners to utilize the verbal portions of their brain.

Writing a book not only helps your potential clients see you as the obvious expert, it actually contributes an important first-step in your seeing yourself that way.

> **"**
>
> *According to legend,* Woody Allen *once said that 50% of writing is putting the first word on a piece of paper.*
>
> *Indeed getting started is what stops most people from writing. These tips can help you get going:*
>
> **1** *Start anywhere. You don't need to begin at the beginning. You can decide later what goes first. Just write.*
>
> **2** *Don't worry about grammar and flow. You, or you and your editor, can buff it later.*
>
> **3** *Outlining is okay. Write in a loose form; you can always change it.*
>
> **4** *Once you have started, keep going. Before you know it you will have finished the hardest part—the first draft.*
>
> Mary Westheimer **"**

For more information on
Publishing Books and Reports, visit:

www.obvious-expert.com/books

More Than One Way To Write A Book

Would you like to write a book that helps many people and makes you a lot of money, but you don't have a topic? Do what I have done and show people in your industry (or another industry) how to solve a major set of problems.

I've written sales script books that show people in different industries how to handle the toughest objections, questions and resistances they encounter. One of my books has sold more than $1 million and another sold more than $250,000 worth of copies.

If you don't have the answers to the problems or objections, interview the top experts in the field. I wrote one sales script book with the top financial planner in the world, Tom Gau, CFP. We give his exact words for handling the toughest objections any financial planner gets. These are the words that enable Tom to earn more than $3 million a year while working part time. We've sold more than 1,000 copies of this book at $250 each.

By showing companies hundreds of the exact scripts that lead to closing sales, we have been able to increase their sales by hundreds of millions of dollars. For doing this writing, I have been paid a few million dollars. This is truly a win-win solution for all parties.

DONALD MOINE
http://www.DrMoine.com

Wordsmithing Fundamentals

Like most activities, writing is a process that comes more easily for some people than for others. If you are not in the group who can effortlessly produce written masterpieces, don't despair; you are in the majority. But being "word" and/or "grammar-challenged" does not have to prevent you from writing a book. Following some simple guidelines can make the process much easier.

Writing your first book is your chance to see how much you remember about the wisdom of your high school or college English teachers. Wouldn't they be flattered to know you were drawing on the information they tried so relentlessly to pound into your brain? More importantly, isn't it good to know that most of what they told you was dead-on target?

> *I've written three books and revised two of them. Before you start, make a clear, specific outline and stick to it. You will save days of time. Even plan about how many pages you'll make each chapter. And that will get your book out. But what you really need to do when writing it is be calling anyone who might want to use your book, write about your book, sell your book or have you want to speak about your book. That way when it's done, you are ready to go.*
>
> Claudyne Wilder

#1 Organization

 Start by organizing your thoughts. There are a few people with such awesome wordsmithing talent that they can sit down and let the ideas flow, with the end product being a Pulitzer Prize for literature. Everyone else needs to start with an outline. (See how much this already sounds like high school English class?) Begin your outline with the intended title of your book.

◆ **Next write a thesis statement.** This key sentence forms the crux of your book; it is what you know that other people want to know.

Example:

You can effectively rid your home of harmful environmental allergens in six easy steps.

Break down your thesis sentence and analyze it to see if the words say exactly what **you want to say.** Study the boxed example on the next page to help you better understand how to analyze your thesis statement; it is the most important concept of your book—it is the backbone of all your text.

◆ **Compare your thesis statement to your intended title.** Do they mesh? Do you need to adjust one to match the other? For this particular book on allergen control, perhaps the title is: *Six Proven Ways for Pet Lovers to Rid Their Houses of Environmental Allergens Without Moving Out or Hiring a Maid.* Do not be afraid to hammer and pound away at your thesis statement and title until they express precisely what you want them to convey to your reader and they interlock perfectly, supporting each other. If you can get the thesis statement, the title and the points or arguments of the outline to flow logically and say what you really want to say, then your written word will almost always be clear and logical. Following this plan, if you do have problems with the book, they will typically be small problems and will not require major rewrites.

#2 *Structure*

◆ Set aside the beginning of your book (probably the first chapter) to suggest what you are about to explain to the reader. Include your thesis statement and your personal story—this is the collection of experiences that qualifies you to write the book. Your personal story is also what keeps you from preaching to your reader and puts you in the position of sharing with the reader. Done correctly, your personal story is what makes you and the reader intimate; it causes the reader to identify similarities between your life and his or her own.

◆ The next chapters are easy; they are the problem and solution sets that back up your thesis. Each chapter represents one or more problems that you (and your research sources) solve for the reader. In our hypothetical book on allergens, we offer the reader

EXERCISE

Analyze the following sentence to better understand how a thesis works:

> ### *"You can effectively rid your home of harmful environmental allergens in six easy steps."*

"You"

(The word "you" is your subject) Your subject means the reader, the book buyer. Does the subject of your thesis statement match your intended reader?

"can effectively rid "

("can effectively rid" is your verb and adverb) Your verbs show the action you are telling your reader how to accomplish. Your adverb describes the action of the verb.

"your home of harmful environmental allergens in six easy steps."

("your home of harmful environmental allergens in six easy steps" are your prepositional phrases and the objects of the phrases.) Prepositions and their objects narrow and define the range of the intended action. Choose each of these words carefully; they are the meat and potatoes of your book. If your book, for instance, includes ways to get rid of allergens at your home and your office, then your thesis statement should reflect this. If you plan to include chapters on food allergies, then say so and do not narrow the thesis statement to only environmental allergens.

six problem and solution sets. Think of each chapter as being your answer to the argument the reader might raise when you say, "Your environmental allergy problem can be solved in six easy steps."

◆ Finally, wrap it all up. Give your book closure. In a sense, say, "these are the problems I said I would solve and these are the solutions I offered." Then offer your reader a bit more. Recommend books, websites and seminars. A confident author never shies away from sending the reader to other experts.

◆ When you have completed your simple outline, you have given your book logical structure to follow that will make it easier to read. You will have also made the book much easier to write, which is the next step.

#3 *Appearance*

◆ Create a computer file that represents your entire book. Format this file as a manuscript. Choose "print layout" or a comparable setting, to view your work so that your pages always appear like book pages—reinforcing the message to your brain that this collection of words is your book.

Even if you plan to typeset your own words, while you are initially writing, keep your formatting style very simple. Be a writer only. You can be a typesetter, graphic artist and publisher later.

◆ For your working document (a book in progress), left justify your text.

◆ Chose a simple serif font like `Courier New`. This font is not what you want for final print, but for a working document, it is a particularly good choice. Each letter width is exactly the same as every other letter, helping you get an accurate count of the letters and spaces in your document.

◆ Using `12 point, Courier New` font, set your page margins at one inch all the way around and your paragraph spacing at "exactly 25 lines." You will create pages with a consistent number of spaces, from one page to the next. This formula results in approximately two hundred and fifty words per page. Based on this standard, figure:

> 200 pages × 250 words per page = 50,000 words
> 75,000 words yields 300 pages, and so on.

When your word-processed book is typeset and font selections are made, along with the addition of headings, titles and other elements, your words per page count will change. Large print books average about 250 words per page, academic books may go up to 600 words per page, and everything else tends to run between 325 and 400 words per page of printed text.

Most book publishers suggest you need at least one hundred book pages to create a product that feels like a book and not like a booklet to the purchaser. Is your book long enough that the book buyer will feel they have paid for something of value?

How Long Should Your Book Be?	# Of Pages
Qualifies for U.S. Postal Service "Book Rate" mailing	8+
Qualifies for Library of Congress card catalog number.	50+
Qualifies for listing in *Books in Print* by R.R. Bowker.	50+

EXERCISE

Outline
Title

I. **Chapter 1**
   a. Introduction (what prompted you to write this book)
   b. Thesis statement (what is the idea/philosophy/argument/suggestions that drive this book?)
   c. What will you discuss to back up your argument?

II. **Chapter 2**
   a. Problem
   b. Solution set to back up the thesis statement.

III. **Chapter 3**
   a. Problem
   b. Solution set to back up the thesis statement.

IV. **Chapter 4**
   a. Problem
   b. Solution set to back up the thesis statement.

V. **Chapter 5**
   a. Problem
   b. Solution set to back up the thesis statement.

VI. **Chapter 6**
   a. Problem
   b. Solution set to back up the thesis statement.

VII. **Chapter 7**
   a. Problem
   b. Solution set to back up the thesis statement.

VIII. **Chapter 8**
   a. Conclusion
   b. Wrap up; summary of thesis statement
   c. Closure to book

During the writing phase of your book, the less formatting you add, the less you or someone else laying out the book for you, will have to replace later. Besides, this is the stage in developing your book to think about your words, not their finished appearance. This is the time to focus your thoughts and just write!

When all of your words are in place, run spellchecker and grammar check. Print your document, read it silently then read it aloud and make corrections. Then find a trusted, knowledgeable friend and let them take a red pencil to your masterpiece-in-progress.

Parting Thoughts:

> **"**
>
> *Years ago, I was asked by a friend to help a friend of his write a book about Elvis Presley. The man with whom I was to work was an associate of Presley's when the King began to climb the ladder of success. We agreed I would write as he told his story. The result was a fairly successful and honest book about Presley. We both enjoyed the experience, and we even made some money. Look for opportunities! I went on to a career in publishing. My retirement is now spent writing, working as a foreign rights consultant and traveling to many interesting parts of the world.*
>
> Leslie Slawson Smith
>
> **"**

> **"**
>
> *There is no better way to prove your expertise than by publishing a book. My expertise is women in the workplace and breaking the glass ceiling. My first book,* More Power To You, *showed women how to succeed by being effective communicators. This led to a host of media interviews, speaking engagements, and a second book,* Swim with the Dolphins. *Additional books have followed including* What Queen Esther Knew: Business Advice from a Biblical Sage. *Use your books to establish your credibility and expertise. Carve out a niche as the leading authority in the field. Lucrative speaking engagements and media opportunities will follow.*
>
> Connie Glaser
>
> **"**

CHAPTER 4

Speak Out:
Join The Lecture Circuit

WAR STORY #4 *I was headed home. 250 newly printed self-published books sat in the back seat of my car, and I was feeling great. Then it hit me, just how am I going to get my books in people's hands? I can mail them to some folks, but I can't send them to potential clients I don't know about.*

At that same moment I saw a billboard along the highway that proclaimed, "Welcome to Fresno". It featured the logos of twelve different service clubs in the community and listed the locations and times of their meetings. I had driven past it many times before—and this time, I almost missed its relevance. But the thought struck me, Wait a minute! I can get the word out by creating a free lecture to offer to clubs in and around my hometown.

I turned my car around, drove back and pulled off the highway. With traffic whizzing past me, I sat calmly parked on the side of the road, copying names of clubs and the locations of their meetings.

When I arrived home, I started calling the restaurants where each club met, asking for a contact name for that service club. The people to whom I spoke almost always referred me to the club president and gave me a phone number. I called each contact and said, "Hello, Mr. Jones, this is Elsom Eldridge and I have a new, entertaining and educational program which I think your members will enjoy. Who is in charge of booking speakers for your meeting?"

The club president always referred me to the program chairperson and gave me his or her

A Speaking Marketing Machine

When I moved my consulting practice from San Francisco to Palo Alto, about one hour south, my business started to slow down after a few months. I turned on my "speaking marketing machine" by contacting every professional group and Chamber of Commerce in the area.

As a result I got six or seven speaking engagements over a three month period. Doesn't sound like a lot, but I was diligent with my follow-up and when I tallied my results six months later, I had gained 26 new clients in 26 weeks.

This formed the heart of my practice and things haven't slowed down since.

ROBERT MIDDLETON
http://www.actionplan.com

phone number. Then I would call each program chair and say, "Hello, Mr. Smith. Mr. Jones asked me to give you a call. I have a new lecture I believe will be of great interest to (name of club); it's a free twenty-five minute talk. The topic is: The Seven Secrets for Scoring Higher on Every Test We Have to Take in Life, Guaranteed! I understand you are in charge of all the bookings. What do you think?"

That very afternoon, I called all twelve service clubs. Nine of them asked whether I could mail them some information about my lecture. One group had merged into another. The other two groups said they didn't have a speaker scheduled for the following week and invited me to speak. My entry into the lecture circuit was born.

Before long, I was speaking before five to six groups each week. In the course of the following year, I gave lectures to two hundred and seventy-five clubs within a twenty-five mile radius of Fresno. I was not only a published author, now I was a prominent guest lecturer in my community.

EE Jr.

> . . . Of the nine books I have written, three have landed me speaking engagements, seminars, workshops and many radio interviews. At one of my speaking engagements ten years ago, I was told that I needed a book. I hurriedly put together a twenty-one page booklet and the books expanded from that initial effort.
>
> Ida Greene

Start Talking!

There is no quicker way than the lecture circuit to build the perception that you are an expert. We are not talking about traveling around the globe to speak before crowds of 10,000 people. We are talking about addressing groups of fifteen to one hundred people right in your own community, usually over breakfast, lunch or a chicken dinner.

If you can draw the larger crowds, you can start calling yourself a keynote speaker and command top dollar. And while becoming a keynote speaker is not what happens to most public speakers, such fame could develop for you in the future. In the meantime, concentrate on the local lecture circuit. You will be donating your time—that means "No Fee". But that's okay, because the payoff can be enormous.

As the highly respected motivational speaker, Dottie Walters, points out, "There are many reasons for presenting for 'No Fee'. The majority of speeches in the world are done for no fee; the payoffs are prestige, publicity and fine public relations."

Do not balk at the idea of giving your time away without payment. Think about how fortunate you are that you can run a business and market your product without having to hire an ad agency, develop TV and radio commercials and buy airtime. You can market your product for no greater expense than the investment of your time. Even if you do electronic media or print advertising to promote your consulting services, think of your efforts on the lecture circuit as real bang-for-the-buck self-promotion. Certainly your time is valuable, but how much can you object when the product you are promoting is your reputation?

Where To Speak

In almost every city and town, there are hundreds of service clubs, associations and organizations that need speakers for their meetings. To help you target your best audiences, think about what kinds of services you offer and who might benefit from them. Your local Chambers of Commerce and public library typically have directories of clubs in your area. Your local newspaper usually publishes announcements of upcoming

Life Saver

The local service club lecture circuit saved my life each time I moved to a new city. I would get out the paper, look in the calendar section and call the RSVP number. I'd ask whoever answered for the program chair contact information and I was on my way.

Not only did the service clubs give me a physical platform to strut my stuff, they announced my name in the newspaper and in their newsletter. The experience provided me with an opportunity to network, which brought me an endless stream of retainer and consulting clients and it jumpstarted my social life as well.

I am truly grateful and very appreciative of their role in the community and in my professional and personal life.

RALEIGH PINSKEY
http://www.promoteyourself.com

A Speakers Directory

In 1992 I started a print publication called, *Speakers for Free & Fee Directory* in the Los Angeles area. I knew that if professional folks were given an opportunity to speak before an audience of ten to one hundred, that they could garner business through their speaking. I also knew that no one was offering a connection between the speakers and audiences.

The Directory was successful within six months, a win-win for the speakers and program chairs. In 1994, we began our online version: speaker services.com.

In 1999 we let go of our print publication and are now entirely on the web.

Over the last 10 years, we've trained thousands of folks in the art of public speaking and marketing. Speaking should be part of your marketing plan. It can provide you with multiple streams of income.

SUSAN LEVIN
http://speakerservices.com

meetings. On the Internet, you can go to **www.google.com** or any other efficient search engine and search by your community, region, state, or by club, associations or organization. You will be pleasantly surprised at just how many potential speaking opportunities you will uncover.

Organizations you might want to put on your list include: Alumni associations, American Society for Training and Development, Board of Realtors®, Business and Professional Women, Chambers of Commerce, Elks, Independent Contractors Association, Jaycees, Kiwanis, Lions, Manufacturers Association, National Association of Women Business Owners, National Association of Women in Construction, National Network of Commercial Real Estate Women, Optimists, Rotary, Society for Human Resource Management, Soroptimists and Zonta.

Service clubs usually meet once a week and many business and professional associations meet once a month. For each meeting the groups need a free speaker with about twenty to thirty minutes worth of something interesting to say. The more interesting the speaker, the more accolades the group's program chairperson receives, which can also work to your benefit when opportunities for referrals arise. After successful speaking engagements, always be sure you ask the program chairperson (or the president) to give you a testimonial letter that you can use to promote your program to other organizations.

Remember what it is like to have the program chair's job? In organizations in which you have been active, you may have had the responsibility of recruiting lecturers. Guest speakers don't grow on trees! Your offer to speak will typically be well received, and if it's not, be persistent and follow-up later.

Polish Your Skills

Lecturing is a quick, proven way to build your reputation as an expert. If you are one of the many people who is deathly afraid of speaking in front of groups, there is help. An easy way to gain more speaking skill is to get involved with Toastmasters International® **www.toastmasters.org** in your area.

Toastmasters® groups usually include twenty to thirty people who coach and support each other as they advance their speaking skills. The groups are made up of business people just like you, which means Toastmasters offers good networking opportunities as well as great training in public speaking.

Deliver A Good Speech

Once you've confirmed your speaking date on the service club lecture circuit (or even before), you need to start preparing. Keep in mind that your goal is to provide an interesting, informative lecture, and that doing so promotes your business.

Know your audience. Stay abreast of your local news, and if possible, read organization newsletters. Keep your comments as timely and as personalized as possible to the listening audience. There is no such thing as too much knowledge about the groups that are hosting you as a speaker.

To enhance your chances of getting follow-up business from your lectures on the local circuit, we recommend the following:

Give your lecture an interesting title. When people see the title of your upcoming speech in the group's newsletter, you want them to say, "Oh wow, I can't miss that one." Your title can be humorous or serious, but it must capture the imagination of anyone who might be attending the meeting. Remember, keep your audience in mind.

Write your own introduction. Type it on a 3×5 card or a piece of paper and give it to the program chair or the person who is going to be introducing you to the audience. With a pre-planned intro in hand, the person can introduce you in a manner that lets club members understand they are about to

Start A Domino Effect

I have been able to make the most of my speaking engagements through free publicity. It started when I spoke at a workshop that was hosted by my local township. An acquaintance of mine took a picture of me speaking at the workshop and sent it to the township—that picture and an article about the workshop were in the township newsletter that went to hundreds of homes in the area.

People saw my picture and my name, and contacted me to speak to their groups, or to hire me to help them get organized. And the more often I speak, the more opportunity there is for publicity. That one article really started things rolling.

SUE BECKER
http://www.pilestosmiles.com

hear from a very, very important speaker—an obvious expert.

- If you don't write your own intro, the program chair may stand up and say to the audience, "It's good to see you all here today. Here's our speaker. Good luck."

- As an alternative, you want the person introducing you to say something similar to: "I am so pleased to have the honor today of introducing to you our speaker, test-taking skills expert, Elsom Eldridge Jr. He is a consultant and author who teaches people how to achieve higher test scores—without cheating—and develops strategies through his on-going research that will bring us better scores on each of the tests of life we face daily. He's going to share today, *The Seven Secrets for Scoring Higher on Every Test We Have to Take in Life, Guaranteed!* Please welcome with me, Elsom Eldridge Jr."

- Or how about this one, "We are so happy and privileged to have with us, Elsom Eldridge Jr., expert on how to get higher scores on every test you will take—not only in academia, but in government, business and many other aspects of your life. There are seven strategies Mr. Eldridge has developed through his research, that he reveals in his books, and that he will share with us today. Please join me in welcoming, Elsom Eldridge!"

Create a good speech It doesn't have to be the Gettysburg Address, but it does have to be interesting and informative. Begin by telling the audience members what you're going to say, say it, and then conclude by telling them what you said. In addition, our formula includes: Sprinkle humor throughout. Don't resort to old, tired jokes the audience might have heard before. Try to say something humorous about your topic or recent experiences.

Lunch And Learn

I love to teach, so "Lunch and Learn" seminars at local bookstores, health clubs or office park conference centers are a favorite way to offer my services to the community.

Seminar topics include:

- stress management techniques

- improving organizational skills

- maintaining a work/life balance

- the art of skillful communication

- overcoming fears.

These complimentary seminars are very popular and usually produce a client or two.

BONNIE MORET
http://www.themoretway.
wmnsnetbiz.com

- Give them some facts they've heard before. This helps develop rapport and shows the audience members you know what you're talking about.

- Astound them with some new facts. This information should be something they have not heard about before or at least a different twist.

- Mention two or three clients in the process of your talk. This triggers the thought that you are an expert for hire. You don't have to mention them by name, and should do so only if you have permission from the clients, but at least mention them by circumstance. Be aware, however, that if you mention only clients that are multi-million-dollar corporations, it might backfire on you. The people in your audience will think you're out of their reach unless they also represent multi-million-dollar corporations. Again, keep your audience in mind.

Give the audience members something tangible to take home. We call this our interactive outline and it's different from what other speakers hand out. Most people who speak in front of service clubs give audience members brochures, flyers or business cards. As soon as the members leave, they lose those—or, worse, they leave them right there on the table to be cleaned up along with the dirty dishes. You want them to hang on to your information so they have it when they need it later.

- To create this effective marketing piece, use a folded 8.5×11-inch sheet of paper. At the top of the first page should be the title of your speech. The rest of the booklet should contain an outline of your lecture. On the back page, print your name and all of your contact information. Your name, address and phone number should go at the bottom of all the other pages of this booklet, as well. The key is to leave some blank spaces for the audience members to write information as you're

W.I.I.F.M.?

Here are some valuable tips:

- As an expert, you need to make sure you are introduced properly. Write your own introduction in full. Make it typed, double-spaced, in a large, clear font. Make sure the person introducing you can pronounce your name properly.

- Establish the importance of your topic. Create a context and give a concrete example of how the immediacy of the subject relates to the audience's current interests. Explain how your subject will help them to reach their specific goals and objectives. Spell it out precisely: WIIFM (What's In It For Me).

- Highlight the speaker's (your own) qualifications to present on the particular topic. Say things that are true and relevant to the listeners. Never lie or stretch the truth. Negatives should be turned into positives. Avoid private jokes

- Speak and move effectively. Today in business, what you say is not as important as how you say it. Words account for only a small part of the total message we convey to others. The rest comes from our style, use of voice, body language and other non-verbal forms of communication.

Greater competition requires that we all become better presenters.

PETER BENDER
http://www.peterursbender.com

A Toast To Toastmasters

This is a testimonial to the many benefits I have received, professionally and personally, since joining a local Toastmasters Club over five years ago. At that time I had no clue how to approach speaking professionally. I have now delivered over eighty speeches, with several of them earning me a paycheck as the keynote speaker. The skills I have gained in Toastmasters also aided me in writing and teaching an accredited college course for my local community college.

Toastmasters has enhanced my organization and leadership skills. As an entrepreneur/marketing consultant, this has proved invaluable, as I am always trying to engage in more projects than I have the time to effectively manage. It has taught me invaluable delegation skills and helped me to manage my time and resources more efficiently.

All Toastmasters Clubs operate off the same basic fundamentals of helping develop the individual, so the individual can in turn "source and serve" their respective communities. In the end, I believe Toastmasters has helped me achieve my USP (helping individuals unlock their unlimited potential) better than any organization, or self-help program I have ever participated in. I would highly recommend joining a club to anyone who wants to improve their communication and leadership skills, thus getting more of what they want out of life.

ERIC STEELE
http://www.ericsteele.com

speaking. Periodically during your speech say, "This is important information, so you might want to write it down in your action outline." Once the person's handwriting is on the pages, that document will find a home in his or her office. It is not likely to be thrown away or left behind.

> **"**
> *. . . Rehearse your opening. You have only thirty seconds to grab the interest of your audience. Don't waste it.*
> *. . . Low energy and monotone will kill any presentation. Show genuine enthusiasm. Be visual. People remember what they 'see' in their imaginations. Paint a vivid picture in story form . . . Have a strong closing.*
>
> Patricia Fripp
> **"**

Turn Audience Members Into Clients

Speaking in front of service clubs does not always bring you an immediate stampede of business. We have found that every time you present your lecture, you can expect roughly ten percent of the audience members to respond over a period of time—assuming, your lecture was relevant to the group and that your audience can actually use your services.

But considering you are speaking before a captive audience and there is little to no up-front investment on your part, you're getting good exposure for minimal investment. And the more you deliver speeches, the more your speaking skills improve and the better you become at identifying viable target audiences. Each audience you face presents potential clients of different backgrounds, businesses, economic situations and, most importantly, consulting needs. You will soon start to spot which types of audiences hold the most potential for you.

Think about this: five lectures per week introduces you as the obvious expert to approximately 6,500 people in one year, many of whom will be the leaders in your community. You never know who will be on the other end of the phone the next time you offer your services to speak, or who will be sitting in your next audience, but they could be the next person seeking an obvious expert—and they'll be asking for you.

> " *When you attend club meetings, you need to be sure you are seated in the expert's seat. There are four of these in every meeting room. The only seats where an obvious expert should sit are located in the corners of the room. If you sit in the front left, the front right, the back left or the back right chair in the entire room, then when you stand up, everyone in the room can see you.*
>
> Fred Gleeck "

A SPECIAL CONTRIBUTION FROM
Dottie Walters

Is There Money In Your Mouth And Gold On The Tip Of Your Tongue?

Dottie Walters began her tiny advertising business on foot, pushing a broken baby stroller. With determination and hard work, she built that business into four offices that employed almost three hundred salespeople. Dottie sold this large business to concentrate on her own speaking, giving seminars, writing, and publishing her news magazine, *Sharing Ideas for Professional Speakers*. With us, Dottie shared just how her success-story got its start:

Apply TWO Rules: Passion And Marketing

Rule 1 Have something to say. Something you're passionate about. A topic or issue that comes from your bones. And when you say it, be it. Be your message. Allow it out of your pores, out of your heart, out of your deepest feelings and beliefs. Let it shine from your eyes, be reflected in your stance and your glance, radiate from all your fingertips. Be so enraptured by your feelings and desires that you magnetize your audiences before you even open your mouth.

Rule 2 Be a marketer first, an expert next, a speaker last. (Marketing is creating conditions by which others decide on their own that they want what you've got.) Many fine speakers do not survive because they think the world is going to welcome them with open arms. Sorry, no cigar. You've got to be so dazzling, charming, entertaining or brilliant that audience members all but lose control, are beside themselves, go ape in your presence. Frank Sinatra and Elvis had that rare quality. Most speakers don't.

BURT DUBIN
http://www.SpeakingBizSuccess.com

Increase The Number Of Seminars You Give

Speaking to groups of potential clients at business meetings is a well-known technique for promoting consulting practices. After doing so as an amateur in the early 1990s, I realized that I enjoyed the profession of speaking and my audiences were enjoying it, too. To advance that career path, I wrote and delivered public seminars around the United States, doing more than 150 per year. That experience catapulted me to a recognized national speaker level and cultivated an appreciative clientele.

Today, my client list includes corporations, professional societies, and trade and business promotion groups. I speak to clients around the country on how to save money through smart purchasing and negotiation practices.

ROBERT MENARD II
http://RobertMenard.com

*I*f you love to tell stories to your friends, you no doubt have what the Scots call the "Gift of Gab!" But you may not realize you can use that gift to promote your business, and then progress to being paid high fees for speaking, too.

I know a florist shop owner who speaks at luncheons for service clubs such as Kiwanis, Lions Club, Rotary and many others. The time slot is usually between twenty minutes and half an hour. My florist friend gives a presentation on the names and meanings of flowers. At every plate, she preplaces a form explaining her new, "Service For Those With Short Memories But Big Hearts."

She keeps on file the dates and names her clients want to remember during the year. She sees to it that flowers are sent on time to mark birthdays, anniversaries . . . and other special occasions, and she charges the client's credit card. No more missed important dates! With her charming talk and the helpful service, she has built a very large business. Cost to her? Zero.

A businessman who was active in the Boy Scouts decided to apply the Scout's Creed and other systems to his business. Results were very successful. Now he speaks for several thousand dollars per program (plus all transportation costs) to business conventions across the country. He talks about what he believes in and enjoys not only the fees he earns, but also the numerous thank-you letters he receives from members of his audiences.

A good way to put together your beginning talk is to base the outline on your right hand. Begin with a light, funny (clean) story that ties in with your topic. That is your 'light' little finger that stands for humor. The next three fingers are the three points of your talk. Explain what they are one at a time, and illustrate each one with a grand story. Repeat the point. Your thumb is the heavy finger on your hand, and it stands for heart. Close your talk with a story your audience will never forget. It can be one from your own life, or your family, or a heart-touching story from history. If the president of the service club asks you to cut your time slot just before you speak, look at your hand and decide which of the three *middle finger points you will leave out. When you come to that point, just say, "I have so much more to tell you, I hope you will invite me back again! And now for my closing story . . ."*

Friends of the Mind Speaking *has been a magic carpet in my life. I have no college education and my father deserted my mother and me early on. But I have always been an avid reader of biographies. When my sweetheart came home from four years with the U.S. Marines, we married and bought a small home and a dry-cleaning franchise, and soon we had two beautiful babies. Then recession struck. We had no idea that dry-cleaning is one of the first things people cut back, or cut out, when times are tough. We weren't bringing in enough to make our house payment.*

Then I got an idea. In high school, I had been advertising manager and feature editor of our student newspaper. One of the features I wrote was a Shoppers Column *about the local stores. Each store paid for its part in the column. But I did not have a typewriter, or typing paper or a car. Even my baby stroller was dilapidated.*

Because of my reading, I have loved the encouraging words of great accomplishers. As I was thinking of all our problems, I thought of my "friend of the mind," Albert Einstein. He said to me (through a book I had read about him), "Stop thinking of problems. Concentrate on solutions!"

So I borrowed my neighbor's typewriter—she even gave me a ream of paper, bless her—and I typed a sample Shoppers Column *using the display ads in the paper for copy ideas. Then I got out the rickety baby stroller. Oops! It was built for one child. Our two had grown. They would not fit! Thinking of Mr. Einstein, I ran to the bedroom and grabbed a big pillow. I got out the clothesline rope and tied the pillow onto the back of the stroller to create a second seat, put my typed sample* Shoppers Column *in my purse, and off we went.*

Our little town was mainly filled with chicken farmers. There were very few sidewalks. Suddenly, ka-plop! Down on the ground went the wheel of the stroller. I remember standing there a minute, ready to give up, but then Mr. Einstein nudged me and I got an

Virtual University For Speakers

In 1997, I started the first virtual university for emerging professional speakers.

My faculty (three national experts) and I offer ongoing teleclasses that help authors, coaches, speakers and entrepreneurs launch a profitable speaking business. My background as a 13-year owner of a national speakers bureau provides me with the expertise and credibility to offer these classes.

If you have a special niche or skill that other people need, teleclasses are an excellent way to promote what you have to offer. You can tape your teleclasses or your speeches (with permission from your audience) and sell these tapes on your website or in the back of the room during events.

I offer a six-pack audio cassette program on *How to Succeed in the Speaking Business,* which was created from live teleclasses.

SANDRA SCHRIFT
http://www.schrift.com

One Thing Leads
To Another

I gave a digital camera presentation to the Kiwanis club that
went great. It was a lot of fun. I
found out later via email that
the President of the Kiwanis
spoke about me and my seminars to the President of the
Georgia Podiatric Medical
Association and recommended
offering my digital camera seminar as a fun spouse event for
the annual convention in Atlanta

SUSAN CHAMBERS
http://www.susanchambers.com

idea. I took off my shoe and hammered the wheel back on.

When I reached the county newspaper office, I stopped. On the door was a big sign that read, "No Help Wanted." I had thought they would offer me a salary to write the Shoppers Column. My heart sank.

At that moment, another of my "friends of the mind," newspaperman Benjamin Franklin, whispered in my ear. He explained that the sign did not mean they did not want to hire me, it meant they had no money to pay me. He said, "Go in and show them your high school press pass. Ask if you can buy ad space from them at wholesale, sell it at retail to the merchants in the form of your column, and I promise you, you will have the money for the house payment in two weeks."

Ben was absolutely right. That is exactly what happened. But then I ran out of cardboard for my shoes. The rocky roads had chewed them until they were past repair.

The next morning, after the newspaper was thrown on my front porch, I ran and picked it up and spread it out on my kitchen table. There in front of me was the answer! There were articles about the service clubs in town having luncheon meetings. Each gave the names of the officers, which I recognized as the owners of local businesses. Then each story told about the speaker who had addressed that group at the luncheon.

Ben Franklin whispered in my ear, "Observe!" (I had noticed that he used that word a lot in all of his letters and books.) Then I saw what he meant! If I could create a subject these merchants were interested in, I could speak to a room full of advertising prospects!

I arranged to trade baby sitting with my neighbor, and I borrowed her car. Then I called the president of the first club and told him I would like to speak to their members on the subject of "What Does Your Customer Really WANT?" I gave myself a moniker, calling myself "Dottie Walters, Your Customer." My talk was about customer service. I brought along a little basket and asked them to place their business cards in it so that I could have a drawing for a prize I had gift-wrapped and brought with me. They all did it.

I had also brought along sample copies of the newspaper, which I folded with my column on the outside and placed at each seat. Later that afternoon, I used the business cards I had collected to sell my Shoppers Column via phone calls. This is where that beginning talk has led me.

My merchant customers asked me to start my own advertising business, and they each paid me in advance to begin it. They opened branches in other cities, and my business followed. Within two years, I had four offices, 285 saleswomen and 4,000 advertising accounts.

People at my speaking programs began asking me to speak to their employees, and they paid me a speaking fee. Since there was not one book at the library about women in sales, I wrote one. Prentice Hall published it as, Never Underestimate the Selling Power of a Woman. Then I was asked to speak for larger and larger groups, and conventions.

When my speaking customers asked me to find additional speakers for them on other topics, I began Walters International Speakers Bureau, and then I began publishing our speaker's magazine, Sharing Ideas. I have spoken in Japan, Australia, England, Mexico, Canada and all over our beautiful United States.

If you had seen me with that rickety baby stroller and the cardboard in my shoes, would you have imagined what lay ahead for me? Speaking and writing is a wonderful way to grow your business locally—and eventually take it global.

Dottie Walters

For more information on the
Lecture Circuit, visit:

www.obvious-expert.com/lecture

Transcribe Your Seminars

If you don't have time to write your book, try letting your words speak for you. To do so, tape your workshops and seminars, speaking engagements and phone conversations when you work as a consultant. Or create an outline and have an associate interview you as you talk onto a tape. Then hire a transcriber to transcribe your tapes, and turn what you have said into your chapters.

GINI GRAHAM SCOTT
http://www.giniscott.com

Bait Piece

One of the surest ways to build a reputation of expertise in any chosen field is to become a guest speaker at local organizations. When you speak to a group, give the audience members something tangible to take home. We call the handout we use when speaking, an action outline, or a **bait** piece. Our bait piece supports our speech as an outline for the audience, it provides a way to keep the audience members interacting with us as they take notes, and it allows us to slip a piece of subtle self-promotion into the audience members' hands.

Standing Ovations Are Great For Business
The Fastest And Surest Way To Make Your Expertise Known To Those Who Care!

Service Club

Plus

Plus

How To Locate

ELSOM ELDRIDGE, JR. • 5703 RED BUG LAKE ROAD, #403
WINTER SPRINGS, FLORIDA 32708 • 407-678-7928

Front page:

Title that is intriguing, exciting, entertaining, and leaves the audience wanting to know more.

Subtitle further engages the audience's interest.

In our talk we list some organizations (like Rotary, Kiwanis, etc.) with check boxes beside them so the listener can mark those relevant as potential speaking targets for them. Under the category of *"Pluses,"* we discuss fraternal organizations, church groups and trade and professional organizations, with a place for the listener to note these as we name these.

Thankfully, sometimes, simple is best and a good bait piece is simple to create. Start with an 8.5×11-inch sheet of paper and fold it in half so it creates a booklet of four pages, front and back.

On the front page, start with your speech's title, followed by the subtitle.

The front of your speech should be at the top of the first page. The next two pages of the booklet should contain an outline of your lecture. Leave some blank spaces for the audience members to write information as you're speaking. Finally, the last page of the booklet is your personal (or your company's) marketing material.

A speech's title must be:

◆ **Intriguing**

◆ **Exciting**

◆ **Entertaining**

◆ **And leave the prospective audience with the advance thought,** *"This is a speech I don't want to miss!"*

The title should be crafted to appeal to general interests, unless the audience is a specialized group—then you can create a specialized topic.

One example of an intriguing subtitle is:

> *Surprise! Surprise! Surprise!*
> *Absence of Planning Equals*
> *Surprise! Surprise! Surprise!*

Use your subtitle to tell a little more of your story. Include your name, address, and phone number at the bottom of page one, as well as on the bottom of page two, and of page three.

Example:

The examples that follow show the pages of a bait piece that we use during some of our thirty-minute talks.

Example of the front cover, page 1 of a bait piece on the topic of how lecturing can help position the speaker as an obvious expert.

On the lines provided under "How To Locate," the audience for this speech might fill in notes about where they can find lists of community organizations for public speaking. This source list would include: the phone book, the library, Internet searches, Chambers of Commerce and newspaper calendar listings of upcoming meetings and events.

Throughout your speech, look for ways to incorporate lists of important points. Leave plenty of blank space on a bait piece—make it easy (and necessary) for your listener to take notes.

Pages 2 and 3 of the bait piece deal with the body of your speech or talk; they are the outline of what you will be saying. These pages list the specific points that correspond to the subtopics within your speech. For example, when we are discussing public speaking, we remind our audience (as one of our first points) never to leave their introduction as a guest speaker to chance. We suggest that speakers provide the person who will introduce them, the speaker's own typed introduction. Include: title, business name if relevant, and a memorable thought that will stick with the listener and make it clear to them why this speaker is the obvious expert. Page 2 of the example (below) shows how we include our information about credibility-enhancing introductions in our bait piece.

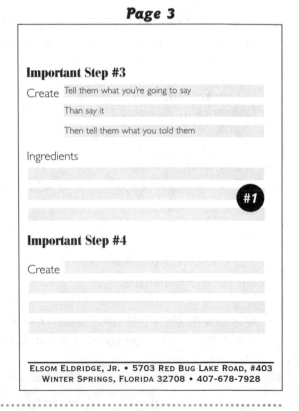

Page 2

4 Steps = Success

Important Step #1

Create

Important Step #2

Create
Establish Your Expert Position

Example   The Seven Secrets for Scoring Higher on Every Test

We Have to Take in Life—Anytime—Anywhere—Guaranteed!

with test-taking skills expert Elsom Eldridge, Jr.

Introduction

I am so pleased to have the honor today of introducing to you,

our speaker, Test Taking Skills Expert, Elsom Eldridge Jr. He has

written six books on how to achieve higher scores without

cheating—and continues through his research . . .

ELSOM ELDRIDGE, JR. • 5703 RED BUG LAKE ROAD, #403
WINTER SPRINGS, FLORIDA 32708 • 407-678-7928

Page 3

Important Step #3

Create   Tell them what you're going to say

Than say it

Then tell them what you told them

Ingredients

#1

Important Step #4

Create

ELSOM ELDRIDGE, JR. • 5703 RED BUG LAKE ROAD, #403
WINTER SPRINGS, FLORIDA 32708 • 407-678-7928

In this bait piece, the answers the listener would fill in for the 4 Important Steps are:

 Create a Great Title

 Create a Great Introduction

 Create a Good talk

The ingredients of the Good Talk (**see #1**) would include some familiar facts to help build speaker rapport with the audience, some brand-new and awesome facts, some humor (but not cheap or corny jokes) and a client story or two.

 Create a Memorable Bait Piece

Remember An effective speech should have entertainment value throughout. It should not try to sell the speaker's services or any product during the speech—that will take care of itself just by the speaker being recognized as the obvious expert in a specific field. Here's a good formula to apply to speech writing:

$$\textbf{\textit{60\% information}}$$
$$\textbf{\textit{(with as much new news as possible)}}$$
$$\textbf{\textit{and 40\% upbeat, engaging comments.}}$$

Example of the back cover, page 4 of a bait piece on the topic of how lecturing can help position the speaker as an obvious expert.

Master Sales and Marketing Specialist Elsom Eldridge, Jr.

co-author of

The Obvious Expert Advisors Book Series, inspires you to find the obvious expert within yourself so that you magnetically attract the riches of wealth, success and personal satisfaction.

ELSOM ELDRIDGE, JR.
5703 RED BUG LAKE ROAD, #403
WINTER SPRINGS, FLORIDA 32708
407-678-7928 • FAX 407-678-8173
EECONSULTS@AOL.COM
PERSONAL COACHING AND CONSULTING

Page 4—Back Cover

Back page—print your name, your company, your address, all of your contact information, maybe your photograph, a list of the different consulting services you offer and perhaps a special offer (email or call for special report, audio tape, etc.). Your name, address and phone number should go at the bottom of all the other pages of your booklet (your bait piece) as well.

Remind your audience members throughout your talk to use the bait piece for note taking by saying things like, "Now this is important, you may want to add this to your notes . . ."

Make sure everyone in the meeting room has your bait piece in hand.

Make sure that the audience members write their notes on the bait pieces so that your booklet goes home with them and winds up in their files not their 'file 13'.

Secrets for Successful
Seminars and Workshops

CHAPTER 5

After mastering the lecture circuit, we were ready to launch our first test preparation seminar. Such seminars proved to be an invaluable way to introduce me as the obvious expert to hundreds of people at a time. As a bonus, the seminars became a very lucrative sideline.

We expanded into career prep exam seminars and into sales and marketing seminars, which eventually led me to doing consulting seminars in conjunction with Howard Shenson. Over the years, we have seen over one million participants at our seminars.

One of my passions in life is helping people grow. Seminars are one of the most effective and efficient ways to accomplish this. You can do either public or in-house seminars and reach your market.

When we were first starting sales seminars we wanted to work with a Fortune 500 company, but with no track record, we needed a unique approach. I contacted a Regional Manager at RadioShack® in New Hampshire and said I wanted to offer them a day of training with the company's salespeople, free of charge. All I wanted in return was for the company to track the salespeople for thirty days following the seminar and send me a letter afterward, letting me know the results.

A month or so after I conducted the training, I received a letter from the Regional Manager, now a Vice President. The letter read, "Thanks for the finest sales-oriented seminar that I have

Increase Clients And Referrals

I get about 30% of my clients from seminars and keynotes. Some clients have never heard me speak but saw me in a seminar catalog. A number of my best clients have come from referrals from people who have seen me speak. It's not just a business source: *You get clients for life.* They join my free newsletter, buy my products, refer me to colleagues and hire me for long-term contracts.

One client, the founder of a start-up, contracted my services for more than a year. The media coaching work we did together helped position her as a strong spokeswoman for her products, which was a key factor in getting her company acquired for a hefty sum. She never needs to work again.

SUSAN HARROW
http://www.prsecrets.com

ever attended! Being a Supervisor for RadioShack® for over twenty-five years, the six hours that you spent with my sales managers were VERY productive. And, best of all, the two districts that participated in your training session have experienced a forty-two percent sales gain since your training!"

That first positive experience got me interested in turning sales training into one of my niches. I positioned myself as one of the leading retail sales trainers in America. Bear in mind that some retail companies are hesitant to train their retail sales staffers because such a high percentage of the sales staff turns over every year. Retail companies don't want to spend money this year training next year's competition. So I fine-tuned my position and defined myself as, "the trainer who works with salespeople who stay in a job long-term and sell to customers who return again and again."

Not only did the free training I had offered launch me into a new niche, increasing my earning potential, it also expanded my influence as the obvious expert in several ways.

Because I had audio-recorded the RadioShack sales seminars as I taught them, I was later able to have them transcribed, creating a complete record of the workshop. I broke the information into thirty chapters detailing the habits an effective salesperson needs to know. But some things about my workshops did not translate well to text. The problem was, they were such interactive events, and so specific, that it was hard to capture everything that was taught and learned, based just on the audio version of the workshop. My material did not offer enough different examples to justify a whole book.

I decided to expand my book by including the comments of other experts. I got the names of the fifty top salespeople in the RadioShack® company and, with RadioShack's permission, began calling them. I asked, "What makes you so good at what you do?" They were more than happy to share with me. Now I had enough information to integrate with my own to make an effective book.

Besides gaining the nuts and bolts for a book, I used the letter from RadioShack® to open the door for me to set up more seminars and workshops inside other companies and organizations that employed salespeople. The difference was this time, I was being paid for the seminars. Even though my original work with the client, RadioShack, was offered free of charge, it developed into multiple avenues that helped me market myself as the obvious expert and create many worthwhile revenue opportunities.

EE Jr.

Room At The Top For You

No other method of marketing your consulting business has as much potential for expansion into other forms of marketing as teaching seminars and workshops. In other words, this is a sure way to establish your reputation, build a client base and substantially boost your income.

An outstanding seminar has the potential to a generate six-figure income or higher each year, and that's with relatively little initial investment. The income potential comes not only from the fees participants pay up front, but also from the spin-off of consulting services, speaking engagements and the follow-up sales you can make of books, tapes and CDs. Seminars also help you build your client list and serve as a test-marketing tool for your products and services.

Another good bit of news is that the seminar business stays fairly steady under any economic conditions. When the economy is good, people attend seminars for ways to branch out. During bad times, seminars offer people ways to change their lives and their situations. You can market your seminars successfully under either set of circumstances.

And there's plenty of room for you in the seminar business. It's really part of the larger industry of adult continuing education. National figures place the total value amount of

Teach Classes By Email

Why leave your home? You can teach classes by email only. I surprised even myself by creating the idea of a 5-week, email only class, and charging people a preposterous sum each to be in it. They got 5 emails from me, one a week, and were asked to do some homework and return it to me, again by email. In my first eclass, 16 people signed up. I made $24,000 with one email announcement of the eclass. I made $112,000 in one year.

I've taught others to turn their current talks and classes into ecourses. One person made $17,000 the first time he taught an eclass. Another made $15,000. Yet another has taught his eclass 5 times and made over $112,000. Because I apparently invented this new form of eeducation, as a result I've also been interviewed in numerous national publications, making me famous as well as rich. Pretty cool, eh?

Long live the Internet!

JOE VITALE
http://www.MrFire.com

continuing education at $4 billion to $6 billion a year. There are a lot of people out there making money on seminars, and there's no reason you can't be one of them.

Create The Program

Think about all of the people you have seen giving a presentation before a group: teachers you have had in school, discussion leaders at corporate training sessions or speakers at local service club luncheons. Even if you are untrained in the ways of professional public speaking, you can recognize who's prepared and who's not, or whose presentation is effective and whose is not.

As a seminar or workshop presenter, your job is to make sure your workshop is a cohesive product that is well prepared and well delivered. According to seminar obvious expert, Paul Karasik, as described during an IGPC certification bootcamp, the seminar business requires that you possess three competencies:

Seminar design or instructional design The seminar must have structure and not come off looking like the stream-of-consciousness ranting of an absent-minded professor.

Marketing You must know your target audience and where your seminar fits into the needs of that audience.

Delivery A good seminar, presented poorly, is as ineffective as a poor seminar. Content will not save a bad delivery.

On the next page, are ten essentials you must consider in planning your workshop:

Build Your Customer Base

The quickest and most efficient way to build your customer base with paying, ready-to-hire-you customers is through workshops. From a recent 3-hour workshop on *Small Business Marketing,* 29% of the attendees responded in this way: by joining my coaching program or purchasing the marketing materials I had available. As the instructor you are looked upon as the expert. Don't disappoint. Give sound advice, specific examples, and lots of information in handout materials the attendees can immediately use in their businesses.

DAVID CLARKE
http://www.clarke-kennedy.com

10 Keys For Seminar Success

YOUR TOPIC
This must be relevant to the audience.

GEOGRAPHICAL AND REGIONAL VARIATIONS
If you don't consider these factors, your whole presentation could fall flat.

PRICE SENSITIVITY
Know what your audience can afford, and how that is relevant to the value of what you are offering. By the way, never automatically assume your audience (or your client or potential client) is as broke as you are.

LOCATION
Make sure your site is easily accessible, comfortable and free of distractions and interruptions.

TIME OF DAY, WEEK AND MONTH
You determine depending on your target audience. For instance, you don't want to conduct a seminar for tax accountants in early April when they're on deadline with federal income tax returns. Nor do you want to compete with holidays, long weekends or major (or locally important) sporting events. Many seminar conductors have found that Sunday or Monday are the least preferred days by business people, while the general public tends to least prefer attending seminars on Friday or Monday.

LENGTH OF PROGRAM
Again, keep your audience in mind. Sometimes a jam packed half-day seminar can have more impact than a slower paced full-day session.

PROMOTION AND ADVERTISING
Getting the word out in just the right way will help you draw the audience you need.

YOUR REPUTATION
Everything you do will have a bearing on this. Even if you don't rely on repeat business for your seminars, you want participants to recommend you as the obvious expert to other people.

YOUR PROFESSIONALISM
Just as with your reputation, the manner in which you conduct your business reflects the quality of your program.

THE SUCCESS RESULTS OF YOUR PROGRAM
If participants see noticeable difference in their business after attending your seminars or workshops, they will bring you or send you more business.

Address Your Audience's Important Problems

If you are speaking at a conference, try to find time to be there for the whole conference even if it is for two or three days. You will make a lot of valuable contacts, but what is far more important is that you will know in considerable detail the key issues facing your audience. Frequently I can adapt my presentation to precisely reflect the concerns that my audience has expressed. Audiences sit up and take notice if you start your presentation with the words, "I hope in this short address to help you to solve your most important problems . . ."

If you choose to offer seminars, remember the late Howard Shenson's remark: "Be an entrepreneur, not an academic." Audiences want to know three basic things: how to make more money, how to keep more of what they make, and how to get a better return on what they keep.

Stick to these general themes and you will have them begging for more.

TOM LAMBERT
www.centreforconsultingexcellence.com

Take Responsibility For Your Seminar's Success

As someone who sponsors several guest presenters a year, I would like to offer the following tips to ensure a successful long-term relationship.

1 Do not bother the host organization with details that you can handle, such as directions, handouts, etc.

2 Do not embed a five-minute sales talk in your seminar; instead, give a tape/book as a door prize.

3 Arrive at least one hour prior to the start time of your seminar in case the room needs to be re-set and to test equipment.

4 Take time to meet the early arriving participants—it makes a big difference.

5 Be dynamic and wake up your audience with surprises.

DEBRA LEOPOLD
http://www.takeaclass.org

Choose Your Audience

If you've never taught before, the whole idea of presenting seminars might sound intimidating. But what could be easier than talking about what you love to do in front of a group of eager faces? If you choose your target audience wisely and send out brochure invitations to people you think could benefit from what you're teaching, you should be able to get one hundred people in the audience. But even if you start with twenty-five or just ten your first time, that's okay.

The two kinds of audiences to target:

Private You gain a private audience if you contract with a company to teach a seminar to its employees. The audience members are captive. Their employer is paying them to be there and expecting them to learn something that will benefit the company. The seminar also may indirectly benefit the employee, but the main goal is to improve the worker's value to the employer.

Public The audience members are attending your seminar of their own free will to learn something that will benefit them directly. They have a vested interest in getting as much out of your presentation as possible because they paid for the seminar themselves. They heard about the seminar through some form of marketing or advertising you produced for the purpose of getting them there.

Either kind of audience could be lucrative for your business. You must tailor your presentation to meet your group's needs.

Choosing your target audience wisely is more important than any other aspect of setting up a seminar. If you don't bring in enough people, you'll lose money on the costs of renting a location, printing workbooks and advertising the event. If you bring in an audience that does not appreciate your presentation and cannot find immediate benefit from it, your reputation will suffer. If the audience that could benefit most from your seminar cannot or will not pay for it, then you've wasted your time and money preparing for nothing.

Take a look at the kind of audience you want sitting in front of you. What is the age range of your ideal participants? What kinds of occupations and income levels do they represent? What kinds of households do they come from, and are they more likely to be found in urban, suburban or rural areas? Once you figure out the answers to questions like these, you'll have a clearer picture of where to direct your marketing and advertising materials and how to prepare your presentation to best fit the people who will be attending.

Oh yes, and then there is that one other kind of audience—that very, very important kind—**the non-paying audience.**

The audience that you teach without charging them or a sponsor a fee, can sometimes turn into one of your most profitable. Use opportunities to present your seminars (or a mini-version of them) to build new clients, attract new markets, test new ideas and generally get your foot in doors that might have previously seemed closed and locked.

Sometimes you may decide to invest dollars in producing a free-to-the-attendee seminar, just because it is such a powerful marketing tool. But if you are creative, you may be able to offer this option at little or no cost to you, other than the investment of your time.

Consider finding a business, such as a department store, that will provide you a meeting room at no charge because they wish to increase foot traffic and offer unique benefits to their patrons. You might try offering a non-fee seminar in conjunction with a trade fair where your offering could help the event coordinators attract more attendees from targeted industry backgrounds. Or simply partner with other seminar providers, sharing costs and mailing lists and expand the marketing outreach of all the

Host Teleseminars To Become A Trusted Adviser

Advance from 'stranger' to 'adviser' by making yourself visible to your prospects as often as possible. The least expensive way to do this is by hosting teleseminars, which permits you to prove your knowledge and become a person to your prospects. Rent a telephone line, called a "bridge," from a company such as: www.voicetech.com or www.teleclass.com.

A few minutes before the scheduled seminar, everyone calls a single phone number and is instantly connected to each other. Bridge rental costs are based on the length of the call and the number of participants. Costs range from $20 and up for hour-long bridge rentals. I had planned a series of three weekly one-hour teleseminars, but the individuals who signed up switched to one-on-one coaching. Rather than cancel the time, however, I invited everyone on my 2,500 email list to attend a free one-hour question-and-answer session. The first session, three prospects called in. The second session attracted seven callers; the third, eleven. More important than the numbers, is the fact that the calls generated more than $10,000 in new business—from people who were already on my mailing list but had never purchased.

ROGER C. PARKER
http://www.OnePageNewsletters.com

presenters involved. The point is, once you develop your seminar or workshop, it is yours to use in any way that benefits your immediate or your long term business goals.

Choose A Topic

The topic of every seminar you conduct should be close to your consulting specialty. After all, the reason you're giving seminars is to increase the visibility of your consulting business. You can vary the titles and content to fit a specific audience, but you have to stay true to your expertise.

For example, a financial consultant can give one version of a seminar to retirees and another to business owners. Their investment and spending needs are very different, but both groups can benefit from some of the same information.

Look at the other seminars that are already available in your area of expertise. If someone else is regularly presenting seminars with a similar topic, then your venture into the business is low-risk. You already know the demand is out there. Your potential competitors have done the market research for you.

In choosing a topic, you also need to consider geography. For instance, a seminar that works in Los Angeles might not be relevant for audiences in the Midwest.

Another important point to consider is the timeliness of your seminar or workshop. Wil Horton, NLP obvious expert and IGPC faculty member, was teaching a workshop called *"Critical Incident Stress Debriefing."* He altered his subject matter after September 11, 2001, to use it to train mental health professionals who were dealing with the nation's grief over the terrorist attacks that brought down the World Trade Center towers in New York and a part of the Pentagon in Washington, D.C.

Market And Advertise Your Seminar

The audience you're targeting often determines where you should advertise your seminar. For general audiences, you might

Create An Interesting, Effective Workshop

After publishing my book, *The Courageous Follower,* I hired a course designer to help create a workshop on Leader-Follower relationships. A professional video company became interested in my book and paid for the rights to develop a training video on the topic. I did everything possible to ensure the video was high quality and then I incorporated it into my workshops. I also designed a self-assessment instrument to help participants understand their current followership style and in what ways they need to develop themselves. I rounded this off with a good set of Microsoft PowerPoint® learning aids. In the end, I had an interesting, effective workshop to offer organizations that sought my expertise.

IRA CHALEFF
http://www.exe-coach.com

try the local newspaper. Specialized business audiences might be more likely to respond to magazines and journals that cater to their business interests. Combining one of these types of advertising with direct mailings to specific lists of people can be very effective.

If you're planning a seminar or workshop outside your hometown, you might need help determining which newspaper covers your targeted region. Go to the local library and look for a reference book published by *Standard Rate and Data Service* of Skokie, Illinois. It's called the *Newspaper Circulation Analysis*; it will help you determine where to place your ad.

Next look in a second reference book called *Newspaper Rates and Data,* published by the same service. You'll find out when a newspaper is published, who handles advertising, how much the ads cost and information about the newspaper's circulation.

To find trade and specialty magazines, consult a third volume by *Standard Rate and Data Service* called *Consumer Magazine and Farm Publication Rates and Data.* If there is specific placement that you think will be beneficial to selling your event, give the publication a call. Many major publications, such as the *Wall Street Journal,* offer regional edition placements that will sometimes be worth your investment. Always check contract rates and remnant rates when you purchase your print advertising; they can offer you a way to make a real splash while paying a discounted—sometimes deeply discounted—rate.

To create your print advertisement, look at other ads in the type of media you're planning to use. You can hire a graphic artist or you can craft something yourself. You can create a very effective ad with copy only and no images. Most newspapers and magazines will actually build an ad for you for a small charge if you provide the words and some general instructions about what you want.

Do not hesitate to tell your contact at the newspaper if you are unfamiliar with ad construction; they will be happy to explain to you the exact graphic specifications required for your

Use Your Book To Sell Seminars

After writing my book, I was smart enough to publish it myself. I went to a local Kinko's and duplicated the pages myself, and then I bound them myself. I started calling people I knew to get me in touch with their human resources/training departments. I then offered my one-hour free crime prevention seminar. I made $50,000 in six months! I stayed busy with referrals.

MIKE WILLIAMS
willgp2@yahoo.com

Offer Free Gifts For Participants

My seminars and products help change the mind to the positive through pop music songs. I send out my demo tapes along with a special positive jingle that I write especially for a particular convention's theme and the promoters love this unique gift. Also, I hit the seminar circuit in the USA and did many small workshops in major cities for two years. I then went on and did much larger free seminars in all of the cities I had been. I offered some of my products as gifts to people at the workshops, and then I stayed in contact with these wonderful people and kept them updated with special offers on my website.

MICHELE BLOOD
http://www.MusiVation.com

ad. Even if you think you understand the specs, it is always best to double check the details. Also ask where on the page your ad will appear; sometimes preferential placement for higher visibility on the page is simply a matter of first come, first serve. We always request *upper right thumb placement*.

Be sure you also inquire if the paper runs special interest editions. In many communities a business section "extra" will be included in the paper once or twice each week; this could be the ideal placement for your ad. Or, perhaps another section would afford you greater exposure to your potential clients, such as a weekly special section on food and entertainment, education or any other topic that is appropriately related to your potential audience. Also, don't forget the daily sports pages. If your seminar is particularly interesting to men, and they represent your primary attendees, then try placement of your ad in the sports section. Just remember to ask for help; newspaper advertising departments have vast amounts of readership profile information available to them and they are generally eager to share helpful suggestions and insights with their paying advertising customers.

And here's one more interesting tip if you are designing your own ad: as you experiment with different layouts, fonts and point sizes of words and perhaps logos, you may lose confidence in your ability to determine what 'works' and what doesn't. After too much laboring over an image, you will lose your intuitive eye to spot design flaws. To gain a fresh perspective, simply look at a printed copy of your ad held up in front of a mirror. Whatever is out of balance will immediately jump out at you because your brain is now registering a new and different image, one to which you have not become visually desensitized.

In the end, the single most important factor in the appearance of your ad is for the topic to stand out in large, easy to read type. Your headline or key words must be interesting enough to hook the reader into delving further into the ad.

Your advertisement includes:

- Features of the seminar

- Benefits to attendees

- Testimonials from people who have worked with you before or attended your seminars

- Information about the materials and presenters

- Time and place

- Guarantees and refund policy

- Registration information with a toll-free number and a coupon for mail-in registration—advance registration and prepayment is a good idea!

The next consideration is timing. A magazine's deadlines dictate when your ad is due—at least several weeks in advance for a monthly publication, sometimes a full eight weeks. Newspaper ads, on the other hand, generally are most effective if you advertise a maximum of one week in advance of the seminar, but you must still make sure you meet the publication's ad placement deadline.

> 66
>
> *Do you know that when an address is on a sticker, or label on the envelope, there is usually less than a 30% chance of the letter even being opened? Type it directly on the envelope and the rate can go up almost 50%. Use a window envelope with the recipients address showing through from where it is typed on your letterhead; you will get closer to 70% of recipients opening your letter instead of tossing it as junk mail.*
>
> *When I first learned this, my next typical mailing went from the usual response of less*

Find A Need And Fill It

I have always heard "Find a need and fill it." I was sitting at lunch with a friend one day wondering why my business was not growing at a faster rate, and she asked me "Whose needs are you meeting?" I thought about that question all day and decided to create a seminar that had never been done before. "Imagine 2002," the first-ever Latino success forum, was born. On March 21, 2002, that dream became a reality. Many people had thought of having this forum, but I was the first to find the need and fill it. Never underestimate your ideas and how powerful they and you can be!

DANIEL GUTIERREZ
http://www.acceptyourgreatness.com

*than 1% of the people responding by
contacting me for more information to over
3.25%.*

Robert Bayliss

Seminars Lead To Publicity And Sales

Teaching seminars nets your business great free publicity. I can pay thousands of dollars to advertise in the *New York Times* or *Los Angeles Times*—or teach one class in the *New York* or *Los Angeles Learning Annex*, and reach the same number of people. Plus, they'll be in "buy" mode when they see my course and business description. Some people disdain doing adult ed because it doesn't always pay well. But if you're a dynamic speaker, you can sell hundreds of dollars of books and special reports at each workshop. And every workshop leads to other opportunities. Give it a try!

FERN REISS
http://PublishingGame.com

Direct mail pieces contain much more information than paid advertisements. For instance, you could have a registration card along with a brochure that includes testimonials, endorsements, presenters' biographies and listings of items you will have for sale at the event, such as your books, tapes or reports. We recommend mailing at least eight to ten weeks prior to the seminar or workshop dates.

Just as with designing a print ad, you can design your direct mail piece yourself, employ a freelancer or turn to a print design service to help you. Think backward in your planning process. Consider first the number of pieces you plan to mail, and then learn the different rates for mailing pieces of different sizes. Check to see if bulk rate mailing is an option. Consider paper weight and whether you plan to use a self-mailer (a folded flyer that bears an address label) or if you prefer to use an envelope.

Research your options; you have several choices to turn to for help. For your design, printing, mailing lists and mail distribution, you may go to a direct mail service, graphic design company or a print shop—any of which may offer you some or all of the services you will need, including renting or selling you a mailing list, envelope stuffing, affixing of labels or postage and actual posting to the mail for delivery on pre-targeted dates.

For mailing lists, you may turn to online direct mail sites. Some sites offer you the option to enter target zip codes, plus your target client profile characteristics and receive a count of the number of persons who fall under your specifications. You then have the option to pay to receive these names for one time use or multiple uses as a mailing list. Like their counterpart services in the bricks and mortar world, different online direct mail services offer a different variety of products, so it pays to spend time shopping around for the service that best meets your needs. The list supplier who has been the most helpful to us for several years is AccuData. To learn more about them visit their website: **www.accudata.com**.

Valuable information is also available in another *Standard Rate and Data Service* book, *Direct Mail Lists Rates and Data*. This is the original source of all mailing lists sold and rented in the United States. The lists are broken down by specific—and we mean very specific—characteristics. You can get demographics listings that tell you who subscribes to which magazines, holds what jobs and at what earning level.

Whichever route you choose, just plan to ask a lot of questions, get several itemized price quotes and then pick and choose the services you need.

No matter which advertising medium you choose, here are some tips for making your ad effective:

- Pretend you're answering a question

- Use clear, direct language

- Be enthusiastic, friendly and memorable

- Keep it interesting

- Tell the truth—just make it fascinating

- Tell facts, the more you tell, the more you sell

- Tell readers what benefit your seminars will have in their lives (or their businesses)

- Convey the message "This ad is about you, the reader"

- Include testimonials, which make the ad more believable

- Give the reader some helpful hints or advice

- Write the ad in everyday language

- Generally use short words, short sentences and short paragraphs

Fill A Need By Teaching At A College

As colleges and universities face declining enrollments, increased competition and budget crunches, there is an increasing interest in the use of adjunct faculty to reduce payroll and benefit costs. This is true for both credit-bearing courses and non-credit or continuing education programs. Because of their education and real-life experiences, consultants make ideal candidates for these positions. And for consultants, not only do we gain valuable training experience, but we also have the opportunity to introduce our skills and services to a wide range of prospective clients who are or will be employed by the organizations where we want to market our services. As someone who parlayed his consulting experience into a full-time position with a university as Director of the Center for Corporate Education, and as interim chair of an academic department, let me assure you that as I now re-enter the world of full-time training and consulting, I am positioned with a whole new set of skills and credentials to bring to my clients.

EDWARD HENDRICKS
http://www.ignitespirit.com

> *I like to excerpt snappy sentences from my fan mail and put them together on a sheet of testimonials. If you want to use someone's words as a printed testimonial, courtesy requires that you ask for their permission. Most people are delighted.*
>
> Barbara Winter

Make Your Workshops Interactive

Many people think if you know something you can teach it, but I don't agree. Designing a good workshop is an art form. People need to be engaged in the material; they need to have an experience. I make my workshops very interactive. I get people talking in the first few minutes, and I ask a LOT of questions. People learn more from coming up with their own answers than from hearing what you have to say. Instead of lecturing, I act as a coach and facilitator to send the learning in the right direction. Not only does this kind of learning 'stick' better, it makes people more likely to hire you later because they get a chance to experience you in conversation.

C.J. HAYDEN
http://www.getclientsnow.com

When it comes to marketing and advertising, it's up to you to think creatively. Remember you don't have to take on the whole project yourself. It is possible to establish an alliance with a third party, or several non-competing partners, who will actively promote the event. For example, you could give a seminar as part of a local adult education school. Once an established organization puts their stamp of endorsement on your seminar, the community can easily identify you as an obvious expert.

Kevin Hogan, with whom we have done a number of seminars, says he once was preparing a seminar about drug prevention and self-esteem awareness for a junior high school. The local Rotary Club liked the idea so much that it contributed $1,000 to pay for it.

The Seminar Set Up

To make sure you stay on track and cover everything you want to say when you teach a seminar or workshop, we recommend that you write out a complete script. You shouldn't read your script verbatim during the seminar—that would be boring for your audience. Instead, use it as an outline and improvise according to the response you get from seminar participants.

A script will help you walk through the seminar ahead of time to determine how long it will last. It will guide you in handing out presentation materials at certain times during the seminar. And it will convince the people in your audience that you are in control of the situation and that they are, indeed, getting their money's worth with a professional presentation.

Ahead of time, prepare a workbook that contains relevant information you want participants to take home from your presentation. Be sure to include a page with your contact information and plenty of room for participants to take notes of their own.

Whatever you do, don't read to participants straight from the workbook. This insults their intelligence and gives them the feeling they are not getting what they paid for. Instead, create a dialogue that follows the structure of the workbook and ask them to turn to specific pages with you to write in their notes or perform specific exercises.

Worksheets in the workbook are helpful because they personalize the information and enable participants to apply what you are teaching to their own situations.

Creature comfort is important. Be sure to include breaks during the seminar so people can use the restroom, make phone calls or simply stretch their legs. Always arrange for water stations. You may also want to have refreshments on hand, including an assortment of beverages and possibly light snacks. If your workshop is conducted in a hotel or conference center, refreshments are typically available at a package price that includes facility staff taking care of your refreshment set up and clean up. When you book your location, ask about coffee service for your group.

If you are using a facility where this service is not available, be thorough in your planning. Make sure you have all the little amenities like coffee stir sticks, plenty of paper napkins and conveniently placed waste receptacles. Refreshments do not have to be elaborate, but if it is an all day seminar or a weekend bootcamp, include some options for your attendees, along the lines of coffee, tea, fruit juice, soda and bottled water as beverage selection. Morning breaks may include pastries and bagels and perhaps fruit trays or cookies for the afternoon. Just

Keep In Touch With Participants

Here's what I've learned about doing my Winning Presentations Seminar in companies. I get the participants' email addresses and put them on my list to receive my monthly *Presentation Points Bulletin.* People love it, and every month they are reminded of the workshop and my services. I meet several people in the organization and keep in contact with them so if one contact leaves I have another source. I have now spun off a separate one-day seminar on *Creating Impactful Presentations* from my two-day seminar. I put so much work into my materials that I now license my seminar to companies and consultants. This way I make money from the materials when someone else is teaching the seminar.

CLAUDYNE WILDER
http://www.wilderpresentations.com

Stamp Of Approval

My success as a real estate investor and consultant began when I first started teaching in the continuing education departments of area colleges. There are many advantages when you become associated with the continuing education lecture/ seminar circuit. A degree of legitimacy is conferred on you. Your audience and everything you need are assembled for you. The 15,000 or more brochures the college sends out to the community promote you as the acclaimed expert in your field. Most of my business contacts come from this milieu and remain my clients. It pays to let institutions of higher learning stamp their approval on you as the expert in a particular field.

GEORGE ANSONG
geoansong@hotmail.com

factor the cost of this into your pricing and make sure you keep your audience hydrated and energized.

Pricing

If you are conducting your seminar to generate revenue, (and not solely as a marketing technique) and you need to realize a profit, then make sure you have at least as many people in the audience as it takes to cover your costs plus. To do this, take into account how much it is costing you to set up the seminar.

Add your expenses, including:

- Room or meeting site

- Advertising

- Printing and postage of brochures and other direct mail material

- Printing of workbooks and worksheets

- Refreshments

- Room decorations, such as rented plants or flower arrangements

- AV equipment rental, should there be any

- Travel—airplane, gasoline, hotel, dining, tips

- Fees for your assistant

- Shipping of seminar materials to meeting site

- Telephone calls

- Your fee—remember to pay yourself for your time and your talents

On the subject of fees: we have found that giving discounts for early bird registrants is worthwhile to help you get a pre-planning headcount on projected attendance. Another pricing plus is increasing your attendance by offering discounts to group registrants, or options like a discounted rate when someone signs up and enrolls a friend.

Each attendee is a seed planted in your garden of future business. They are your potential consulting clients, your repeat customers for future workshops and the buyers of your books, tapes and reports. They are also your very best recruitment-by-testimonial to hundreds and thousands of people who learn from someone they know and trust that you are an obvious expert.

Site Selection

Many consultants rent public meeting rooms from hotels because catering services are available, parking is convenient and the location is easily accessible. If you choose to do this, look for a hotel with comfortable meeting rooms. Check out the room ahead of time to make sure it will hold all of the participants who are scheduled to attend. Decide how you want the room arranged, such as theater style, where everyone is facing you, or in tables of small groups, where participants can interact with one another during discussion parts of the seminar.

Ask about other groups meeting in nearby rooms and the type of noise and activity you can anticipate from them. Make it clear that you do not wish to rent the facility at the same time a high school cheerleading, youth baseball, drummers convention or other rowdy meeting might be scheduled. Be especially cautious about what type of activities are scheduled on the other side of a breakaway wall. Ask this question in advance and ask again the day before your meeting. Our own worst seminar experiences have happened when we were adjacent to wedding receptions, bridal shows and dance shows.

While it is great to be able to work directly with the catering representative from the hotel to arrange refreshment service in the room, it is not the best idea to plan to serve lunch. Organizing lunch usually turns into a whole job in itself. Simply build a lunch break into your schedule and then make known in

Expand By Taking Massive Action

I first began teaching seminars at a couple of the community colleges in my area. The hardest part was getting into the first few schools, but I was persistent. I began to expand from the local colleges to some others farther away. At first I was doing seminars that were within 200 miles of my home. When I decided to quit my job and do seminars full-time, I knew I would have to expand to a regional or national market. I began teaching at schools and corporations across the southeast. I called more than 200 schools and businesses every semester. I paid my dues and took some lumps. I remember traveling more than 200 miles to do a seminar for two people, and one was the school's program director! But I got a great referral letter from him. Through action and persistence, I now have developed a seminar business that includes more than 50 schools and corporations in eight states. I have developed my own seminar called *Back in the Black: Creating a Debt-Free Life!* The key to developing and expanding your seminar business is to consistently take massive action with lots of phone calls, faxes and emails, and to regularly follow-up with every lead.

GEORGE LUCKE
http://www.debtfreesolutions.com/
gelcore

advance to attendees some of the nearby options for dining, but that the meal is not included in the workshop.

Another option is to rent other types of meeting space (perhaps a school or public building) and hire a caterer to handle refreshments.

Suggestions for such sites include:

- Vacant office space that is for rent by the day
- Vacant shopping center spaces that are for rent by the day
- Restaurant banquet rooms
- Church halls
- Museum meeting rooms
- Municipal facilities
- Local meeting facilities such as bed-and-breakfasts or historic buildings
- Retail stores that have a meeting space
- Corporate offices
- Banks or financial institutions
- Community colleges
- Schools
- Continuing education community schools
- Trade schools
- Libraries

A different approach to a workshop in a hotel or conference center is teaching your seminar as part of an established learning center, such as a community college. Aligning with an academic facility offers you the advantage of implied credibility.

Move From Lecturer To Teacher

When I first began studying for my Master's in handwriting analysis, some of my instructors cautioned me to keep secret how and what I do. That made no sense to me and, defiantly, when I finished my Master's program, the first thing I did was tell others how I do what I do. My lectures were entertaining, but they became teaching sessions as well. I applied to teach at various community colleges, much to the surprise of my speaker colleagues. They often asked why I would want to teach at our local community colleges. They were amazed that I would want to spend so many hours for minimal compensation. In addition to the great pleasure I take in sharing my knowledge with others, I receive many hidden monetary rewards for my efforts.

IRENE LEVITT
http://Irenelevitt.com

The Right Choice

You might think it's most effective to link with a prestigious, big-name public or private university, but that's not always the case. Depending on what you're going to teach, it may be more lucrative to sign on with a business school or a community college. Many such schools have a substantial enrollment of working adults. This clientele is already earning a paycheck and is looking for a way to boost their income.

Consultant and seminar entrepreneur, Ed King says he has actually stopped people on the street and asked them which learning institution he should approach. He has asked managers of gas stations, dry cleaners and restaurants, for example, "Where do you go to get a practical, specific, reasonably priced class? I'm not from this area, and I'd like to take a class in business to get some practical information."

Make The Pitch

Once you've decided where you'd like to teach your seminar, it's time to sell the institution on the idea. When you go to make your proposal, you should stress that your course can provide the school with three things:

Recognition in the community. You will be providing a needed service for the population and you'll be giving the school free publicity as you promote your course.

A quality program. You might be helping small business owners improve their earnings or helping people decide whether to become entrepreneurs. The course you're offering adds a dimension to the school's curriculum.

Pure profit. You should offer the school a percentage of what you gross from attendee fees. The school isn't going to get rich on what you bring in, but it's money the school wouldn't have otherwise. Make sure the institution understands that your course will be offered at no risk to the school.

Keep Growing To Offer Participants More

Your expertise can expand and contract as you develop seminars. You may start out with one or two areas or topics, and after awhile you'll discover other topics that relate to, or build on, the ones you started with. Then, as you cover more topics, you'll find that you've become an expert in specific types of applications of that topic, and your expertise becomes more focused on that specialty. After awhile, you get interested in different aspects of your specialty, and your range of topics broadens again. My seminars—and the tremendous amount of consulting work that has come from them—have followed this process of expanding and contracting. I started out with teambuilding and communications, broadened my focus and redefined my expertise as "work relationships," and later specialized in managing high-risk employee behaviors before they escalate to violence. I wrote a book on the topic, appeared in national media, and gained recognition in this specific field. Then my focus broadened again to include managing anger and stress as part of the preventive process. Throughout all the expanding-contracting cycles, you keep learning, growing and having more to offer your participants and clients.

LYNNE McCLURE, PH.D.
http://www.McClureAssociates.com

Conducting Seminars Helps You Be Seen As An Expert

Many good inventions, as well as, games begin with something you create for your family, child or friend. Mine was no exception. My 7 year-old wanted to play our piano, so I devised a method where all he needed to know was the ABC's and three colors.

I tested the book in 25 schools in Cincinnati and every teacher endorsed it. Eventually, I sold my method and now I write and have published thirteen teach-yourself music books. I took my books to the national music, toy, book and education shows and taught myself what was out there and where the players were.

I am now referred to an an expert on early childhood music and I do musical workshops all around the country.

NANCY POFFENBERGER
http://www.funpublishing.com

Ed and dozens of his CPA and accountant licensees who have purchased the rights to present Ed's, "How to Start Your Business Seminar," have used this approach for years with great success. "A lot of academic facilities have lost money with various classes in the past, and they're very skeptical about the whole thing," he says. "So if we can come in there and say, 'Look, we can provide a good experience to the community. We can publicize the fact that you're providing this basic information that people need, especially now with the economy turning down. At the same time, there's no financial risk to you whatsoever. As a matter of fact, we will give you ten percent of the tuition.' Most universities will go along with it."

It's possible the institution might say, "We don't work that way" and instead offers to collect the tuition and give you a percentage of the proceeds. They might offer you $35 or $50 an hour for each class, which is much less than you'd make if you charged each participant yourself. Many consultants would just walk away from this kind of offer. But before you do, stop and think, especially if this is your first time teaching your seminar for a fee. You might want to accept the school's offer just to build up your credibility.

Another benefit is that the class can offer you an avenue for promoting and selling your materials and books. Or you could just increase awareness about the services you offer through word of mouth because of all the people in the community your attendees will know.

When you're making your pitch, it's a real plus if you have teaching experience—even if it's in the form of presentations you've made to a board of directors, or speeches you've given at the local Rotary Club. Emphasize this experience and your communication skills.

Ed, who also teaches at Wayne State University, says he takes along a mock-up of an advertisement he will put in the local newspaper, or a workbook he has put together for the course, even in a draft format. "Go in there well-prepared," he says.

"Make sure the school knows you weren't just driving down the street and then decided you'd stop off at the universities and see whether they're interested in this idea. Rather, that your plan is well thought out. Let them see the quality."

And remember, if one person says "no," that doesn't mean you won't be teaching at that school. If the Continuing Education Director at a university turns you down, for example, you can try the Business School or the Small Business Development Center at the same university.

Teach The Course

Teaching a class over a period of time instead of for only one day or one weekend has some real advantages. Give students a chunk of material in a smaller period of time, such as three hours, and then assign some homework. In the following class, go over the information before moving on to the next subject. This method gives people a chance to absorb the information, apply it to their lives and businesses and then ask questions. Just as importantly, it gives you and your students a chance to bond, which is helpful when you're trying to build your business.

> *You get thirty or forty people in a room and you spend some time with these people, and they start to name their dogs after you and invite you to play golf.*
>
> Ed King

"You really become a part of their family. When you give lectures and teach classes, people come to you and ask for your advice and your services. You're not out there peddling your services like the old days when salespeople were selling miracle tonics off the back of a truck."

The Value Of Teaching

As an artist I have many skills to offer my clients. However, I find that as a teacher I can share these practical skills with a broader audience.

Those who want to enhance their lives can take classes and workshops for better understanding into almost any subject. Any success I have in life is because I believe the brain must sustain a balance between the giving and receiving of knowledge to function effectively. From a business prospective, teaching someone is a very personal interaction and becomes a wonderful link to many other people, through word of mouth.

CHRISTIE KNIGHT
christieknight333@hotmail.com

Climb The Ladder By Teaching

Having always been told that I have a unique teaching style, I began positioning myself as a personal technology expert by teaching courses at a local training center called *The Knowledge Shop* in Atlanta. My first course was a fun seminar on digital cameras. I added additional personal technology courses to my offerings each quarter. Teaching courses automatically gave me credibility when seeking speaking opportunities with local service clubs. Next, I pursued publication of magazine articles and eventually wrote my first book. My friends have taken to calling me the "Martha Stewart of Personal Technology". Well, I don't know about that . . . but, I do know that personal digital technology is exploding around us and it's exciting to see so many people participating in it.

SUSAN CHAMBERS
http://www.susanchambers.com

Get Feedback

To continue developing your status and your skill as the obvious expert, you want to ask seminar or workshop participants to give you feedback on your presentation. The best way to do this is through a survey form.

Print an evaluation form ahead of time, preferably on one side of one page, and leave the questions somewhat open-ended. You want to get information, but you don't want to ask participants to write long essays after just sitting through your presentation. Have the participants drop the forms into a box in the back of the room, where their comments can remain anonymous.

Ask participants to tell you what they liked best about the workshop. Ask them what kinds of information/experiences they would like to see more of in future workshops. Do not ask negative questions that cause your participants to analyze or over-analyze, searching for complaints that they perhaps did not realize they had.

If you ask, "What did you enjoy most about the workshop?" you will learn all of the positives. Any attendee who really does have a complaint, will voice it one way or the other on your response sheet. If, on the other hand, you ask, "What did you like least about the workshop?" you will drive all of the responders to search their thoughts, looking for criticisms. The question implies that there are negative aspects to the workshop and that your participants should be able to think of them.

The result of this question, is not that you learn more about how to structure your programs, but that you cause your workshop to end on a negative note. Attendees will leave the event with their parting thought being, "what was wrong with this workshop." And that is certainly not the marketing message you intended!

Remember, you have five goals in setting up your seminar or workshop:

1   To establish yourself as the obvious expert.

2   To get the audience members to request your consulting services in the future.

3   To (at least subtly) make back-end products available to the audience.

4   To line up more seminars or speaking engagements from this one.

5   To actually make a profit from the seminar.

Be sure to include a place for attendees to add their endorsement testimonial for your seminar. Let them know that what they are writing may be published in your future seminar information and will be credited to them by name. Many people gladly oblige, some just because they enjoy seeing their names in print.

We have found that an effective way to personalize the workshop or seminar experience, while providing a valuable service to your attendees, is to make them aware of a sign-up sheet where they can put their name down for a free ten to fifteen minute consulting session with you. After the seminar (each day or on the final day) meet with those attendees who have—just by signing up—prequalified themselves as your potential consulting clients. You gain the opportunity to interact one-on-one with typically about twenty percent of your attendees and learn more about their individual needs.

Saralyn Collins, a Business Consultant and Personal Coach who owns the Training Bridge, says conducting seminars works for her. "I see my job as two-fold: to get audiences totally motivated and excited about their potential to be successful; and to provide as much knowledge as possible for them to absorb in the time available.

"If people have paid a fee for your course, they are there because they have serious interest in the topic," she explains. "Then they go back to their business, and when they have a

Prospects Galore

I prefer to reach large groups of people as often as possible. I like to teach and give seminars because it gets me in front a large community of people interested in what I am doing. By teaching and giving seminars you can provide people with what they need immediately, build your mailing list, keep in touch with prospects that you know are interested in who you are and your expertise. This is a very cost effective marketing method.

ORLANDO BLAKE
http://www.blake-group.com

concern or they need help, they're naturally going to think of you as the obvious expert."

For more information on teaching
Seminars and Workshops, visit:

www.obvious-expert.com/seminars

Be Interactive

Participants retain more information longer and enjoy the process much more when they are actively involved in their learning. Ensure your programs have relevance and are engaging to mind, body, and emotions. Get them thinking and moving so they feel the message through their cognitive, affective, and psychomotor senses and remember Confucius "I hear and I forget, I see and I remember, I do and I understand". After the interaction, leverage every engagement by offering to reinforce the message through learning tools such as CD's, books, ezines, teleclasses, coaching, and additional training on similar topics in order to be memorable as the obvious expert on that subject. Making your workshops creative, fun, and fresh will anchor your message and serve your audience well.

GAIL HOWERTON
http://www.funcilitators.com

Seminar Planning

Presenting Your Seminar

The following pages provide you an excerpted version of the IGPC 21-DAY ACTION PLAN for Seminar and Workshop Preparation.

Many consultants can't wait to get started on the public speaking circuit but are overwhelmed by all of the detailed steps necessary to get their seminar business off and running. This checklist will help you get your seminar planning off to the best possible start. Use these pages as a guide for some of the pre-planning work.

Your Seminar

Give yourself plenty of time to plan and organize your seminar. Make your best estimate of how long planning seminar events will take you—especially if you hit a few logistical snafus—then build a cushion of a few extra days into your planning period.

 ## Determine Seminar Date And Time

Experience has shown that seminars do well on both weekdays and weekends. While the seminar can be held at any time of the day, evening sessions are recommended for weekdays and mornings or afternoon sessions are better for weekend days.

 ## Determine Location

Use the questions on the next page as a guide to help you choose your seminar site.

 ## Book Location

Send letter of confirmation to Site Coordinator. Make at least one follow-up call to the Site Coordinator before your scheduled seminar date.

SITE SELECTION CHECKLIST

Ask yourself these questions:	Notes and Comments	✔
1. How much will it cost to rent the site?		
2. Can adjustments be made to accommodate more or fewer people than expected?	More people? Fewer people?	
3. Does the room size meet your needs?		
4. Is the room temperature comfortable? Is there adequate air conditioning and/or heating?		
5. Is there adequate lighting?		
6. How much flexibility do you have in terms of room setup?	Can the room be set up: Theater style or tables? If tables are available, is the size/ shape of the tables acceptable?	
7. Does the facility furnish everything you need?	Blackboards, dry erase and/or easel? Extension cords? Adequate electrical outlets? (where are they located?) Adequate parking?	
8. Can ice water be provided? Other types of refreshments? Are there convenient facilities for attendee to break for a meal, if the seminar is scheduled longer than a half day?		
9. Are restrooms available? Are they conveniently located?		

Establish Program Budget

Estimate what you must spend in order to attract students for your seminar, supply them with materials and conduct the seminar successfully.

PROGRAM BUDGET

	Projected	Actual
Meeting Room	$_____	$_____
Sleeping Room(s)*	$_____	$_____
Meal(s)*	$_____	$_____
To/from-site travel	$_____	$_____
In-town travel	$_____	$_____
Teacher's fee*	$_____	$_____
Advertising		
Newspaper display ads	$_____	$_____
Newspaper classifieds	$_____	$_____
Flyers	$_____	$_____
Other advertising _____	$_____	$_____
Public Relations		
Postage	$_____	$_____
Printing	$_____	$_____
Direct Mail	$_____	$_____
Telephone	$_____	$_____
Other costs		
(specify) _____	$_____	$_____
(specify) _____	$_____	$_____
TOTAL	$_____	$_____

Items marked with an asterisk (*) are optional expenses that you probably will not incur if you conduct the seminar yourself and your program site is relatively close to your home.

MARKETING & PROMO PLAN

1. _____
   _____
   _____

2. _____
   _____
   _____

3. _____
   _____
   _____

4. _____
   _____
   _____

5. _____
   _____
   _____

6. _____
   _____
   _____

7. _____
   _____
   _____

8. _____
   _____
   _____

9. _____
   _____
   _____

10. _____
    _____

Determine Promotional Objectives

Calculate how many participants you will need to enroll in order to make back your expenses. You don't have to make a profit from your seminar, but it is always good to know how many bodies in chairs it takes to break even. You will also set a goal for the total number of participants you would like for your marketing/promotional efforts to attract.

Enrollment is the "bottom line". You can never have too many seminar participants. (If you run out of seats, find a bigger room in the same facility or schedule a second seminar the next day—don't turn away interested people!)

The first step in establishing your promotional goals or objectives is to figure out how many students you need in order to make back the money you spent promoting the seminar—your break-even point.

Here's how to determine that magic number:

Establish A Break-Even Point

◆ **Determine Total Costs** (Advertising, materials, fees, travel, etc.)

◆ **Divide Total Costs by Seminar Fee**

◆ **Result is the Number of Students Needed to Break Even**

Determine Preliminary Marketing Plan

Frequency of exposure is very important. When you use a well-coordinated variety of marketing and promotional strategies you create a synergistic effect; your message has a much more powerful impact because of the combination of strategies.

List a minimum of ten cost-effective marketing and promotional strategies that you will use to attract students to your next program. Plan for each strategy to pull at least three registrants.

List the specific marketing/promotional strategies you will use on the chart on page 102.

Draft Contact List

Make a list of everyone you know who may be able to help you fill the seats at your program. Include:

Prospective participants—individuals who may be interested in attending your program.

Influencers—people in positions of influence who could encourage others to attend your program.

Media contacts—print and broadcast media. List anyone you know who works for local papers, radio stations, cable TV stations and other media outlets.

CONTACT LIST

Prospective Participants	Influencers

CONTACT LISTS

Newspapers _____

_____

_____

_____

_____

Magazines _____

_____

_____

_____

_____

Trade Journals _____

_____

_____

_____

_____

Radio _____

_____

_____

_____

_____

Television _____

_____

_____

_____

Be 100% prepared! Know how you will handle all types of inquiries that could come up about your seminar. It might even be to your benefit to prepare and write out your responses to each.

EXERCISE

Prepare in advance, answers to the following questions:

1. Do you give discounts for more than one person from (an organization/the same family) attending a program?

2. I'd like some more information on your seminar.

3. I'm calling to cancel my registration.

4. I have a (brochure/flyer) on your seminar and would like some more information.

5. How does your program compare to the one offered by your competitor?

6. I want to attend your program but we don't have the money.

7. I would like to know more about your instructor.

8. I'd like to speak to someone who has attended your program.

9. I'd like to know more about your organization.

10. I'd like to speak to the instructor.

11. Can anyone attend your program?

12. I read your (brochure/flyer) and I'm not sure if your program is for me.

13. I have to leave early; will I miss anything important?

14. We're interested in having your program in-house.

15. I attended one of your programs and was very unhappy with it.

16. Can the press attend for free?

17. Do you give scholarships?

Publish Your Newsletter, Painlessly

CHAPTER 6

WAR STORY #6 *Now that I was starting to build a list of clients and potential clients, my obvious expert, Howard Shenson, had another idea to help my business grow—start a newsletter about my niche in educational testing.*

I could send the newsletter to the same people who were receiving the complimentary copies of my book with my brochures or flyers tucked into the back cover. The newsletter would serve as a gentle reminder to potential clients that I was still out there in case they needed my services.

I created a four-page newsletter right away, and I called it a monthly publication. The first issue was good. The second issue was great. Business started coming in as a result. In fact, business became so good and I was so busy with my new clients, that I did not take time to produce the third issue. The newsletter deadline crept closer, then passed, and I missed it.

Several readers called to inquire about the newsletter—had their names somehow slipped off the mailing list, they asked? A few readers wrote letters to make sure we had their correct address. Another week passed by and then many readers were calling. They were disappointed they hadn't received their third issue.

I was getting my initial contact with potential clients and it wasn't exactly starting on a positive note. What was I supposed to say? I did the only thing a responsible consultant could do under the circumstances—I told them they would shortly be getting a newsletter, twice as large as the old one—as a quarterly publication!

I had learned an important lesson: When you're starting a newsletter, think carefully about how often you promise to publish and how lengthy your newsletter really needs to be. Publishing less often or on an intermittent schedule, or even frequently publishing just a fact-filled, one-page newsletter will not negatively effect the perception of you as an obvious expert. But failing to fulfill a promise to your readership absolutely will.

EE Jr.

Use A Newsletter To Build Credibility

Few things build your credibility and status more than a really useful newsletter. When researching *High Income Consulting,* I found that top earners used newsletters to establish their authority, involve key decision makers in their business and even to make money. My mentor, the late great Howard Shenson, developed a really useful newsletter with a readership of 250,000 consultants across the globe—at a subscription of $149 a year. That is a major business in its own right!

Tom Lambert
www.centreforconsultingexcellence.com

Your Message In Print

No marketing brochure in the world can give you more cost-effective marketing than does a newsletter with your name listed as the editor or publisher. A newsletter is a very powerful piece for lofting you to obvious expert status.

Think about it: A newsletter acts as a showcase for your expertise and it finds its way to the desks of major decision-makers at regular intervals, depending on how often you publish. Many marketing and advertising brochures don't make it past the secretary's desk, but no administrative assistant is going to toss a newsletter that might contain valuable information the boss wants to see.

Publishing a newsletter can be incredibly easy. It doesn't have to be twenty pages; it can be just one. It doesn't have to have photographs or any artwork at all; it can be just text and your company's logo. And it doesn't have to be professionally printed; it can be photocopied onto heavy stock paper.

Your newsletter doesn't even have to be in physical form; it can be sent via email. Each version has its benefits. You might even want to publish both.

One word of warning: Don't back yourself into a corner by promising a timetable when you decide to publish a newsletter. If you say it will come out the first of every month and it doesn't, you lose credibility. And if you say it will come out monthly, Murphy's Law will ensure that you get slammed with consulting work after your first publication and you'll wonder where in the world you're going to find time to continue the newsletter.

You might want to start with publishing every other month, or even quarterly, and see how it fits into your schedule.

Getting Started

Before you start a newsletter, you need to determine:

- Who are your target readers?

- What do your target readers have in common?

- What subjects and issues interest your target readers?

- What concerns and problems do your target readers share?

Answering these questions will help you narrow what content to put into the newsletter and how to develop your mailing list. A public relations consultant would likely concentrate on articles involving personal and professional image, publicity and media trends. A financial consultant would probably stick to items about investing, spending and saving.

Content

Some items you might want to consider including in any newsletter:

- Original articles (by you)

- Reprints of newspaper and magazine articles that are relevant to your business and your client (Be sure to credit the source, even if you use only part of the article.)

- Client success stories and case histories that show off the different services you provide

Sell Your Products While You Sleep

The creation of online electronic newsletters (ezines) has positioned me well. More importantly, it has demanded that I write consistently in three formats every week. The benefits? I now have almost 13,000 subscribers who want to hear what I have to say each week. They are members of corporations or associations who use speakers for their conferences, meetings and executive retreats. They are purchasers of books, tapes and teleseminars. They are my best advertisers!

Two exceptional results: My most recent book was a very easy-to-do compilation of the best of one of the ezine's contents. I was able to bring 13,000 potential listeners worldwide into the negotiations when I signed the contract for my new two-hour weekly talk show on Internet radio, "Optimize Life Now!"

If you want to fill your pipeline and sell product while you sleep, build a quality ezine and provide practical, immediate tips and strategies to improve the success of people in your market.

ROBERTA SHALER
http://www.OptimizeLifeNow.com

Build Clients' Trust Through An ezine

I started writing and publishing online newsletters six years ago. The newsletters were about a variety of educational or writing topics, with personal essay-style introductions.

Soon I noticed a pattern: When my chatty personal section of the newsletter was particularly meaty, hits to my site went up. Later I realized that readers were most of all interested in what I wrote about my personal life, mainly parenting stories and anecdotes. This led to my creation of "N's Zine," a magazine for women age 25 to 45, the target market for my publishing company. Readers visiting my site to read my ezine trust me for information. By extension, they trust me to provide them with quality fiction.

NATALIE THOMAS
http://independentmysteries.com

- Testimonials from clients about recently completed projects

- Reprints of press releases and articles that may have appeared about you

- Excerpts from your own books, tapes and speeches

- News of awards you recently received

- Your speaking schedule

- Welcoming of your newest clients

- Surveys and questionnaires that will help you define and direct your business

- Humorous quotes, jokes and reprints of cartoons relevant to your area of expertise

If you're not sure what to write in your newsletter, keep track of any interesting material you read that might be valuable to your clients or people in your field. Mark it, and go back and ask the author whether you can include it in your newsletter with attribution to him or her. Most writers will give you permission because they appreciate the publicity, although you should always ask.

Your articles should be short, to-the-point nuggets that busy business people can read on the fly. If an article happens to be an excerpt of a longer report you have written, or something else you want to market, you can put a referral line at the bottom for readers to call your office and ask for the report to be sent to them.

This tactic accomplishes two things: It lets you disseminate more information about your services in an easy and inexpensive way, and it puts you in contact with potential clients. When a reader calls and asks for the report, you can take that person's name and address and then start a conversation. You might tell the person you have another report on a similar subject that you'll also send. And while you've got the person on the phone, direct the conversation so that you can glean information that will help future newsletters and your business.

One of the biggest advantages of having "editor" or "publisher" next to your name is that you can ask people questions as part of your research. If a person calls you to ask for a report, you could ask whether it would be okay to interview him or her for an article or a survey to be published in an upcoming newsletter. You will almost always get a "yes".

In your 'interview,' don't ask specifics, or the caller might think you're trying to give him or her a hard sell, when what you hope to do is develop a **rapport**. Just ask general questions about the caller's industry and the problems it faces. From your conversation, you should be able to gauge whether the caller has ever hired a consultant—a question you may want to ask outright. You'll know from the answers you receive whether or not this person should go on your list as a potential client.

There's one other factor to consider when you're deciding on the content of your newsletter: Think about your competition. If there are already newsletters in your industry, yours must fill a niche and stand out as different.

Fred Gleeck, master niche marketer and consultant, also the author of *Secrets of Self-Storage Marketing Success Revealed,* noticed that other newsletters in his industry were geared toward general industry concepts. He concentrated on content that answered the questions every business owner wants to know, like: "How do we get more customers?" He made the content specific to self-storage owners and operators. That tactic helped establish him as an obvious expert.

Design

Be sure to give your newsletter a name that will capture the reader's interest, and then print a tagline under the title that explains what the newsletter is about or tells something about its readership. (For instance, we published a newsletter which we

Reader's Humorous Content

After collecting the worst sales experiences of entrepreneurs and salespeople, I created a website to collect more stories online. My newsletter is now read worldwide by more than 6,000 people.

Why do they send me their stories? I bribe them! Stories that make the newsletter receive one of three gifts from me: a watch with my corporate logo, which is the chalk outline of a dead guy, or a poster of a noose with a humorous sales message, or a copy of my book of the best of the worst stories, *The Death of 20th Century Selling.* This wildly successful ezine is being called a cult hit among sales folks by *Sales & Marketing Management Magazine.*

DAN SEIDMAN
http://www.salesautopsy.com

Incorporate 4 "E's" Into Your Content

Too many people seem to consider a newsletter an advertisement and fill the pages with blatant come-hither and hard-sell promotions. When created in the right manner, a newsletter can be a welcome addition to the mailbox. Consider these "E words" in deciding what you want your newsletter to achieve:

1 *Excite* The information should be new and interesting.

2 *Educate* The reader should glean something new and useful from your words.

3 *Encourage* Your publication should spur the reader to do something, such as choose one product over another.

4 *Endear* The information you provide should endear readers to you and your business, and perhaps make the reader want to keep the newsletter.

T.J. Reid
http://www.tjreid.com

started in 1994 called, *PowerLines: The Ultimate Consultant & Seminar Business Report©.*)

Put your name in the banner as the editor or publisher. This reinforces your status as an expert.

Include the month and year somewhere at the top of the first page. Don't put Volume 1, Issue 1, because this sends a message that you are a new expert. On the bottom of every page, include your company's name and contact information, address, telephone number, email address and website—it is a plug for your business, and for you as the obvious expert, while you are keeping your readers informed.

Our newsletter, *PowerLines,* also has a small-print paragraph at the bottom of the first page telling readers that all of the content is copyrighted and what the annual subscription rate is. List the full retail price of your newsletter, even if you send it at a discounted rate or send it with your compliments to some of your clients. The price helps communicate to your readers that they have something valuable in their hands. They will be more inclined to read it and keep it or read it and then pass it along to friends and associates, than to toss it.

Layout the newsletter on your desktop computer using one of any number of programs on the market today. Most will allow you to drop copy and artwork into a standard template. Microsoft® Publisher, for example, contains more than thirty templates, and guides you through every step of the process, including sending the file to a professional print shop if you want to do that.

And here's another hint we picked up along the way: Punch three holes into the left side of each newsletter (or purchase pre-punched paper) to encourage people to insert the newsletter into a three-ring binder. This will increase dramatically the number of people who keep your newsletter instead of throwing it away when they're finished reading it.

Distribution

Deciding who should receive your newsletter is easy. Send the newsletter not only to your current clients but to anyone in your contacts list, business address book or marketing database who could use your services at some time or who might know someone who can. Keep adding to your list as you meet people or receive referrals from people you know.

If you are looking for a larger circulation list, check the public library for directories of mailing lists published by *Standard Rates and Data Services* or check online **www.srds.com**. You can purchase or rent mailing lists that offer very specific demographics by interest, geographical location, profession or other features.

For example, if you decide your best potential targets are chief administrators of acute care hospitals that have more than one hundred beds but less than two hundred, have cardiovascular units and are located in coastal cities with populations of less than eighty-five thousand people, you can get a mailing list of precisely those people.

More Tips

You'll find a printed newsletter comes in handy as more than a mailer. Here are other ways distributing a printed newsletter help define you as an obvious expert:

- Distribute your newsletter at your speeches, seminars or trade shows to generate leads. When people see your name and perhaps your photograph on the newsletters, they are more likely to seek you out to talk about information from the newsletter. People who might be able to use your services will make personal contact with you, saving you the trouble of picking them out of the crowd.

- Send your newsletter to media contacts, editors, columnists and radio personalities to generate publicity

You Never Know Who Will Read It

When I began speaking professionally full time, I published a brief one-page newsletter with copy on the front and back. I mailed it to key influencers I had identified and, of course, friends and colleagues.

I still don't know the exact route one of those newsletters took to reach a book publisher in New York, but she contacted me and asked for a one-page book proposal. She said anyone who could write so clearly and concisely certainly should be able to write a book. I responded, and the result was the publication of my first book, *Teambuilt: Making Teamwork Work*.

The key to hard-copy newsletters and enewsletters is to demonstrate expertise rather than just advertising your services. You never know what will happen!

MARK SANBORN
http://www.marksanborn.com

Start Off With An Email Newsletter

If you aren't comfortable writing your own newsletter, or email newsletter get a freelancer to interview you or to polish your words. Get another consultant to help you with the small details of online design, and/or mass emailing it.

Still, your costs will be considerably less than with a traditional mailed newsletter. You can 'mail it' more often, offer a poll, and lead your subscribers to a website where they can learn more about your business.

To jumpstart the introduction of your newsletter, offer a prize drawing for people who submit their email addresses to you. Let subscribers know you will maintain their privacy and not trade or sell your list of names.

CHRIS MCCLEAN
http://7lessoncourses.com

and increase your chances of being quoted in the media. Often, media professionals are seeking solid information to fill their news pages and broadcasts. Your information could come at the right time. Once they get used to seeing your name regularly in print, they come to think of you as an obvious expert.

- Insert your newsletter into other mailings as an added bonus for your current and potential clients. They will see it as a gift and will look favorably upon your business. Also, they might pass it along to other people who they know can use your services.

- Use your newsletter to help fulfill the desirable goal of following up with client prospects and other key clients, twelve to twenty-four times each year. It is key to stay in front of people who might become clients, and newsletters are a non-threatening way of doing it. Clients are not obligated to respond with a 'yes' or 'no', as they would be with a sales pitch. All they have to do is sit back, read and enjoy. One word of advice: Weed out your list occasionally. It is a waste of money to continue sending your newsletter to people who are not going to give you feedback and who are not interested in your services. If you haven't seen results in six months, recruit some help and give your newsletter a serious critique.

- If you are not confident in your writing ability, consider buying a 'canned' newsletter that covers your industry. These are pre-written by companies that write generic articles useful for many people, with topical themes, such as for doctors, dentists or attorneys. Add your business name to the front page and then send the newsletter to your contacts. A word of caution: Be sure the canned information will not conflict with your own values or beliefs, or support products you would not recommend, and that your competition is not using the same information sources.

- When you see articles in other publications that you think would interest your readers, call or email and ask the publishers for permission to reprint the articles in your newsletter. Most publications will agree as long as you attribute the article to them. Now you can fill space without having to do all of the writing yourself.

- Include some articles people can clip and save. Checklists such as "how-to" and "top ten" articles are especially handy. They give the reader quick glimpses into a situation or problem without requiring a lot of thought. Readers tend to save the articles for future reference.

- If you want to publish a monthly publication without investing a great deal of time, try a one-page, two-sided newsletter. Focus each month on one topic that you can write about in six hundred and fifty to seven hundred words, which is long enough to establish your credibility, but short enough that you don't need a Ph.D. to write about it. Include a resource box where you tell readers you are available for further help. Roger Parker is now using his innovative concept of the one-page newsletter with great success—in fact, he tailors his newsletters for custom audiences.

  Roger once published a newsletter for three months for employees he would be training at a U.S. auto manufacturing plant. By the time he entered the training room, the attendees were familiar with his work and receptive to him. The company has since asked him to return to conduct more training.

- Archive all of your newsletters on your website. Roger does this, and says it helps him beef up his website's content. It also provides a service for clients and

Use Advertising To Pay Your Costs

Starting my email newsletter is one of the best things I've done to make myself known. I started by emailing one of my articles to a dozen friends and asking them to pass it along to others who may be interested. I quickly started receiving requests from complete strangers, asking to be added to my mailing list.

Today, I broadcast every two weeks to thousands of subscribers. I still include my own articles, and I also include articles from guest authors. By creating two spots for sponsor ads and a place for a handful of classified ads, I get a steady stream of advertising revenue that more than pays for the hosting and database maintenance services. Overall, a great investment!

GARY LOCKWOOD
http://www.BizSuccess.com

Draw People To Your Website With A Newsletter

I operate the largest online marketplace for opt-in email lists and marketing services. My email newsletter, *Email Marketing Results,* is a critical component of the marketing strategy for the website. Every time I send out the newsletter, I can count on a 20 to 25% surge in traffic on the website. Email newsletters I've created for clients have achieved similar results.

AL BREDENBERG
http://www.emailresults.com

prospects by giving them access to his articles, so that they can benefit from his expertise long after the newsletter has been published.

● Write articles that probe into the expertise of people who could be your biggest potential clients. This will give you exposure to these prospects you could not get otherwise. Think about what kind of reception you would get if you called people's offices and asked for an appointment to talk to them about the consulting services you offer—they wouldn't give you the time of day. But ask those same people to grant you an interview for your newsletter, and they will roll out the red carpet.

● After you've published articles quoting people who could be potential clients or good contacts for you, send each of those people twenty copies of the newsletter. One is for the quoted person to keep, and the other nineteen copies are for them to send to people they would like to influence or impress. This technique gets your name circulated among people who also might someday want to pay you for your services.

● Once you've established contact with the people you interview, they will most likely remind you at every opportunity that they are open to being quoted again in your newsletter. In other words, they think of you as a friend and remember your name when they need your services or know someone else who does. Many business and professional people have had the experience of being misquoted or represented in an unflattering light by media services. If you can establish yourself in their eyes as fair and friendly, as a venue where they know they will always get good press, then you find they typically beat a path to your door hoping for future publicity.

Electronic Newsletters

Email newsletters follow many of the same guidelines as their print counterparts. Articles and items should be short. Electronic newsletters are designed for busy people, who are going to file it aside to read later if it contains more than four computer screens (pages) of information. If your readers get too many back issues piled up in their queue, they may unsubscribe.

But electronic newsletters have an advantage that print versions do not offer: They can contain hyperlinks, which are website addresses embedded into the copy. Hyperlinks make your newsletter dynamic. The reader can click the address and go immediately to your website, perhaps for more information on an article—but certainly to find out more about what you offer as a consultant.

You can send a simple text-only email. Or you can email your newsletter yourself, directly from your own database. Remember, sending attachments creates potential formatting discrepancies between what you create and what the viewer may see. You also run the risk of your newsletter simply being deleted by computer users who are virus wary.

When you send a text-only email, be sure to start with your most important story at the top, along with an enticing headline. Make it clear where one article stops and another begins. Do this through use of headlines and spacing.

Distribution of an electronic newsletter can be as simple as sending out a mass email to targeted people. If you chose this route, be sure to use the "Bcc" function on your email—that stands for blind carbon copy and prevents any recipient from seeing any other recipient's email address. Or, simply create what many email management programs call a "personal distribution list" or "group" list, which permits you to list many names under one title and transmit a document to every email address on the list by entering a single title.

As your newsletter grows in popularity, or if you're starting

Readers Love Personal Details

Today's ezines are the advice columns of yesteryear. The more meaty the info you can provide, in a down-home style, the more readership you'll build. And people love personal details—especially if you're funny. *My Publishing Game* ezine complements my books and other writing and publishing offerings. And keeping my customers and friends reading keeps them ordering.

FERN REISS
http://PublishingGame.com

Try A Newsletter Postcard

For the past four years, I have consistently built my business on a small 4.25×5.5-inch postcard with business tips. Here are my guidelines:

1 Make your postcard newsletter timely, short, easy on the eyes, informational (give tips, not teasers), upbeat and personal. You should offer discounts but limit advertising.

2 Build a nugget library of typical business tips, which are 75 words or less.

3 Build your mailing list, even if you start with only 50 names.

4 Send it via snail mail, and I recommend you do it monthly.

5 Use a balance of graphics and words, even if you use clip-art graphics.

6 Mail it first class.

7 Carry extras with you to all networking opportunities.

LINDA L. FAYERWEATHER
http://www.lindafay@lindafay.com

with a large subscriber list you may find emailing from your mailbox to be inconvenient. There are email list hosting providers that will do the job for you for a fee.

When you sign up, you give the hosting provider a list of recipients. Send the provider a copy of the newsletter when you're ready to publish, and the provider takes care of the rest. That includes maintaining your subscriber list. Anytime you want to add names, you just email them to the provider. When readers want to unsubscribe or to change addresses, they can automatically email the provider, who updates the list.

Just as with a print newsletter, you want to make sure your publication has a catchy title at the top, along with a descriptive tagline. At the bottom you need a paragraph containing all of your contact information.

And here's an added bonus: Electronic versions typically contain more biographical information about you and your company than print newsletters. This could include a description of your business, information about how to purchase your latest books or reports, and referrals to your other specialties, businesses or newsletters. In other words, you get to highlight what makes you the obvious expert to publish this newsletter.

Kevin Hogan publishes a very effective weekly ezine called, *Coffee with Kevin*. He chose the title because he wanted to convey the feeling of an intimate conversation between two friends or business associates over morning coffee.

Kevin shares his tips for publishing a weekly ezine:

● Keep your typestyle simple so every single recipient can read it. That way, you don't have to worry what fonts the person's computer can recognize. Your newsletter can be several screens long but will appear as one continuous page with a hyperlink to other websites sprinkled in.

- Publish early in the week so people can look forward to getting the newsletter and can put your information to work right away. If it comes out on Friday, for instance, they might forget about it by the time they returned to work on Monday.

- Develop your own formula and follow it every week so your readers know what to expect. For instance, start out with your lead story, and then have a question-and-answer segment, followed by the week's industry news, and wrapping up with housekeeping items such as your upcoming calendar and contact information.

- Keep the content focused on your areas of expertise. If you do stray from that topic in an article, try to tie it into what you do so people understand why you feel compelled to write about it.

- Start off talking about something a little controversial. The point is to try to get the reader to respond in some way, even if it's to email you with an opposing viewpoint. There's a fine line to walk here—you don't want to insult any of your readers. Be sensitive and present both sides, but choose one position and explain why.

- Mingle in comments about what's going on in your life. You might ask why people would care. But think about the impression you give when you tell them you've just returned from London or Charlotte or Sacramento. It implies you're the obvious expert because someone paid you to go there. If you mention you just recorded three new CDs in a studio, your readers may be motivated to purchase them.

- Briefly tell the readers where you're going to be next. Say "I'll be teaching January 26 in Minneapolis and then

Get A Start With Your Newsletter

"I don't think I would have had a business if I did not start a newsletter. My first was a simple double-sided page, photocopied and mailed to 300 people whose business cards I had painstakingly collected. It changed my business overnight. When I met people, I would say, 'May I send you my free newsletter?' and they would happily give me a card. I added to my classified ads: 'Call for our free newsletter,' and the responses skyrocketed. People passed copies on to friends and posted them on bulletin boards. Now my newsletter is an ezine and goes to many thousands of people, but I still get phone calls from clients who first learned about me from that old newsletter."

C.J. HAYDEN
http://www.getclientsnow.com

Make It Easy For Your Readers

These elements will give your newsletter a professional appearance and help grow your subscription list:

1 Make it easy to subscribe by publicizing your newsletter on your website, in your email signature with a hyperlink, with subscription instructions on your print materials, with verbal invitations to groups you address, and in information you hand out during seminars. Also make it easy to unsubscribe.

2 *Use viral marketing.* Consider cross-promotions with non-competing newsletters targeting the same audience. Text newsletters are the preferred format for most types of reader software.

3 *Make your newsletter interesting* and newsworthy with content-rich articles.

4 *Publish at least once a month.* For email newsletters, let readers opt in and don't spam them with unwanted information. State your privacy policy regarding email addresses. Include your reprint policy and your concise signature/byline with at least three ways to contact you: phone, email and website.

JANET DELPH
http://www.expertmagazine.com

January 28 in Philadelphia." Tell them the subject matter. That way, if you're appearing in their community, they can come hear you speak. Give them a hyperlink to your website, where they can register online.

- Keep the ezine content-powered. You want to have so much information that they can't wait to read it and can't bear to stop once they've started. Throw in excerpts from your latest speech, or how-to articles that would interest most of your readers. For instance, I've written about self-confidence, procrastination and sales techniques, including tools people could use for self-improvement.

- Near the bottom, include a special offer for a seminar you're teaching. I advertised a nine-week ecourse, and I had seven people sign up at $2,000 each. Even if no one signs up as a result of your ad, the promotional piece has given readers proof that you are the obvious expert.

- Close by listing your website address at the very bottom of the page. One of my readers asked me to do that. It makes finding your website convenient.

Kevin says it takes him about five hours each week to produce his ezine, but the effort pays off in product sales, contacts and new clients. He estimates his ezine brings in at least $1,000 to $2,000 weekly in additional income.

Publishing an ezine is also a good way to let potential clients know about timely services you might be offering. Soon after the September 11, 2001, attacks on the United States, Wil Horton was scheduled to teach a seminar on the timely topic of "Critical Incident Stress Resolution."

He was hesitant about using the U.S. mail to promote it because so many people were concerned about dangerous contaminants being spread through postal envelopes. So Wil used his ezine to get the word out.

He emailed his electronic magazine to his fifteen hundred subscribers—what happened next was very interesting. So many readers forwarded the email to people they knew, that Wil's mailing list grew right away by five percent. His seminars, presented in five cities in the East and Midwest, filled up quickly. Even though he was charging only half of his normal cost in an effort to help the economy, Wil was still pleased with the results.

The examples from Kevin and Wil point out another sure sign that you're the obvious expert: when your marketing tools actually help you bring in revenue.

A SPECIAL CONTRIBUTION FROM
Roger C. Parker

Frequency Is Important

Roger C. Parker is a best-selling author, speaker and consultant with a background in sales and marketing. He has written thirty-one books which have sold over a million and a half copies and authored hundreds of articles. Roger has presented hundreds of design and marketing seminars throughout the United States and Australia and his clients have included Apple Computer, Hewlett-Packard, John Deere, Microsoft, Shearman & Sterling and Yamaha.

A two-sided, one-page newsletter sent to customers and prospects once a month is a far better alternative than larger issues that appear bimonthly or quarterly.

One-page newsletters focused on a single educational topic are easy to prepare and distribute. They can be distributed for no cost when small quantities are printed on your desktop printer for hand

WIN-WIN-Win

The best way to reach your customer base and demonstrate your super expertise and knowledge is to create a monthly free ezine.

- Publish religiously on the same date or dates every month.

- Include lots of great content and how-to information that's very useful to your audience (customer base).

You'll establish a rapport with them and can promote yourself and your products to them. Win-win-win. Get started today!

ERIC GELB
http://www.PublishingGold.com

Consider Personalizing

Newsletters offer a prime example of a communications element that can be well-served in a digital format. First, development and distribution is much less expensive than print. Emails average roughly .15¢– .30¢ per message, vs. $1.50 for a single direct mail piece. The receipt of information is immediate, and delivery/ response rates are fully trackable. Each individual newsletter can be personalized, which can dramatically increase the read rate.

JENNIFER ZICK
http://www.reside.biz

distribution to key customers and prospects. Other copies can be sent as email attachments. Most importantly, one-page newsletters can enrich your website by driving traffic to it each month.

Archiving past issues on your site adds useful content for your readers and makes your site more attractive to search engines.

I prepared my first one-page newsletter to arouse advance interest in an upcoming presentation at an international conference. I sent it as an email attachment to three previous clients, one of whom was a program manager at Microsoft®. Soon after sending it out, I left for lunch. When I returned to my office, there was an email Request for Quotation from Microsoft asking for a week of my consulting time. If my one-page newsletter hadn't been in the program manager's email inbox that day, I would almost certainly have missed out on an important consulting opportunity.

For more information on
Publishing Your Own Newsletter, visit:
www.obvious-expert.com/newsletter

Write Copy That Communicates

A SPECIAL CONTRIBUTION FROM
☙ David Garfinkel ☙

David Garfinkel is the President of Overnight Marketing in San Francisco. His firm specializes in results-driven direct marketing for Entrepreneurial Businesses. David is a marketing consultant and a master copywriter. He has worked with businesses in eighty-one different industries. When he is not busy helping clients turn their adverting efforts into more sales and more profits, he is frequently busy granting interviews to *The Wall Street Journal, USA Today, Fast Company, Home Office Computing* and dozens of other newspapers, magazines and trade journals.

There are twenty-six letters in the alphabet that can obviously be re-arranged in vast combinations to form words and word groups. While the possibilities seem infinite, in fact, the number of words that are common and frequently used in social language tend to mark the rather limiting parameters of our communications boundaries.

Words within those boundaries come and go with the times, making the nucleus of our communicative language-set even smaller. Somewhere, someone had to make a decision, whether or not: "things go more pleasantly with your favorite soft drink," your sport shoe should inspire you to, "just take action," or if you, "deserve a respite today."

When advertising and marketing language, or what is commonly called "copy," is weak, obvious expert David Garfinkel points out, it hurts your business in two ways:

◆ **Your business has wasted the money spent to create the copy and artwork, not to mention the money spent to send, buy the space for, or host the promotion.**

◆ **Clients who were already looking for what you have to offer have chosen to go with your competitors who have better, clearer copy.**

BULLETPROOFING YOUR COPY

Analyze the following Sentences	✔

Read your copy aloud.

When you speak the words you've written, you'll come across errors and clumsy word combinations that will often escape you when you read the same words silently. Reading it aloud helps you check the language 'flow.'

Show your copy to a child.

This is a valuable and little-known technique. It's especially worth doing if you are planning to conduct a large mailing campaign. A ten-year-old child will tell you what's unclear with greater accuracy than the best professional editor. If a child understands it, then your busiest and most distracted adult reader will be able to understand it, too.

Show your copy to a client or prospect.

Nothing puts your copy to the test better than showing it to your 'profile' client for their reaction, but here's a warning: Some people feel compelled to become instant literary critics or hypercritical English professors when they are put in this role. You don't want this. Tell the person reading your copy you want to know if they understand what your copy is about and if they are interested in what you are offering. All you are looking for are 'yes' answers, not suggestions on how to 'improve the grammar' or 'make it more businesslike.' Such suggestions are well intentioned, but if you act on them, they will usually take the 'teeth' out of your copy.

Put your copy through this final six-point checklist:

- Will your prospects understand what you're offering them?
- Will they understand what you want them to do?
- If you have an order form, is it quick and easy to fill out?
- Could a busy, distracted, irritable person fill out your order form with a minimum of effort?
- Is the type big enough to read (typically about 12 point)?
- Are words, sentences and paragraphs short with roughly no more than 4 lines per paragraph, with spacing between each paragraph?

Result:

"You may have lost the lifetime value each of those clients would have spent with you. Weak copy steals money from the future of your business."

To address the problems many of us have with writing powerful, concise copy, David has developed his trademarked, *Copy Optimizer*™.

The *Copy Optimizer*™ explains:

Good copy will

◆ get the right prospect's attention.

◆ create or intensify desire.

◆ develop trust and conviction.

◆ prompt the prospect to take action.

Try to eliminate these five copy weaknesses:

◆ Copy written too hurriedly.

◆ Copy doesn't 'speak' well.

◆ Language too jargon-y.

◆ Copy not focused on prospect's hot-buttons.

◆ Copy missing basic elements of success.

DAVID GARFINKEL

More Tips:

Change all sentences in your copy that start with the word "It" or "There". Any way you re-write the sentence will be stronger and more effective than if the sentence begins with either of these two words. If you are writing a book, or even a report, you will sometimes find it unavoidable to structure your sentence to eliminate first-word use of the words, "It" or "There," but in advertising or marketing copy—when every word is crucial—don't waste any sentences with this ineffectual beginning.

Eliminate the word "the" as much as possible throughout your copy, along with the words "which is," and "who is". Many times these words are unnecessary in the sentence.

Write your copy with the adverbs and adjectives (these are your descriptive words) you choose—then take the red pen to your paper and eliminate 50% of them. One powerful, descriptive word beats the heck out of a string of semi-effective words.

When you need to check many lines of type against something already written, try working backward. The psychological principle known as closure often causes us to read words as we intellectually presume they are—not what is actually printed.

Example:

If you saw the written words, "No purchase necessary, must be eighteen years of age or odor to enter," you may assume you have seen the word "older". This happens because you have read this grouping of words so frequently that you don't actually **read** each word. Spellcheck programs in word processing software will let you write **odor** when you mean **older**. Spellcheck does not care if your copy stinks. If you let the error slip past, blame closure.

E X E R C I S E

Using your most recently written newsletter, brochure, flyer or ad, rewrite the copy applying the tips in the worksheet. When you are finished, compare the results. Next, go back to the document and see if you can express the same ideas equally well after reducing the word count by 25%. Shorter is usually better! "You can effectively rid your home of harmful environmental allergens in six easy steps."

Over-familiarity with written word (especially your own words) will cause you to miss errors in your copy. To compare one written document against another, check the words by reading them from the bottom of the page to the top, working backward (or right to left) as your go. Errors or omissions will jump out at you because you are reviewing what you see, not what you think you see.

Get Your Magazine and Journal
Articles in Print

CHAPTER 7

WAR STORY #7 *I learned from Howard Shenson that people do not buy from sales people. They buy from professionals.*

It's not who you know, but how you meet them. People buy from someone they have grown to trust, admire, respect—someone they know professionally who just happens to be able to provide something they need at the moment, not someone who walks in off the street and tries to sell them something.

But if you want to build a business that is more than local or regional, how do you get to know potential clients in other parts of the world? More importantly, how do they get to know you? Mingling with people in other cities, states or countries is not as easy as shaking hands with professionals at the local Rotary Club. It involves a different strategy and one of the best ways to create the illusion that you're standing there in someone's office, offering your services as a trusted adviser, is to publish an authoritative article with your name and perhaps a photograph with it.

Many of my friends and colleagues have seen their careers soar as a result of articles published in magazines and trade journals. Kevin Hogan talks about how he unexpectedly turned a personal health issue he was facing into a thriving branch of his consulting business simply by writing from his heart.

Kevin shared with readers of Hearing Health *magazine the story of how he successfully*

Start Writing Daily To Become A Writer

If you want to get published in magazines, you really should be writing on a daily basis. This may be easier for some than others. If you're an engineer from 9 AM to 5 PM, take out the pen at night. Or let your spouse take care of the kids for a few hours.

Becoming a successful and established writer takes practice. You have to start slowly and work your way up. Let's say you have no editorial background. Offer to write some items for your local newspaper for free. Get some experience under your belt and then approach a magazine for work.

At my last full-time job, I wrote day in and day out. The material was primarily training related, not editorial, but it was still great preparation for what I am doing today. Now I typically write a few career-related articles each month. I am editing a book on business terms for young entrepreneurs. And I write for my own clients. After all my hard work, I am considered an expert at what I do.

ERIN FLYNN
http://flynnmedia.com

battled tinnitus, a severe ringing in the ears. Kevin's article opened new doors for him in consulting. It dawned on readers as they read Kevin's articles that he was obviously the person who could help them if they read his book and learned the technique of self-hypnosis.

Kevin recognized the opportunity. He created products and services to meet the demands of the readers. Six months after the magazine published the first of a five-part series on the subject, he had made tens of thousands of dollars on sales of his products—all because his magazine articles demonstrated he was the obvious expert.

EE Jr.

Your Name In Print—Obviously!

We talked in Chapter Five about establishing yourself as an editor or publisher of your own newsletter. Another way to get your name in print and promote yourself as the obvious expert is to write articles for magazines or trade journals, or newspapers or web-based publications.

Many of the same benefits apply—for instance, leaders of your industry will speak with you if you ask to interview them for a story you're writing in a magazine or trade journal. But these articles have some advantages over publishing a newsletter:

1 They can be one-time shots. You don't necessarily have to follow a set schedule, producing them on a regular schedule as you do a newsletter.

2 You're writing only one article instead of filling an entire newsletter.

3 The circulation of a magazine, journal or newspaper is likely to be substantially larger than that of your newsletter.

Writing articles is a sure way of differentiating yourself from your competitors. Most consultants don't take the time and effort to project their knowledge and expertise in such a public forum.

Getting your first article published can be tricky. Until you've established yourself as a writer or a recognizable expert in your field, magazines and trade journals are not going to invite you to write articles. You will have to 'sell' yourself and your ideas to them. You may or may not be offered compensation for your work.

Roger Parker says he got his foot in the door at a leading trade magazine by striking a barter deal. He knew the magazine would not pay him, but the publication was the perfect vehicle for Roger to get his name out to potential clients. He went to the publisher and said, "I've got a deal for you. I'll write these wonderful marketing articles and advertising critiques, and in return you give me a quarter-page ad."

So every month, readers in his designated target market saw three to ten pages in a one hundred and fifty to two hundred-page magazine with Roger's words on them. His picture and his biographical and contact information ran with each article. He also had a quarter-page ad in the same publication. He couldn't have gotten better publicity if he'd paid for it. And the magazine benefited by having a meaty piece of content it could count on every month.

How To Choose Your Topic

As with newsletters, some of the best-read stories are those that are informative and give readers a solution to a challenge they might be having today. One example is an article listing ten ways to solve a specific problem. Another is to choose a topic that begins with "How to. . . "

IGPC faculty member, Nick Nichols, uses the following strategy when he writes articles for magazines and trade journals. His target audience is small business owners who work at home,

Marketing Through Your Articles

While you can't be everything to everybody, you can be something to somebody! Writing magazine articles Is a great way to niche yourself into being perceived as an expert in your field and in a specific industry. By writing articles supplying practical information, you can reach a specific audience and springboard into other opportunities, including keynote and conference speaking and guest appearances on radio and TV. You can also use the articles as marketing pieces, sending copies of them to clients and prospects.

ORLANDO BLAKE
http://www.blake-group.com

Share What You Know

I've been writing for publications for 29 years. I didn't realize how much knowledge I'd accumulated until 10 or 15 years ago when people started asking for writing advice. I was so busy using the techniques I'd learned from those years of experience that I pretty much took my skills for granted.

New writers' questions however, brought my level of expertise to the surface. And when I discovered how much I loved sharing what I knew, I decided to teach it. My writing workshops added to my credibility as did my two subsequent books, *A Writer's Guide to Magazine Articles* and *Over 75 Good Ideas for Promoting Your Book*. Currently, I enjoy writing articles for a variety of writing-related magazines, ezines and websites. And I often encourage others to share their particular brand of expertise because giving is also a gift to oneself.

PATRICIA FRY
http://www.matilijapress.com

primarily over the Internet, selling their products and services. About four years ago, Nick wrote a magazine article on "How to Create an Offer for Your Web Page," telling readers that most of their web pages give no incentive for people to return again and again. It took Nick only about one hour to write the four hundred-word article, but the effort generated a large amount of feedback and several thousands of dollars of business for him.

Coming up with a topic is as simple as asking people in your area of expertise what kinds of problems they're facing. You can get ideas just by listening when you're at a business luncheon, or speaking with the person next to you on the plane on your next business trip, or reading newspapers and magazines to keep up on the latest trends, or asking friends and colleagues to brainstorm with you.

Nick says he writes many of his articles after becoming annoyed with something that is happening in the business world that he thinks has a direct impact on his target market or on business in general. It serves as inspiration for him.

"Then I just go and write what I feel," he says. "It's almost like a rant—like a Dennis Miller rant. I rant about a specific problem and then I come up with solutions, one or more solutions, for that problem in my article."

Steven Haas says his articles often evolve from notes he's preparing for an important conversation or sales presentation. "Usually it seems that I'm about halfway through my preparation activity and I look down and say, Wow, I've got some information here that would make for a great article or special report someday."

When that happens, Steven sometimes calls magazine editors and publishers to determine whether they're interested at this early stage. If they are, he develops the idea into an article. Sometimes he takes the same idea and writes both an article and a special report—from different angles, of course.

Writing Guidelines

A full-length article for a magazine or trade publication typically is between one and three thousand words. It might delve into a subject from many different angles, taking a more in-depth look at a problem, its history and its solutions. Articles usually incorporate information from more than one source. For example, you might interview several of your clients or other people in your field for different perspectives in a full-length article.

A column, on the other hand, tends to be shorter—usually four hundred to one thousand words and focuses on your opinions or observations about one aspect of an issue. That issue could be as simple as a review of a new book or as complicated as an explanation of how to cope with the latest tax codes.

Steven has a special routine he goes through to write a magazine article, and he points out that the same advice applies to writing reports.

1 **Always begin with the end in mind.** "I ask myself what the readers really need to learn, and then I give it to them in bite-size pieces," he says. "I usually start with a compelling title and subtitle. From there I craft pertinent bullet points that will serve as bull-headers for the article and help the reader dissect the information. This serves as the outline and allows me to assemble pertinent information that flows well for the reader."

2 **Think user-friendly.** "Always lead with a hypnotic introduction," Steven says. "You want to pull the readers into the report and set them up for a meaningful take-away. When you arrive at your first subheader, or bullet point, you should set that up for the reader as well."

3 **Write as if you're telling a story.** "Always be looking ahead and letting the subject matter lead into the following bold header."

4 **Create a compelling close.** "After you've covered all of

Warm Up Your Articles With Personal Stories

Articles that have a human dimension as well as provide valuable 'how to' information are highly sought. Technical information is good, but the article becomes special when you can integrate your experiences (good and bad).

Have a sales tip you'd like to share? Great. Integrate it with a candid and humorous personal story that lets your readers know it's OK to make some goofs along the way.

My article titled *Confessions of a Reluctant Saleswoman* not only continues to be published in numerous Internet magazines, but it generated such interest that I developed a speaker's topic around it that gets rave reviews.

JOYCE COLEMAN
http://www.joycecoleman.com

Cultivate Your Contacts And Clients

Several years ago I sat next to the publisher of a major city newspaper at a business association meeting. I proposed a few topics on marketing, which she agreed to publish. Over the next five years, I published more than 50 articles for the newspaper. Once I was published in the newspaper, it was easy to get accepted for publication in other marketing magazines, newspapers, websites and books. And I discovered a great marketing strategy for my business. Every time I published an article, I would send it out to my database with a small note. Invariably, I would get a new client from the mailing.

DEBBIE BERMONT
http://www.simpleprinciples.com

the pertinent information, bring the readers full circle," Steven says. "Summarize the information you've just shared and then share several strategies on how they might use that information."

5 **Give yourself time to revise.** "When you're finished writing, put the piece down and walk away for at least one day," Steven says. "It's amazing how creative we can be when we've given our brains a rest and look at things from a different perspective."

6 **Include pertinent photos and/or graphics.** If you're not that adept with technology, you could even partner with a printer or a multimedia firm and ask for help in creating something that really stands out.

7 **Get some second opinions.** "When you think you've got a finished project, pass it around to a few trusted advisers within your circle," Steven says. "Ask them to provide comments, feedback and suggestions."

8 **Give yourself credit.** "Before you submit your article or print your report, make sure you include a byline that briefly describes you, your business and a few of your noteworthy connections and/or accomplishments."

9 **Protect your work.** Remember to include the ©. The © serves as a legal copyright. This is evidence that the material is copyrighted and that other people cannot legally claim it as their own. However, if you want to defend that copyright in a court of law, you have to register it.

10 **Include your contact information.** Give the readers several ways to get in contact with you. Provide your name, telephone number, business address, website and email address.

Choose The Right Publication

Deciding where to send your article is actually even more important than choosing the subject matter itself. Howard Shenson came to this conclusion after researching which consultants seemed to get the most business after having articles published.

"Most people who were writing articles and not gaining new clients as a result, were usually writing for the academic, theoretical and scholarly journals," he said. "Who reads those? Graduate students and allegedly their professors. Neither group has a budget for consulting. Neither group has a need for consulting. You may get asked to travel three thousand miles at your expense to present your findings at a symposium of your peers, but flattery is not economically rewarding."

On the other hand, people who were writing articles for trade magazines were getting consulting assignments. "The people who read those are practitioners," Howard said. "They don't have time to go to symposiums, but they do have budgets to bring you to their corporate headquarters to analyze and solve their problems."

Think about which publication or publications would offer you the perfect audience of readers who might be able to use your services. The size of the publication's circulation is not important. Even if its readership is not as large as those of the major U.S. business magazines are, a small trade magazine can be a perfect vehicle for your article if its readers are specifically interested in your field of expertise.

Some authors prefer to approach one publication at a time with an article. They do not want the conflict of more than one publication accepting the article and then having to choose which publication to turn down. Other authors routinely identify to the editor that an article is sent as a multiple submission. This lets the editor know up front that other editors may be reading and vying for the article.

The Best At What You Do

We specialize in retail conference speaking and consultancy with clients in over 15 countries. The key is to be recognized as the best at what you do.

You need credible exposure in the market place. In our experience, the key has been to write an authoritative book that fills a niche in the market place. We wrote *Just About Everything a Retail Manager Needs To Know* and we also aim to get regular columns in the leading trade magazines around the globe. Remember it has to be regular as your audience needs to be constantly reminded of who you are and the skills you can offer. This is then followed up with an enewsletter to targeted clients.

JOHN STANLEY
http://www.jstanley.com.au

Make sure you know in advance if a publisher is willing to look at a multiple submission. Also, be certain when you contact the editor, either by letter or phone, that you tell enough of your idea to sell it, but not so much that an editor can re-work your thoughts and assign a highly similar article to one of their publication's staff writers.

Research And Networking

Do you sometimes need more material for your articles? If so, don't overlook the expertise of colleagues and associates that can add a different and sometimes richer point of view. You can also use this opportunity to expand your network by contacting someone who you would like to know. I was recently writing an article about morale in the workplace and the importance of having fun. I contacted one of the leading authorities on the subject, interviewed and quoted her in the article. I have recently had the chance to meet her when I was in her city and now have a new colleague.

BARBARA **WINGFIELD**
http://www.moralebuilders.com

> **"**
>
> *I was working in the field of higher education when I got frustrated by the lack of business acumen I observed around me. I got interested in the idea of marketing and started to give talks about it through* The Council for Advancement and Support of Education (CASE). *I wrote short articles for their magazine,* Currents. *The Council asked me to write a book about marketing higher education. I worked three years on it in my spare time. They published it. I kept the copyright in my own name. I wrote more books for them and then I started my own publishing company,* Educational Catalyst Books. *From there I published a newsletter (now in its 18th year). Then I launched my consulting business and, as they say, the rest is history. I have been recognized as one of the founding fathers of applying marketing principles to higher education. I am also the author of thirteen books on marketing higher education and nonprofit.*
>
> Bob Topor
>
> **"**

Writers do have some protection (remember the copyright © you added to your work?), and the greatest protection for both writers and publications is that the ethics standards in an industry where everyone trades on the integrity of his or her name, is extremely high. However, take all the steps necessary on your part to help prevent any potential conflicts that could arise from individual differences in perception of what constitutes similar-but-different articles.

Another factor in your choice of publication should be the length of time between when a magazine accepts an article and when it publishes it. Howard said he and a friend were in graduate school when they submitted their first article to a trade journal. It was accepted in two weeks, and the two men rejoiced that they'd soon be famous. But the article wasn't published for another three years. By that time, Howard and his friend had practically forgotten what they'd written.

Many people have achieved publication by submitting stories or columns to web-based publications such as ezines. Some of these publications go out to people who pay to receive them and others are free to the reader. You can find a listing of some ezines and their submission rules at **www.freezineweb.com**, The Free Directory of Ezines.

Most ezines have not yet gained the prestige of their print counterparts, but they offer several advantages you can't get from a magazine or trade journal.

1 Once one of your stories or columns is posted on an ezine, you never know where it'll show up. Often, other ezines will pick it up, and web publishers will use it in their newsletters, so your words have the potential to spread like wildfire.

2 Stories and columns that are posted on the Internet often stay there forever. That means long after the latest issue of your favorite trade magazine is in someone's recycling pile, your words can still be read by people surfing the Internet for information.

Fill The Publication's Needs

My sales horror story articles are appearing in magazines like *Entrepreneur, Realtor,* and *Stephen Covey's Sales & Marketing Excellence,* and many trade publications.

The best technique for pitching and getting a 'yes'? Go online and look at the publication's editorial calendar. You'll see topics for upcoming issues. Call the editors and mention which issue you'd like to write for. They'll be grateful that you know their needs and you'll be off to a great start with a new relationship that will bring tens of thousands of eyes of new exposure to your business.

DAN SEIDMAN
http://www.salesautopsy.com

> " *An easy way to send email queries is to use an email submission service, which saves you the time and expense of finding the names and email addresses of editors and agents to contact.*
>
> Gini Graham Scott "

Find A Publication That Targets Your Client Base

One of my best marketing vehicles has been the column I write for *U.S. Frontline*. It's a magazine catering to Japanese business people, which is one of my target groups since we primarily consult for Japanese-affiliated firms. I've lost count of how many reader inquiries have led to client engagements, and the column also provides great exposure for my seminars and books. And being the only American who writes for them makes me stand out—my photo is with the column, so I often get recognized at sushi bars! The key is to find a publication that targets your potential client base, and develop a good relationship with them so that they will publish you consistently, preferably as a columnist.

ROCHELLE KOPP
http://www.japanintercultural.com

Write Your Query Letter

If you know someone who's the editor or publisher of a magazine, and you have regular conversations with that person, you might be able to pitch an article yourself without going through a formal process.

For most consultants and most writers, the only way to propose an article to a magazine or trade journal is to follow the ages-old tradition of writing a query letter to the editor or publisher who will make the decision.

The query letter is a standard, formatted request that tells the publication what your article would be about, how you would handle the subject matter, why you're qualified to write the article and when you could produce it. In other words, it's a sales letter.

One of the best sources for learning about writing a query letter, and identifying where to send it, is *Writer's Market*®, an annually updated guide with information about publishers and articles about getting published. *Writer's Market*®, also available online and updated daily, **www.writersmarket.com**, lists magazines and trade journals in alphabetical order by category and tells you how each publication expects to receive query letters, provides mailing addresses, information you should include and any special instructions.

Many professional writers consider writing an effective query letter a tougher challenge than writing the article (or the book) that the query is meant to sell. Your letter must convince the editor that his or her readership wants to read the story you want to write, that you will increase magazine sales and/or credibility with your topic and your byline and that, of all the writers out there, you are the best one for the job—and you typically have to accomplish this in two typed pages or less. While this sounds like an impossible task, it is really a learned skill. Here are some tips to help make the process easier:

Pay close attention to the submission guidelines from the publication where you'd like your article to appear. These are available to you by writing and requesting them from the publication or in a resource guide like *Writer's Market*®. Also, more and more publications are posting their guidelines online. Study the guidelines and read between the lines. Be sure you are presenting your article in a way that the editor will see how it 'fits' with their format and philosophies.

Use quality business stationary for your letter, with a complete return address, email address and your phone number. Always include a #10 self addressed stamped envelope. Make the process of getting in touch with you effortless for the editor.

Give your letter personality, but keep it professional. Never be corny: skip the story of how you dream of being published or any implication of how publishing your article benefits **you**.

Address the editor by name not just by job title. Make a phone call to to the publication to ensure that you are sending your letter to the right person and you have spelled his or her name correctly. Keep the tone of your letter professional; make your salutation formal and the style of your letter all business. If you submit by email, format your query in this same business style, but do it in the body of the email, not an attachment.

Reprints

Typically, each magazine and trade journal has a policy about whether it will accept reprints, or articles that have appeared in other publications. Some magazines insist on retaining all rights

Articles Make You More Accessible

I gave a presentation to a local community organization, helping participants develop crisis communications skills. In the class was a fellow who was launching a new magazine to be distributed to every hospital in New Jersey. He asked whether I would write a regular column. I jumped at the chance to be featured every month in front of a group of potential clients for my Crisis Communications/ Media Training Workshop!

Each month, there is my article, photo, and thumbnail sketch mentioning my consulting business and the availability of my book, *Keeping Cool on the Hot Seat: Dealing Effectively with the Media in Times of Crisis.* Hopefully, the next time a crisis rears its ugly head at their hospital, they'll go running for the most recent edition of the magazine and find me!

JUDY HOFFMAN
http://www.judyhoffman.com

Make Your Articles Easy To Use

Seek out trade industry publications, websites, ezines, corporate newsletters, reports, business journals, newspapers and Chamber of Commerce publications. Write in modular form so editors may choose to make a series from longer articles. Sidebars, bullets and quick bites of information are easier to read and will endear you to editors. Display your articles on your website. Make reprinting your articles available free to anyone who credits you as the author. Digitally submit a listing of articles to editors, noting that they can download articles from your website. Offer a value-added bonus such as a tip sheet at the end of the article, and include marketing material or an offer to subscribe to your ezine along with the bonus information, adding to your database of readers. Compiling your articles may eventually lead to your book.

GAIL HAHN
http://www.funcilitators.com

to the article, which means you cannot resell it to anyone else. Other magazines want only first rights, meaning it must appear in their publications first and then you can sell it as many times as you'd like. Some magazines buy first rights in just a region, such as North America. And other publications, especially those that can't afford to pay top dollar for articles, are not particular about accepting articles that have appeared elsewhere.

In any case, you should get an agreement in writing, spelling out how reprints of each of your articles will be handled. *Writer's Market*® gives you information about most publications' policies. Despite their standard policies, some magazines will negotiate with you over the terms of your article.

A magazine might offer to let you retain the rights if you submit the article and take no fee for writing it. When you're first getting started writing articles, it's more important to get your name out there and retain the reprint rights so you can get the most mileage from a single article, than it is to earn income from a particular article.

If the article is written without compensation, magazines usually are more open to letting you include a blurb at the end about you and your business. Fred Gleeck says he takes this descriptive paragraph one step further and includes three ways for readers to contact him: his email address, his website address and his toll-free phone number.

Put Your Articles To Work

Here are a few more tips for making the most of your efforts to submit articles for publication in magazines and trade journals:

● When you can, propose that your articles be published in a series, in order to get your name and contact information into the publication more often. The more they see your name, the more the readers will begin to trust that you are, in fact, an authority in your field.

- Submit a professional headshot with your article. This shows the editors that you know the rules of the game. Hire a photographer to take several portraits of you, head and shoulders only, some smiling and others serious, some from the side and others head on. Look through the proofs and choose the one that best exemplifies the image you want to portray. Have someone help you make the choice, because we don't always see ourselves the way others do. Have several 4×5-inch photographs produced. Your picture will not appear as a 4× 5, but the photograph will print better if the image is reduced rather than if it is enlarged.

- When your article is published, you should receive at least one free copy of that issue. Now that you have your picture with your article, you want to circulate it so other people can see it. Photocopy it and take the copies with you when you speak at events, teach seminars or attend conventions and other events. People will recognize you. You are a celebrity when your photograph appears next to your name and you will attract people almost magnetically.

- Send photocopies of your published article to potential clients. Seeing your name in print raises their level of trust that you are an expert in your field.

- Send photocopies to current and past clients, along with a handwritten note saying why you think they would be interested in the article.

- Keep electronic files of all of your stories. In some cases, you can use a retooled version of an article for another publication without having to start writing from scratch. Frank Candy has created a 'bank' or collection of hundreds of articles within his area of marketing expertise. The articles range in length from half a

Being A Writer Has Its Benefits

Early in my speaking career, I volunteered to write a column for a client's newsletter. Since then, I've always had at least one regular column going, often more than one, some paid, some unpaid.

How do I get them? I ask (with a well-crafted query letter and sample columns.) Benefits?

1 *Increased visibility.* Military spouses are one of my niche markets. The worldwide distribution of my column in the *Army Times* newspaper gave me instant celebrity and added credibility.

2 *New research and material for my work.* With a monthly deadline, I find myself even more active in gathering new material.

3 *Increased opportunity to interview experts.* Most folks like to be quoted. Being a writer gives me greater access to other experts.

KATHIE HIGHTOWER
http://www.jumpintolife.net

She Wrote The Book On It

Our cultural metaphor for an expert is "she wrote the book." So what better way to become known as the real expert than by learning enough about your subject to write a book.

At our communication training firm, 78% of our clients have come to us as a direct result of a published book, an article excerpted from the book or PR associated with the books.

Create your own observations, something new, controversial, memorable.

DIANE BOOHER
http://www.booher.com

column (about one hundred words) up to four magazine pages.

- After you've written at least ten articles, you can compile them into a special report or even a book.

- Keep track of people who call you as a result of each article. You will be able to determine how many of the calls result in new clients. From there, you can measure how many of those new clients buy your services and products, or refer you to other clients. This will help you see which publications have been most valuable to the growth of your business.

- Post your articles on your website, and other sites where you think the material would be relevant, so they can be read long after the publications in which they appeared have moved on to other issues.

- Consider submitting articles to websites along with magazines and trade journals. This is sometimes a faster way to get published. Because websites don't have to go through printing presses and carry their publications via airplane and delivery truck, they often don't have deadlines as far in the future as magazines (which usually work a minimum of two months ahead of time.) Also online magazines have the potential to reach a much wider audience, which is a plus for you.

A SPECIAL CONTRIBUTION FROM
✺ Millie Szerman ✐

No moss grows between **Millie Szerman's** toes! Author, speaker and work-at-home expert, Millie Szerman has been hearing this said about her since her childhood. Whether she is rushing off to appear on Oprah, as she did twice in 2002, speaking at the Publisher's Marketing Association, being interviewed by *Home Business Magazine*, or pursuing her love of mentoring, Millie is always in motion. Millie says that she loves sharing information with others and loves helping others do their own thing. When asked how she describes herself, Millie admits that she is always on the go; her assistant just rolls her eyes at such an understatement and compares Millie to the Energizer Bunny®.

Millie Szerman is the author of: *A View From The Tub: An Inspiring And Practical Guide To Working From Home.*

Be An Unabashed Self Promoter

I've been a work-at-home executive nearly all my life, but only compensated for it for the last fourteen years. That's because when I worked for corporate America, I would always bring work home with me, never earning any more for the extra time I inevitably put into my job.

In 1988, due to some changes in my employment, I started my consulting business, on a shoestring budget, but with energy and enthusiasm in abundant supply! Being a divorced woman, with a teenager to support (and control), starting a business was no easy task.

Luckily, I had always been a good planner in a financial sense, with outside help, of course. It was this outside financial planner

Get To The Point

In four years, the *Made for Success Ezine* has grown to having subscribers in 100 countries, making it one of the largest ezines in the world—certainly in the personal growth industry. My subscribers tell me the main reason they like the ezine so much is that it is brief, bulleted and extremely practical. In other words: Get to the point and make it one they can use! This technique has grown my business such that I have been asked to speak to groups of some of America's finest organizations. The power of this is phenomenal.

CHRIS WIDENER
http://www.madeforsuccess.com

Become A Regular Contributor

I just got my first big break!!! Atlanta Home Improvement Magazine is going to use me as a regular contributor to write their *Smart Home* article (Home Technology Topics). I'll be listed on their contributors page along with a write-up about me and my website. I'll have a byline on each article and a paragraph about me and my website address at the end of each article. They are also listing all of my seminars that relate to home technology in their "Classes & Seminars" listing.

SUSAN CHAMBERS
http://www.susanchambers.com

who referred me to a Money Magazine *stringer*, (outside resource). Money *was looking for people who were successful working from home. In addition, they wanted those whose lives had been changed because of the work-at-home experience. Well, one can say that my life changed drastically because of my home-based business!*

After some basic communications, I was one of four chosen to be interviewed for the article . . . but it was my social skills and knack for limelight that helped land me on the cover! Okay, I'm an unabashed self-promoter! And, the fact that I have a Public Relations consulting business certainly helped!

The magazine sent a photographer to my home. During his tour to establish locations for three different shots, he spied a red telephone in the magnificent master bathroom, located adjacent to my office. (My home office was in the master bedroom—my sleeping quarters were in another part of the house).

My mind raced when he posed his question: "Do you take business calls when you're in the Jacuzzi tub?"

"Of course!" I answered—and saw an opportunity. "You weren't thinking of taking a shot in the tub, were you?" I asked. That planted a seed, but he took only six or seven photos at the end of the roll.

A few days later, I phoned the production director and asked which photos were going to be used in the publication. Again, I mentioned the bathtub shot and how I didn't know if that was what folks wanted to see as a work-at-home lifestyle.

VOILA! I had my hook, and milked it the only way I knew how! It worked, and I landed on the cover of March 1996, Money Magazine. In addition, I was the lead-in to the article, with a two-page spread—all of this representing the lifestyle that the work-at-home environment affords.

That issue is still, I believe, Money Magazine's *number one*

newsstand issue, selling more than any other issue. Since then, I've
published a soft cover book called, A View From The Tub: An
Inspiring and Practical Guide to Working From Home; *it's a*
MUST READ *for anyone contemplating or just starting out on that*
work-at-home journey!

For more information on
Writing Magazine and Journal Article*s*, visit:

www.obvious-expert.com/magazine

Start With Articles

Writing articles is a wonderful way to save money on advertising and present a more credible appearance. Several of my one-time articles expanded into a series or a column.

1 Pick a magazine, newspaper or newsletter that targets your market.

2 Write 5 to 10 benefit tips.

3 Send these to the Managing Editor saying you would like to expand these to an article.

4 Offer to write the article or be interviewed.

5 Request they run your picture.

6 Request they mention your URL, phone number, name and USP in a contact box.

7 Mention your company name and location in the body of the article in case they don't have room for the contact box.

8 Send the article to your database and put it in your Media Kit and on your Web site Media Room.

9 Do it! Promote and Prosper!

RALEIGH PINSKEY
http://www.promoteyourself.com

Your Words In Print

Just because your articles, reports and press releases are non-fiction writing, doesn't mean that they have to read like they were written by the same people who wordsmith the 1040 Tax Form.

Your articles should, like well-written novels, have action and interesting and dimensional characters. You don't have to fictionalize your work to accomplish this, but you do have to research thoroughly so that you have a wealth of interesting facts with which to work.

Action

Apply one of fiction writing's best techniques to your non-fiction article and start in the middle (or at least start where the action is!)

Instead of leading into your article with background information, lead with your most interesting or controversial point. After all, you have to depend almost entirely on your first sentence to motivate your reader to read the second one.

Example:

Suppose your client Bill Stevens, a businessman, has been seeking to get his name better known in the south Florida community where he lives. On your advice, he has become an active member of a local service club. Recently he participated in planning and hosting a pool and patio party for a group of special needs children—an event in which several sports celebrities also participated; interacting and entertaining the children

You could lead into the article talking about the children; everyone likes 'feel good' stories, or you could focus on the athletes because they are another good attention-getter. But neither approach gives you the opportunity to shine the spotlight on your client, Bill. So try something like this:

"Bill Stevens wasn't a bit surprised to find Dolphins in his backyard swimming pool, or even concerned about a couple of Gators on his patio chairs."

How can the reader resist reading on to learn more? You have started at a point of action and you have created an incredible visual image for the reader. Once you have gained their attention, your second sentence can elaborate, explaining that the dolphins are Miami Dolphins football players and the gators are members of the Florida Gators basketball team, and all were involved in creating an afternoon of laughter and fun for some very deserving young sports fans. You can then go on to explain the vital role Bill and others in his service organization played in making this wonderful day a possibility.

You have taken a story that wasn't really about Bill, and validly succeeded in making him a key element in the reader's mind. If you structure your sentences well, you can lead with Bill's name and you can close with your comments on what a great job he has done. On top of that, because your lead sentence focuses on action—some seemingly unusual action—you have taken a sweet, but ordinary article and found a way to gain the reader's attention

E X E R C I S E

Take the following three article topics and craft a fictitious, but possible lead line:

a. You were the guest speaker at a Chamber of Commerce luncheon; your topic was, *Boosting Your Bottomline thru Better Networking.*

_____

_____

b. Trends in your industry have done a complete turn-around since the last Presidential election, and things are not headed in the direction most people assume.

_____

_____

c. De-mystifying databases—you know the secrets.

_____

_____

Practice the active lead-in. Select articles you have previously written and find the true action of the storyline. Can you improve your lead sentences?

E X E R C I S E

Select three people about whom you might be writing. Apply one of the following strategies to each of them. These techniques are skill-builders, not suggestions for your finished product.

a. Interview your subject and prepare the points you anticipate using in your article about that person. Next, interview the person's child. Ask serious, information-seeking questions. Write the points you would include about that person, based on your interview with the child. Compare your results. What new insights did you gain by the process? Can you use the information from the second interview to enhance the article you write?

_____

_____

_____

_____

b. Describe in writing, the personality of a person you know well, writing as if you were creating a movie script based on his or her life. This process requires that you think of the ways a person sounds and moves as well as how the person looks. If you struggle with this, try it from the reverse perspective: pick a leading character from a movie and write about their personal attributes. Actors help make this easier for you because their 'job' is to make personalities become so larger-than-life that they are distinctive and memorable to us.

_____

_____

_____

_____

c. Describe a person you know well without using the person's name or the personal pronouns "he" or "she". You will be forced to describe the person's identity in a new way, each time you mention them in your article. You might, for instance, use such descriptors as: "educator," "parent," "respected community leader," or "avid fisherman" to represent the same person.

_____

_____

_____

_____

Characterization

Most of us can think of a couple of people we know who are so similar in appearance and personality to each other, that we catch ourselves accidentally calling them by each other's name. Sometimes, we find that we blur the details of their lives and wind up wondering, 'Was that Mary or Melissa who likes fish, but never eats beef?' 'Is it Mr. Smithers or Mr. Williams who entertains his clients on his houseboat?'

Typically we need mental identification marks to help us sort and retain accurate memories of people and their personalities. The more distinctive a person's appearance or demeanor, the easier we find it to keep that person uniquely marked in our minds. If you consider how easy it is to confuse personal details of people who we know, see, hear, smell and share experiences with, think about how genuinely challenging it is to define people by written word descriptors only. Write an article and the people about whom you write can quickly become as muddled and manila in the readers' minds as characters lost in the snow drifts of a Russian novel.

Before you write about people:

◆ **Take time to learn the details that makes them unique. Learn to ask out-of-the-ordinary questions in order to gain out-of-the-ordinary facts.**

◆ **Borrow another technique from fiction writers and create profiles in your notes on the people about whom you write. The profiles will contain much more information than you include in your article, but knowing more details, will enhance the way you write about the person.**

Example:

If you know that the businessman about whom you are writing also trained as a gourmet cook, then your article might include some information to the reader about the subject's passion for cooking. Perhaps as you give his 'recipe' for business success, you also throw in his favorite recipe for eggplant parmigiana.

Your article, and your subject become infinitely more memorable to the reader when you reveal bits and pieces of the subject's real persona.

> *You want the editor's attention, so write in an easy-to-read style without a lot of complicated jargon or buzzwords. Offer a new viewpoint and/or valuable content, such as how-to articles or tips. Use a spelling and grammar checker, a tool that is so obvious and still overlooked by many. Don't rely on this tool solely. Instead, re-read and check behind yourself, because you want to be perceived as the expert you are. Your byline information should be concise and include at least three ways to contact you: a phone number, an email address and your website.*
>
> Janet Delph

Use The Media To
Your Advantage

CHAPTER 8

WAR STORY #8 *In the marketing seminars I teach, I often engage the audience— composed primarily of consultants of various specialties—to help me solve the woes of a hypothetical working man. As the audience members create consulting advice for the character in the story, they develop an extensive list of real-world solutions that can expand on their own consulting practices.*

The story opens with our protagonist, a young man of twenty-five who has just been hired as the organist for a large Episcopal church. He is eagerly headed home to share the good news with his wife, who is the mother of their nine-month old son. He knows that her joy over his new employment will be tempered when she learns that his annual organist salary is to be only $3,000. Even in 1963, $58 a week is a challengingly small sum.

The organist's wife, however, has her own news to share that evening over their celebratory dinner of macaroni and cheese and applesauce. You see, she will be telling him that she is pregnant again, a statement that will seem anti-climactic once she informs him that she is expecting twins.

"$3,000," I tell my audience, "and they will soon become a family of five."

"So what can this young family man do to increase his income?"

My seminar attendees always come through; they understand the fine points of no cost, low cost self-promotion.

Hit Your Target

Develop publicity ideas for very specific media targets. Too many use the shotgun approach: sending out stories with general appeal to media outlet. Problem is, everyone is flooded with general interest stuff. A targeted approach is much more effective. For example, we wanted to let bookstores know about our books. All bookstores get *Publisher's Weekly* magazine. So we developed a version of *Sun Tzu's The Art of War* targeted specifically for independent bookstores battling the chains. We only sent out one press release, but it was so relevant, we were called by *Publisher's Weekly* the same day.

GARY GAGLIARDI
http://www.artofwarplus.com

"He can teach piano and organ lessons," someone will suggest. "He should post notices on bulletin boards all over town." "He could establish a relationship at a music store." "He should give lessons through a small college." "Maybe he could write reviews of the symphony for the local newspaper, and work the press and get photographed wearing his organist cassock and sitting in front of the keys. He must become the obvious expert at teaching piano and organ!"

And then I always assure my helpful audience, that I did do those things—all of those things and many more, because, yes, it is a true story and I was the young organist. In fact, I also wrote a weekly newspaper column and produced and directed musicals for the New Hampshire Musicale Society. I even directed and produced an operetta to increase my community visibility and credibility.

I started with zero clients. A few months later I had more students than any other piano and organ teacher around. You see, when your back is against the wall, it is amazing how creative you will become.

I learned at that young age how to market my business and myself; I learned because my personal situation was truly sink or swim. Yet years later, when I became a consultant, I ignored these good survival instincts. I thought I was supposed to do something different. I figured there was some secret advertising formula. The truth is, there is not.

Building a consulting business is all about identifying yourself as the obvious expert and utilizing grassroots marketing strategies, no matter what your consulting expertise, or your particular circumstances.

EE Jr.

Get Them To Talk About You

Getting your name in the media will help you build your reputation as the obvious expert. Every time your name and your business are mentioned in the newspaper, on the radio or on TV, your credibility goes up another notch. People will recognize it, and your name will come to mind when they think of your specialty.

Get publishers and producers to recognize you as an expert. Build familiarity. Unless you already know the reporters who cover your area of expertise, you'll have to do this the old-fashioned way, and that is by using perseverance.

News organizations need news. They're always looking for something interesting and relevant to report. Help them out. Start by sending a press release to your local news organizations every week for the next six months. They won't use all of them. They might not use any of them at first. Don't get discouraged. Remember, if you don't send any out, you definitely won't get in print.

Keep getting yourself and your name out there in public by networking through local organizations. Healthcare consultant Dawn Gay, CPC, CPMC, suggests you get involved with the Chambers of Commerce in your area, or other groups that routinely get news coverage. Eventually, the people who work at your area's news organizations will get used to seeing your name and will begin identifying you as an obvious expert in your field. They might even become inspired to interview you.

Start With Your Press Kit

Chances are you will need to send press releases about your business, yourself or your clients. Take the time to develop a good press kit. Do this because it:

1 will automatically endorse your work as being submitted by someone who is both serious and professional

2 will brand your work in a way that becomes recognizable to

Free Publicity

If you want free publicity, give the media exactly what they want. When I published two tips booklets in 2000, I snail-mailed a news release and a copy of each booklet to editors at national publications, inviting them to excerpt up to 10 tips of their choosing from each booklet. Various media outlets chose different tips, depending on their audience. *MyBusiness* magazine even called for an interview and gave me a full page feature, with a photo. I also consulted *The Oxbridge Directory of Newsletters*, and then targeted print newsletters. I got a three-line mention in *The Kiplinger Letter,* which resulted in about $10,000 in sales.

JOAN STEWART
http://www.publicityhound.com

Invest Your Time

Media relations is a discipline that takes time and an extreme level of patience. However, once you've been quoted as an expert the follow-up opportunities tend to flow on a regular basis. There are several rules you need to be aware of to become an accepted resource:

1 Writers and editors are typically on a tight deadline…they tend to look for people they can quote at the last minute. If you receive a call, return it immediately. In some cases writers will take the first person to return their call, even if what you have to say might have been better.

2 No "BS!" If they ask for something that you really aren't an expert in, tell them so up-front. If they get burned, even once, the word will spread quickly within that community and you may never get another chance.

3 Put together your own list of experts you can refer the media person to. If you do them favors like this, they will certainly call back!

CB "CORK" MOTSETT
http://www.tabjax.com

the recipient, and

3 if done correctly, will so facilitate the process of sending press releases that you will be far more motivated to send many of them and send them often.

Your press kit begins with a pocket folder. These can be custom designed or you can search paper suppliers who offer unique, quality products. Spend some time looking around; visit stationery shops, office supply stores and online or catalogue paper product companies. Talk to printers and graphic designers for tips on your options. Some business people produce great press kit folders simply by customizing a stock folder purchased at an office supply store.

Once you select your folders and embellish them with your graphic 'brand', you will wonder how you did business without them. You will find them not only handy for press releases, but the perfect way to present many proposals, contracts and other documents you use frequently. Just make sure your selection: fits easily in a standard size envelope for mailing, looks professional and holds up well when handled (some paper types show fingerprint marks so easily that they can look shabby from the moment you take them out of the package) and that your folder easily holds several pages of documents plus your business card.

Your press release is the main ingredient in your press kit, but don't forget to include other basics:

● A marketing piece or bio about you (or your business) and your accomplishments.

● A list of questions and answers relevant to your consulting practice with specific questions and answers for each press release you send. Double-space your text and make sure the questions are clearly discernable from the answers. This makes the job of the media person who receives it much easier, and while they may not ask you the exact questions you have listed, at least they can tell where you stand and what types of questions they may want to ask.

- If appropriate, include a couple of headshots. Most newspapers prefer black and white photos and if you have to choose between color headshots or black and white because of the cost, pick the b&w. Use photographs that are at least 5×7; they can always be reduced in size but they rarely enlarge clearly. Your press photo headshots are one place you do not want to pinch pennies. Be sure that you place your head in the hands of a skilled photographer.

- Always include a statement or identifier for a caption line. Type your suggested caption line on a clear or a white peel-and-stick label. Never write directly on a photograph, either on the front or on the back. Never send a photo without a label, unless you are willing to risk seeing someone else's name appear in print, underneath your picture.

- In addition to the actual press release itself, your press kit should always contain a cover letter. Write the cover letter on your letterhead; keep it brief and informal in tone. Let the recipient know what the topic of your release is and why you thought he would be especially interested in receiving it.

- Finally, to make sure you put those snazzy folders with their bios, photos, cover letter and well-written press releases to work often, make sure your mailing list of media contacts is kept on a database. If your kits are put together in advance, waiting on your shelf for only the addition of the next news release, then you can easily develop the habit of adding your current news and putting the kit in the mail.

Spread The Word

Being on the air and in print is an awesome opportunity to spread your message for free. And to make your media effort as effective as possible, capitalize on the before and after.

1 Notify your database of the date and time or issue.

2 Send out a recap or reprint after.

3 Take pictures of you and the host or journalist.

4 Create a Media Room on your website for the pictures, articles; list the station call letters of your appearances.

5 Upload the audio or video of your appearance on your website for all to experience.

6 Make a tape and include it in your Presentation Kit to potential clients.

7 Send the tape to your clients and prospects.

RALEIGH PINSKEY
http://www.promoteyourself.com

Publicity specialist Lynn Stewart recommends you add one more very important element: a souvenir for the person who opens the package.

"I always recommend the client add something interesting, some sort of a tsatske—you know, a specialty or promotional item. Something interesting, clever and suited to the topic. It could be a coffee cup or something more creative."

Lynn and her advertising team were once making a pitch to a client in Los Angeles, and rather than fly the whole team there, each person went to the store and selected a Barbie® or Ken® outfit that would best depict his or her personal style. The doll clothes were mounted in a portfolio—one for the creative director, one for the account supervisor, one for the traffic manager.

"But, of course, the content of the kit is the most important thing," Stewart says. "It has to be compelling copy."

For a radio station, you might even include in your kit a cassette with other interviews you've done so the decision-makers can get a feel for how you sound on the air.

When it comes to promoting your business to the media, having the right press kit is crucial. Lynn says, "The press kit is one of the first things I put together for my clients. You spend the most money on it that you can. You know, if I've got $10,000 in my budget, I'm going to make sure I get the best press kit before I figure out the rest of it."

Writing Your Press Release

Of course, the most import part of your press kit is the actual news release. The one you write may not turn out to be the story the press outlet runs, but if it stimulates any positive press about you and your topic, then it has done its job.

We've said that the appearance of your press kit is vitally important, and that goes double for the press release itself. Make the release look good, in every way from using a quality paper stock, to adhering to a standardized, professional layout.

Make sure your press releases are well written. The media outlet may re-write everything you submit in order to make it read with their particular style, but if the original version is poorly written to begin with, they won't even bother to consider it.

There are many books that can help you see how a press release should look or check **www.obvious-expert.com/media** for examples. You might even want to pay a public relations person to write releases for you at first.

If you plan to write your own press releases, here are some helpful suggestions:

- Some writers try to stick to one-page new releases only, but two to three pages are acceptable if the content is truly newsworthy.

- Start your first page approximately one third of the way down the page. Begin with your headline typed in all capital letters and in bold, centered on your first line of text.

- Double space and full justify your text to create a highly structured, formal appearance. Below your title write your release information. This may say, "FOR IMMEDIATE RELEASE" or say either, "HOLD UNTIL" or "EMBARGOED UNTIL" with your first acceptable release date. Skip several spaces between this line and your first line of the story.

- Begin your release with your dateline/location line. This is when you are writing the release (not your release date) and the city from where you are releasing the news.

- Use at least one-inch margins, all the way around. Two-inch margins are acceptable unless they cause a shorter release to run over onto a second page. If you do have more than one page, type "MORE" at the end of each

One Thing Leads To Another

Having worked as a global management consultant for over 30 years, I've worked with scores of companies in many SIC codes, helping them with strategic planning, marketing, acquisition & trend and new business identification. This led to writing books about economic and future trends. I was often called by the business press for quotes about the future trends that will impact various industries. My experiences working with many different companies gave me a unique perspective that I leveraged into a good consulting, business brokerage, speaking and writing business.

BARRY MINKIN
http://minkinaffiliates.com

page of text. Type the words, "PAGE TWO" on the second page and the subsequent page numbers after that.

- At the end of the press release, type -30- or ### to identify the end of the text. Many writers also type, "END."

- Make sure full and accurate contact information for reaching you is at the bottom of the last page.

Your Radio Show

Do you have a good voice and something interesting to share? If you want tons of free publicity try hosting your own radio show. When I self-published my first book I faced the problem of how to become known as an expert. After being a successful guest on syndicated radio shows, I started the *Creative Health & Spirit Radio Show* on a pay-per-show radio station. The show presented helpful information and included commercials about my books that generated an ever-constant revenue stream. Instantly I was recognized as an expert in my field, media doors opened because I was now part of the media, large publishing houses subsequently published my next books and I now have my own 24/7 Internet Radio Station.

LINDA MACKENZIE
http://www.healthylife.net

Along with the appearance, of course, content is critical. Send an editor a few good news releases and you are probably in for life; send poorly written ones, and no matter how much your style improves later, your releases will rarely gain a second glance on their way to file 13.

Think of your news release as an inverted triangle. Power-pack your headline, then lead with your best shot. Keep your most important information at the very top of your release, in the first three or four lines, working your way down to your less critical points. The media often cuts press releases from the bottom up. Besides, if the first few lines aren't interesting and action-packed, the editor will rarely read beyond them.

Do not generalize. Be highly specific in what you write. It adds to your credibility and to the strength of the story. Skip all the 'hype'. Your story is your story. It is either worth telling as it is or it is not.

Never make your story seem—even vaguely—like self-promotion, or a sales pitch. You will close media doors forever with that approach. If you want an angle to make your news release more likely to be picked up, then try to provide information that readers might need to know. Editors often consider "public need" as significant criteria.

Here is another insider's tip: Editors are, apparently, somewhat trainable. Send your submissions on or about the same time each month. We all are such creatures of habit that an editor can become conditioned to expecting to see a release from you and even start subconsciously planning a space to use it.

Always cite your sources. Inspire the editor to see you as a reliable contact. Use interesting direct quotes, when possible. Of course, follow the journalist basic of including, "who, what when, where, why and how." Never, ever leave an editor reading your release and thinking there are gaps in the story.

Skip the use of jargon, and scrub your story clean of gender, ethnic or culturally specific words. Also, eliminate acronyms and industry language unless it can be easily, clearly defined without bogging down the flow of your story.

Keep It Newsworthy

Your press releases can be about anything that might be newsworthy. The key word here is **newsworthy**. Don't waste the media's time or yours sending out press releases on trivial events, or on anything that looks like a bid for publicity.

Appropriate Press Release Topics:

- changes in a company

- awards

- significant special events

- remarkable business trends

- human interest topics of service work, and of course, stories involving children, animals or how the 'little guy triumphs'

- novel or quirky happenings

- new products

- new facilities

- events with a local, national or global tie

- solutions to problems

Electronic Press Release

Some media outlets are open to receiving press releases by email.

Be Recognized As The Expert

Our PR agent, Stacey Miller, monitors expert source sites like ProfNet. On my behalf, she replied to an inquiry for experts in business attire. An Associated Press (AP) writer interviewed me. I was quoted and the article appeared in newspapers nationwide. *USA Today* interviewed me and *NBC's Today Show* called. Within 2 hours, I flew to NYC for an interview with Katie Couric. During my second appearance, Katie reviewed my book, *Casual Power.* Sales accelerated and *Casual Power* remains a category best seller. We parlayed this into over 100 interviews with TV, radio, national and international magazines, and newspapers, including *Wall Street Journal, Financial Times, Business Week* and *Success Magazine.* Now everyone acknowledges Sherry Maysonave as a communication and image expert.

SHERRY MAYSONAVE
http://www.casualpower.com

Your Radio Talk Show

To position myself as a business expert, I launched my weekly radio show, *Business in Motion*. My interview guests include entrepreneurs, innovators and corporate executives. It paid off in many ways. Prospects differentiate me as the radio show host. I call business leaders to interview them—then they go in my database. After the 30 minute interview talking about their success—they like me.

I can use the lessons learned in my writing, speaking and consulting. I can name drop. A bonus was the development of my interview skills, questioning and listening, something critical in consulting. You can do this too.

My radio show is with the university station. Most colleges and universities have community radio stations and they need talk shows.

GEORGE TOROK
http://www.Torok.com

Before you send yours electronically, check to make sure the reporter, editor or news director is amenable to this format. Many recipients will delete email if they don't recognize the sender because they fear computer worms, viruses, spam, or unwanted junk mail. If your news release contains an attachment, the likelihood that it will be deleted is high.

If you do submit electronically, go for a lighter tone and a shorter release. William Parkhurst explains in his book, *How to Get Publicity, And Make the Most of It Once You've Got It* (©2000, HarperBusiness), says, "Formatting is probably the biggest problem in distributing an email release."

He points out that the message can look fine when you type it, but recipients could be using different kinds of hardware, software or Internet providers that cause your email to appear as, "an aberration of curls, marks, and horrific indentations."

To combat that, you can save your release in a pure text file with hard returns at the end of each line. Don't use tabs, because what you intend as blank spaces might appear as characters, such as open boxes.

- Avoid using complete words in all-capital letters, which are seen as shouting in email. The recipient could think you're being rude or at least annoying.

- Don't direct the recipient to check out your website, as you would in a printed press release, because that's seen as bad etiquette. Instead, include a hyperlink to your site in your signature at the bottom of your email release.

- Start the press release with a heading similar to one you'd put on an interoffice memo. It should include lines of information that start with "TO:" "FROM:" "SUBJECT:" and also "ATTACHMENTS:" if you have received the go-ahead to send one to the recipient.

- The "SUBJECT:" line substitutes for the headline you'd

put on a hard copy press release.

- For the main body, the trend is toward a shorter release such as two paragraphs—or one screen—instead of the equivalent of a whole typewritten page.

- The signature at the bottom should be separated from the rest of the release by a boundary line of dashes. It should include your name, the name of your business, your contact information, your website address and a special note when necessary such as "FOR REVIEW COPIES, PLEASE STATE YOUR PREFERRED MAILING ADDRESS."

How To Get Publicity

Once you've created your press releases and press kit, you are already halfway there. Now it's time to get the media to use them. Your goal is for reporters, editors and news directors to get your name into the media in a favorable way.

"Getting them to call you is the first challenge," says Frank Candy, who knows the ins and outs of the system. "You can do that in a variety of ways."

Try following these helpful tips:

First, develop an effective mailing list. Make sure your press releases are:

- **Appropriate for the media outlet you're targeting.** Does the media outlet usually cover the type of information your press release addresses?

- **Up to date.** A reporter, editor or news director who receives a press release addressed to the person who held the job two or three people ago, can form a negative impression about you and your business.

- **Crystal-clear about the local angle of the story.** Editors should be able to determine with a glance of

You Need A Hook

Some books offer a tougher challenge when it comes to making effective use of the media. Take Mr. Lloyd Pedersen and his first novel, *The Vintage*. Mr. Pedersen realized his first self-published book—all 885 pages of it!—needed publicity. He then turned to us here at *Five Star Publications*.

I told Mr. Pedersen that we needed to come up with a unique angle, since his first attempt at garnering any publicity was unsuccessful. I then inquired about his age. When he informed me that he was 90 years old, I knew we had it! We portrayed him as a first-time author at the age of 90. (He insisted we inform the media that he didn't start the book at the age of 90, but rather at the age of 80!)

As a result of working that angle, several publications and a wire service expressed interest in the story. In fact, the wire service's interest led to a call for a possible interview with Mr. Pedersen from a major late-night talk show. Who could ask for more than that? Sometimes the angle can make all the difference!

LINDA F. RADKE
http://www.FiveStarPublications.com

fifteen seconds or less whether a piece of mail addresses an angle that will be relevant to their local audience.

● **Respectful of deadlines.** Learn each media outlet's deadlines. They might be earlier than you think.

Know your options for sending multiple releases. In some cases, your press releases might be of interest outside your local area. There are ways to send them to multiple media outlets regionally or nationally without having to do all of the research yourself. In her eBook, *Secrets of Effective Press Release Distribution,* (©2001, WhatsOnline.Com, Inc.) marketing and PR strategist B.L. Ochman walks you through the process.

"Target specific media outlets. That's much more effective than blanketing all of the media with your news releases," says B.L., whose website helps those with public relations needs. "You should aim for quality of coverage instead of quantity," she explains in her *Reality PR*™ program.

"We'll take one paragraph in *The Wall Street Journal* over 1,000 articles in papers with circulations below 2,500 any day," she writes. "We believe there is a newsworthy angle or trend story about any business if you know where to look . . . Major PR firms and many clients still measure the value of PR by quantity of press coverage instead of quality. In Reality PR, we work to tailor stories to what the media wants. And instead of shot-gunning journalists with PR-speak releases, we ask them what they want and we give it to them."

When you're trying to get media coverage, you shouldn't ignore the smaller newspapers or the publications in your trade. Any coverage is good coverage. It's OK to start smaller and work your way up to *Wall Street Journal* status.

Follow up after you deliver a press release. The squeaky wheel usually gets the grease when it comes to dealing with the media.

Consider pitching a story over the phone instead of, or before, sending a press release. This is a good way to gauge what the editor might be looking for in a story like yours. It also

Respond Quickly

Be the obvious expert in your market by becoming the helpful subject matter expert for the media that reaches them. Write a personalized letter or email to each editor, reporter, producers and columnist, reflecting your specific appreciation of how they cover your kind of news. Offer yourself as an information source for specific topics. Indicate that you'll help find other experts, as needed. Suggest some timely and timeless story possibilities. Promise to respond quickly. Briefly describe your expertise. Include a 24-hour contact number and email address.

KARE ANDERSON
http://www.sayitbetter.com

separates your news from all of the other proposals that come across the reporter, editor or news director's desk. A telephone pitch works best when you already know the media contact, and when that person trusts your sense of newsworthiness. Sometimes pitching a story on the phone is also a way for you to develop a working relationship with the media contact.

Emphasize what you can do for the media, instead of what the media can do for you. Keep in mind that instead of contacting media outlets and telling them how wonderful you are, Frank says; it is better to write to them and say, *'I have a vast amount of resources available to you.'*

When you've established yourself as one of the experts a media outlet uses, you might be in a position where you're contacted by writers for other television, radio, newspaper, magazine and Internet content providers as well.

"You'll find that these people are very busy," Frank reminds us. "They might have a list of twenty people to contact for a particular assignment, and you might be number 5 or 10 on the list. You must respond to them rapidly and effectively by saying something such as, *Tell me what you want. Tell me exactly how you want it—in what format. What size? What's the spin on it? What's the hook? What's the headline? What's the length? What do you want to accomplish? How do you want your people to respond? Do you want it to be controversial? Which side do you want to take with it?"*

Reminder: If the issue is controversial or two-sided, make sure you take a side you normally would take or it won't serve you and might cause confusion in your business positioning.

When possible, suggest that the reporter speak with some of your clients or former clients. That way your clients can say great things about your work that you might not be able to say yourself without appearing to be self-serving. And they get their names into the media as well, which makes them grateful to you.

Celebrity Counts

Clients beg for "free publicity" but the key thing to remember is that publicity is worthless unless it underscores your expertise and credibility. Credibility is the "magic ingredient" the media has to offer. When people see you on TV or hear you on radio, you are a "celebrity" in their eyes. The fastest way to get free publicity is to look toward your local media. Tie in your book, product or service with something going on in your town. Alert the newspaper and local TV and radio stations. Also, write an EFFECTIVE media release. Make sure that it catches their attention! Tabloid-style headlines are best, and guess what? They don't have a whole lot to do with your book! Be persistent—remember, if you have faith in yourself, others will too!

MARISA D'VARI
http://www.GetBookedNow.com

If you can find a way to serve the reporter and the readers while gaining exposure for your business, then it becomes a win-win-win situation, Frank says.

"Remember, it's not about you. It's about 'us' and ultimately going in with the right attitude. And that's the attitude of service, of giving and of helping."

Timing And Placement

Any day of the week you mail a press release is better than the alternative, *which is not sending one at all!* But if you can, plan for your release to arrive Tuesday through Thursday. Monday is everybody's busiest day, and not the best time to get attention for things sent in the mail.

On Friday, Saturday and Sunday, there are fewer staffers working at most media outlets, so the people there are busier and might have less time to devote to reading your information right away. On the other hand, with a little experience, you might learn the routines of, and develop a rapport with someone on the weekend crew. He or she may be very appreciative to have some news items targeted to his attention, instead of working from the 'leftovers' of the weekday crew.

Use your best judgment and make sure you give the media outlet plenty of lead time to handle your story idea in time to meet its deadlines. Each media outlet is different in the amount of lead time it builds into its schedule, but in general the following timetables apply:

Typical Media Deadlines:

Magazines	Allow 3–4 months minimum	5–6 months is ideal
Daily or Weekly Newspapers	2–3 weeks minimum for non-breaking news	1 week cuts it thin
Radio	1–2 weeks minimum	3 weeks plus if it is a major media event
Television	2–3 weeks minimum	3 weeks plus if it is a major media event.

Reach Mass Markets

Promoting special interest or niche products can be difficult. The key is to translate the niche to reach larger or mass markets. We were successful in gaining exposure for special interest programming in such publications as *People Magazine,* getting our experts on shows such as *Oprah, The Other Half, Weekend Today,* and *Phil Donahue,* not to mention other magazine and trade publications, as well as, national and local newspapers. It is important to know how to create a newsworthy hook, present it in the best possible light and be at the right place at the right time. Good publicity translates into distribution and sales.

LESLIE MCCLURE
http://www.411videoinfo.com

The longer the lead time, the more opportunity you have to send a second or third press release before the actual event. You could mount a weekly campaign for each of the weeks you have available between your original pitch and the date of the event you're pitching.

If you're proposing a news story that is not time-sensitive, you can send in your press release and then just wait several days or a week before you follow up with the phone call to see whether the media outlet is interested.

Send your releases not only to the business editor but also other sections of the newspaper where they might be relevant: local news, education, real estate, art news, health news, features, neighborhood news or national news. A word of advice, however: Try to narrow it to one or two departments for each press release. If every section receives every release, the editors will assume that another department is handling your information, and none of the departments will take your requests seriously.

Place Your Story Before You Write It

For even more recognition in the print media, you might offer to write a column. A column means you have a 'slot' reserved in which to place your words even before you write them. Your slot becomes an unofficial negotiable commodity, because people who also want media coverage will be eager to offer you their goodwill in 'trade' for the print press visibility you now represent.

Sometimes gaining such a slot is easier than you might think. Prepare a collection of your similar previously published words. If you do not have something that is comparable to the column you wish to write, create a sample of a column or two, just the way you would like it to appear.

If you have never previously been published, prepare an entire sample collection of articles and columns written the way you would have done them for publication. Then you must find

Create A Unique Moniker For Yourself

I'd gone from being a garbage man to a sound-barrier breaking U.S. Navy pilot, but it was thirty brushes with near-death and catastrophe that really interested major media. When people started calling me "The Luckiest Unlucky Man Alive," I wrote and published a book by that title and trademarked that unique moniker for myself.

Since people have always been wanting to get lucky since time immortal, I am now in demand as an expert in how you can turn unlucky situations into lucky ones, both at home and at work, to help you achieve greater levels of personal and professional fulfillment. Simon and Schuster took note—they are now publishing my newest hardcover. *There's a Flying Squirrel in My Coffee.* To review my key point: there is something special about you. Listen to your heart and tap into it. Then create a moniker for yourself that helps you to promote your own unique selling proposition.

BILL GOSS
http://www.BillGoss.com

a way to (1) get your written work in the hands of the editor of the publication in which you wish to appear, and (2) you must find a way to make personal contact with this editor and discuss your proposed column. A telephone call may be a start, but try to schedule a meeting, lunch or discussion over coffee— whatever it takes to gain the ear of the decision maker.

If your column takes a Question and Answer format and you are not sure what to say in two hundred to five hundred words, here's an easy idea. Ask yourself: What questions would I ask a consultant who does what I do? Type in those questions. Then research the answers and write them in three or four paragraphs each. Those questions and answers can be the basis for your first column. You can make up the questions for the first couple of columns yourself. Soon, people will start writing to you with questions they are eager to ask.

Letters to the Editor are another way to gain recognition in the newspaper. If you see something about your industry or your area of expertise in the news, and you think you could clarify the subject, fax or email the newspaper a letter with your opinion.

Be careful not to put yourself or your business out on a limb by creating controversy. Keep your opinions on a strictly professional level. Remember that a little of your opinion goes a long way. Reserve your comments for something about which you really feel strongly instead of submitting letters every day or every week. Even better, use Letters to the Editor as an opportunity for shining the spotlight on someone else by noting their exemplary service or actions, something that has gone otherwise unnoticed by the press.

The Interview. When you interview for a print publication, the interviewer plays an interpretive role. In the electronic media, what you say and how you inflect and reflect is right up front for the viewer (or listener) to experience for himself. But in a print publication, your words, personality and the article's

---

Everyone Will Know Your Name

Get publicity, get noticed and get it for FREE! Write articles and press releases, send them to everyone, and, include a picture. Contact reporters when you see an article you like and tell them. Make yourself easily accessible and tell your contacts your areas of expertise.

As an owner of a small computer consulting business, health care is a hot button for me. Since several media contacts know me (because of all my PR), I get many calls for "quotes" and "insight" for articles and TV or magazine specials about benefits and technology issues. Everyone seems to know me, and I like that. You'll be amazed how easy it is to get free publicity to work for you.

ROCHELLE BALCH
http://www.rochellebalch.com

result rests solely in the hands of the reporter. You must develop an instant rapport with the interviewer or risk being misrepresented.

Radio and Television

Getting invited to speak as an expert on a local talk show is a good way to get your name out to the community. To do this, prepare your idea or ideas and then contact the radio and TV stations in your area and offer to discuss a specific topic.

The subject could be a new approach to something, even if it's only new statistics on an issue. It could be a dramatic and different way of handling something. It could be a how-to that will help people benefit from your knowledge of your industry. Whatever it is, it must be a subject that will entice the program's producer to believe listeners will not turn the dial when your interview is being broadcast.

Send the producer a brief résumé before the program. Emphasize your expertise and some of the ideas you would like to discuss. You can even include this as part of your proposal.

Or you can follow the advice of Kevin Hogan, and make a bold move. Kevin recommends you position yourself as someone who can fill in anytime a scheduled guest drops out of the lineup. This works especially well on radio because you can be interviewed over the phone and don't have to look pulled-together the way you do for a TV interview. A radio station can call you with fifteen minutes notice and have you on the air in no time.

"It's so easy to get on the radio, it's unbelievable," Kevin says. "You're a problem solver as an expert. You solve problems. So what problems does a radio producer have?

"Say that I was scheduled to appear on a radio show at noon, but I got sick and called the guy at 9 o'clock in the morning. He's got a problem. Now you are the solution. Why? Because you sent this radio producer a fax a month earlier, that said, 'Hey, by the way, if somebody ever can't make it on your show,

Be Media Friendly

You can be on *Oprah, Regis, CBS Sunday Morning, CNN, TIME* as I have, *WITHOUT* a publicist, by being media-friendly and savvy! Here's 10 of my secrets:

1 Respond immediately to any calls from media.

2 Respect deadlines.

3 Be brief, entertaining, flexible.

4 Leave audiences with TLC: thinking, laughing or crying.

5 Give your audience value, not just a sales pitch.

6 Sell yourself and your products every time you speak, by making a positive, lasting impression.

7 Be humble, sincere, confident and helpful.

8 Listen and learn from other speakers and professionals

9 Articulate, refine and maintain your professional, public image always.

10 Never compromise your personal or professional integrity/values on or off the camera/air.

ANGI MA WONG
http://www.wind-water.com

and you need a last-minute fill-in, twenty-four hours a day, seven days a week, call me at this number. It's always answered. I will fill in for you.' "

>
>
> Reader's Digest *did a short condensation of my book,* How to Get Kids to Help at Home. *Their PR person asked me to do talk shows. During the month that issue was on the newsstands, I did 30 talk shows from my office via telephone.*
>
> Elva Anson

Use What's Available

I was a pro guitarist back in the late 1970s, which as usual meant I also offered guitar lessons. I found out the public library was working with the cable TV company to offer some educational programming, and thought it'd be cool to offer basic guitar lessons on TV. So I offered; they accepted, and I recorded some episodes of basic guitar instruction for them.

GEORGE PRICE
porge@rocketmail.com

Getting the fax number for a radio show is as simple as calling the station and asking for it, Kevin says. Introduce yourself over the phone and tell the receptionist you're interested in being an on-air guest and that you'd like to fax the station some information about yourself.

Your fax should outline what topics you could discuss during an interview. For instance, it might say you could show audience members in five minutes, or twenty minutes or some amount of time, how to do something specific, such as get a raise or get a great deal on the next car they purchase. Include a list of all of the issues you could discuss. Once the station receives your fax, it will go into a special file because you're always available.

The Radio Interview. Depending on the program, radio interviews can offer you the luxury of a long conversation on the air. You might be able to express your views, sell yourself and even answer questions from callers. But don't let the length of time you might be allotted fool you. Keep your answers short.

Show interest in your interviewer. Don't feel that you have to stay on a single topic because it happens to be what you're 'selling'. Let the interview be dynamic and flow in a manner consistent with friendly conversations.

Prepare for any radio and TV interview by practicing what you will say. Work with a friend or two. Have your friends ask you questions so you can think of ways to answer them. Practice in front of a video camera or with a tape recorder. Don't gamble on inspiration of the moment or you might not come across as the expert you claim to be. Your friends should ask you the hardest questions possible, and you should record the practice sessions so you can rework any of the problem areas of your answers.

While you're on the air, keep your energy level high. Be yourself. Show that you appreciate being there and that you respect the host. Listen carefully to each question so you give the proper answers. Make your answers fit the questions asked, as much as possible. When you can, structure your answers to give the interviewer a logical lead to the next question you hope he will ask. If he does not ask what you expect, keep your cool and go with the flow.

"You don't have to be amazing to be on the radio," Kevin says. "All you have to do is be interesting. And the way you're interesting is to have tons of material prepared for the audience, and you get rid of the word 'I.' In other words, every time you're ready to tell something about yourself, you instead have a message that says, 'This is how you can do it.'

The Television Interview. A TV interview usually is shorter and more rigid than an interview for radio. Make sure you take a few 'cleansing breaths' inhaling deeply and exhaling slowly before you begin. This is a great way to squelch the jitters that may be noticeable in your voice. Enunciate clearly, speak slowly, and for most people, it is good advice to deepen the tone of your normal speaking voice slightly.

Keep your answers brief and never let your sentences trail off without completing them. Don't interrupt or talk over the interviewer. Just try to come across as pleasant and confident.

Keep Them Updated

Publicity experts estimate I have received over $1 million dollars in free publicity, by submitting weekly press releases to TV, radio and newspapers about any new company: accomplishments; activities; affiliations; awards, celebrations; contracts awarded; discounts offered; donations made; equipment purchased; ideas or positions presented; office space added; personnel changes; publications or surveys completed; services offered; and special lectures attended or given. Many times I am ignored by a specific media, only to be pleasantly surprised to see a 1/2 or full page feature story, or receive an invitation to appear regularly on a special talk show.

JOE TEAL
DrJoeTeal@aol.com

Focus your eyes on the interviewer—the camera crew loves it when you look and act as one normally would while having a one-on-one conversation. They can then orchestrate their shot calls in a normal manner. Since you are looking only at the interviewer, you won't risk looking wild-eyed or shifty because a cameraman caught you in a moment when you were rolling your eyes around the room.

Be prepared for interruptions while the crew works to coordinate all of the people on the set as well as the complicated equipment. Remember that a TV interview set is the appearance of an oasis of calm, when in reality it is a hub of camera and lighting crew chaos. Try not to be distracted by the sounds and activities around you.

To increase the chances that your name, business, website address or other information appear correctly in graphics, you should fax or mail it ahead, a few days before the show. Then bring along business cards to hand to anyone on the crew who might need a last minute refresher on your name and its correct spelling.

Press interviews of all types can be tricky and unpredictable. You are usually speaking about a topic or event you know inside out, which is the very reason you may omit the obvious or speak as if your audience has more basic knowledge on the topic than they actually do. Combine that with the fact that you are often speaking with someone, who is directing the questions, but may have little real knowledge about your topic. Expect the unexpected!

One consultant tells us that she learned her lesson for life about dealing with the press in her first interview—which happened to be for television. She was one of two people in a thirty-minute spot to discuss an educational program she was helping implement in a public school system.

She went into the interview believing that she was 100% prepared. She had done her homework in advance and she and the interviewer had also talked at length about the interview.

Distribute Your Media

Getting into the media is only half the trick. The other half is to let everyone know you are going to be in or that you were in. You can do this by email. My favorite is to send photocopies of the article to my database. This does two things. When they see me they state, "George I see your name everywhere." Often they do this when we are in ear shot of others. And they seem to 'see' my name in the media even when it was not there.

GEORGE TOROK
http://www.Torok.com

However, she could not have been more surprised when during the show, the interviewer did not ask her one single question she expected him to ask. She was caught off guard, fumbled with her information and had trouble working in the concepts she really wanted to discuss. While the interview was—in her eyes—a failure, it was not because the interviewer was trying to make her look bad. In fact, just the opposite was true; the television newsman was her own husband!

Many years and many successful interviews later the consultant attributed her skills in being interviewed to what she learned in her very first one: Never assume you can know the interviewer well enough to be able to let your guard down before or during an interview. Prepare! Prepare! Prepare!

Focus On Your Goal

Don't worry about the size of the article or broadcast spot that results from your press release or request for coverage. Whether it's one paragraph or a half-page in the newspaper, whether it's a one sound bite TV quote or a half-hour radio interview, you are getting your name out there. Enjoy sharing what you know and pat yourself on the back because when you are being quoted in the media, you are the obvious expert.

For more information on
Making Effective Use of the Media, visit:
www.obvious-expert.com/media

Be True To Yourself

In media interviews, meetings or sales calls, you'll often be asked a question you don't want to answer or don't know the answer to. Here's a simple technique called "bridging" that will keep the focus on the message you want to give. Say, "I don't know about that, but what I do know is . . ." then answer with information you want your audience to remember. Formulate your key messages ahead of time. Then don't allow yourself to be swayed from your core knowledge. Stay with the subject material you know and you'll always be perceived as an expert.

SUSAN HARROW
http://www.prsecrets.com

Making The Most of Your Media Interview

A SPECIAL CONTRIBUTION FROM
☀ Patti Wood, MA, CSP ☀
INTERNATIONAL SPEAKER AND TRAINER

Patti's career path began its turn toward public speaking when a college professor of a poetry class—which was at that time her major—remarked on Patti's outstanding skills in oratory. It was just the nudge in the right direction Patti needed to be off to such successes as becoming the 'go-to' expert on the topic of body language interpretation for *Cosmopolitan, First, Seventeen,* and many other publications, as well as *CBS* and *ABC* radio news, the *BBC* and *PBS.* While the world may look to Patti to tell them what everyone from politicians to movie stars are silently saying, Patti explains that she gives interviews and speeches because she believes each word a person says is so very important, and because it is "fun—really, really, really fun."

You've probably spent many years becoming an expert in your field. In order to share your expertise with the public, you need to also spend some time becoming media-savvy. Being in the spotlight means you gain recognition for your knowledge, talents or skills, and it's a way for you to teach others about your field. If you can be dazzling in a media interview and then learn how to follow-up, you'll find opportunities will keep knocking. Here are few ways to get your name out there, where members of the media can find you.

Prepare for a Potential Interview

Have the following checklist ready when the phone rings with a request for a broadcast or magazine interview. Usually the journalist, producer or host of the show is making quite a few calls to potential guests and will be in a big hurry. They will typically speak quickly; if you can shoot off your questions and requests quickly, they'll appreciate it. Do not expect to gab.

Interview Tips	Expert Insights	✔
List yourself in the expert directories, which you can find by browsing the Internet. For example, *The Yearbook Of Experts* **www.yearbooknews.com** offers a listing in their bound directory and their online site, as well as special online press releases available for a yearly flat fee.	Patti lists all her credentials as a body language expert, ensuring she gets many radio and magazine interviews with no additional effort on her part.	
Send out press releases. Can you link your expertise to a newsworthy event? Are you hosting a special event? Are you part of an unusual celebration? Are you speaking at a prestigious institution? Have you recently written a book or an article?	When *ABC* and *CBS* radio news asked Patti to analyze Gary Condit's body language in the famous Connie Chung interview, she followed up those interviews with a press release to 500 media contacts with the lead line that her expertise was used by the two networks.	
Apply your expertise to something new and different.	When Patti hit upon the idea of using body language expertise to analyze a national entertainment event—the Oscars—she received the national magazine coverage she wanted. Patti sent out a press release saying she could analyze the body language of the stars on the red carpet or as they received, or did not receive an Oscar. That led to more than 20 radio interviews, and entry to mass-market magazines with a broad appeal, such as the *National Examiner, US* and *Cosmopolitan.*	
Offer—for free—something you have written that they could use on the air.	Create a quiz or test or a sheet with 10 things people want to know about your topic or ten questions people always ask about this topic and send it out to media lists. Make it short, content-rich and fun.	

You should ask the critical questions in your first phone call, but the following questions can be addressed later via email.

You may want to make a copy of this sheet and keep it by the phone or on your computer. In the event that you receive a call asking you to go on the air immediately, do not accept the offer unless you are a very experienced interviewer. Otherwise, you could end

Critical Questions	Expert Insights	✔
What time is the interview and what time will you call?	Request they email you confirmation of the interview, including the time the interview will start, as well as other details.	
What is the topic and what do you hope to find out?	Tell them how you would like to be introduced to the listeners and request that they announce your website address for further information.	
Will you call live on the air or will there be a wait?	Give them your phone number and an emergency back up number. Have them email you the station call letters, numbers and the name of the show as well as the contact's name, phone number and address.	
Approximately how long will the interview be?	Tell them if you have other interviews or obligations near the show time so they will get you on and off quickly.	
Do you typically run on time?	Ask if they have a website. If so, suggest they link their website to yours and tell the listeners about the link.	
Who else will be interviewed (or has been interviewed) on this topic on your show?	Tell them if you have a book (and offer to send one), or an event, product or service particularly applicable to their audience. Request that they mail you a tape of the show.	

up looking like less than an expert and it could hurt, rather than help, your chances of getting future interviews.

TIP:

Often, you'll be told that tape requests must be made separately to someone else at the station. If so, be prepared to give the station name, call letters, time slot of the show and your start time. This will give you a record of what is said. In addition, you can sometimes use the recording for future promotion. However, this is illegal unless you've received written permission from the station. It's rare that your request would be turned down, but keep in mind that 99% of stations will NOT grant permission to sell the interview as a product. Ask them to confirm these requests via email. In addition, request their email address, then confirm everything on your end via email. That way, you'll have all the necessary information in print, and you have all their contact information in case you want to contact them again with a story or show ideas in the future.

Personal Preparation Interviews are really fun, but they are extremely time-consuming. The following tips will help you get your ducks in a row before you begin this process so you don't waste energy.

Patti sometimes offers a free hour of her time to a contest winner, which includes an analysis of their body language for interviews, or public speaking coaching session. The station gets a great give-away prize, and Patti gets to let listeners know she coaches as well as speaks.

It takes more than simply knowing your material in order to have a smooth, successful interview.

There are additional considerations for radio broadcast that can make or break your interview.

Secondary Questions You Should Ask	✔
What kind of show is it (news, comedy, entertainment)?	
How many people does it reach? What is the market (city or cities)?	
What is the editorial slant (conservative, liberal, controversial)?	
Who is the interviewer and what does (s)he prefer to be called?	
How familiar is the interviewer with your topic?	
Would they like any other information about you?	
Let them know you maintain a list of questions past audiences have asked and find out if they would like to see the list. Make the offer only when you believe it will be well received.	
If you have a book, product or service that you can offer for free, ask them if they would like to give it away to callers during your interview, or perhaps later as a contest prize.	

Get Your Ducks In A Row	Expert Insights	✔
Know your topic inside and out.	If you have an hour or a day or training material on the topic or you have read a few books, or written an article on it, you probably do not have the depth or breadth of knowledge for an un-scripted interview.	
Be familiar with all the current books, research and media buzz on your topic.	Go to **Amazon.com** or another on-line book source at least once a month and find out what is out there on your topic and read it. Get any periodicals related to your topic so you know what is hot. Go to your favorite search engines at least once a week; put in your key words and see what comes up. This will also let you know who the other experts on your topic are. Perhaps you'll want to write together or quote each other.	
Get in touch with other experts who are being interviewed.	Develop an expert network to share information.	
Get clarity about your image and your business goals.	Ask yourself: Why are you doing interviews? What are your goals? What image do you want to project? How do you want to be perceived by your audience? How do you want your information used by the media? How do you want it used by your audience?	
Decide what you will and will not talk about, as well as what types of shows you will and won't participate in.	You may find that certain shows are (in your view) morally ambiguous, strange or distasteful.	

Logistical Tips	Expert Insights	✔
Even if they are sending a tape, tape the show on your end.	You can buy a recording device from RadioShack that will tape both sides of a telephone call. Or use an old tape recorder and capture only your answers. You may also record onto your computer and burn it to a CD.	
Check your phone for sound quality.	Call a few friends and ask them to give your phone a sound check. Many cordless phones have a background buzz.	
If you use call-waiting, disengage it prior to the interview so it won't make a clicking sound while you're on the air. If you have other phone lines in the room, turn them off.	You don't want your fax line or home phone ringing during the interview!	
Create a quiet place for the interview.	Turn off any background buzzing equipment, and if you're at home, tell everyone you will be on the radio; put a note on the door and put the barking dog outside. Turn the papers on your desk over so you won't be tempted to read.	
Prepare your voice.	Drink water at room temperature. Do not drink caffeine, orange juice, iced or carbonated beverages. Caffeine and cold beverages constrict your vocal chords. Orange juice is acidic and traumatizes the vocal chords. Dairy products make you want to clear your throat. And carbonated beverages make you burp. Just prior to the interview, hum loudly for 3–4 minutes. This warms your vocal chords and enables you to sound as confident in the first 30 seconds as you will later in the interview.	
Prepare a list of questions you think you may be asked and have answers prepared, including key points you want to make.	Write them down—don't rely on your memory.

(continues on next page) | |

Logistical Tips	Expert Insights	✔
If you're selling a book or service, develop pithy quotes that focus on the problem you are helping to solve.	Refine your main points into sound bytes of less than 25 words. Make sure it sounds strong.	
Prepare a list of short anecdotes.	Hone a few of your best stories down to three or four lines. When said aloud, they shouldn't take more than 30 seconds.	
Do not mention your product/service/book repeatedly.	Talk about your solutions and insights.	

Patty's Parting Thoughts & Pointers	✔
Never, ever use a speakerphone for an interview. The sound will be distorted.	
Don't have your radio on in the background. This causes feedback.	
Be relaxed and move around. Most interviewers like high energy interviewees. Stand up and gesture while you are on the air; gesturing increases your vocal variation and creates more memory links so you'll think of more great things to say.	
Discover your interviewer's style and what they want, and match it.	
Make the interviewer look good. Make their questions great questions, and try not to correct their remarks.	
Have some great short tips or tidbits of information ready.	
Keep your answers short, especially if the interview time is short.	
Don't brag.	
Ask a media coach to listen to one of your tapes.	
Celebrate your success! When you're done with your interview, treat yourself to something special. You've worked hard.	

Your Content-Based Website, With Sparkle Please

WAR STORY #9   *The World Wide Web as we know it today didn't even exist when I started my consulting practice in the 1970s. Today I cannot imagine any consultant running a business without it. Even only a few years ago I was a neophyte about using the Internet for my business. At first I kept resisting it, then it became obvious that I really needed to become very knowledgeable about the Internet to stay competitive in the marketplace. So I made it a goal to jump in at the deep end and learn how to use the Internet for business. My strategy was to set a deadline when I absolutely wanted to be up to speed on the subject and then schedule to teach a course titled, "The Secrets of the Internet." Over the next 90 days I had no choice but to immerse myself in everything I could find on the subject, apply everything I learned and seek out other experts.*

By committing myself to teaching, I became a very passionate student (recall from our discussions in Chapter 3, you never have such ownership of a subject as you do after you have restated or rewritten it in your own words). In other words, when the student is ready, the teacher appears.

Fortunately my learning curve was accelerated, thanks to my friendship with the obvious expert on designing websites and marketing on the Internet, Roger Parker. One of his many

Enjoy More Success

To increase your business and to establish yourself as an obvious expert the word is "WEBSITE" —a quality website designed and written by web experts who understand marketing.

At SalesPEAK, the web has positioned us as sales and presentation experts. Sure, we do great work and our website gives us the exposure that establishes credibility in our competitive industry. Many consultants think that being web savvy qualifies them to create their own website. This is the equivalent of performing your own root canal or representing yourself in court. DON'T DO IT! Leave it to the experts and offer free articles and information that helps your potential clients enjoy more success. Then, as the obvious expert—you'll enjoy more success, too!

RENEE WALKUP
http://www.salespeak.com

books, Relationship Marketing on the Internet, *has helped define him as one of the top consultants advising clients on website designs, including how websites do and don't work and what will draw new visitors, while keeping regulars coming back to the site for more.*

Just as with any other form of marketing, your website can be as simple or as complicated as you want to make it. The key is to focus on your client base when you are deciding how to present yourself and your business on the web. The more solid, timely, useful information you are able to offer your website visitors, the more likely you are to develop their loyalty and increase their chances of calling on you for their consulting needs.

My first attempt at a website drew few repeat visitors and fewer clients. Thank goodness I started getting advice from Roger and other obvious experts on the subject. You see initially my website was a patchwork quilt of my service offerings. Every specialty and every niche that I could serve was addressed on that one site. In hindsight, I realize that I appeared to be a one-man-band of consulting services which ranged from educational counseling, test making and test taking preparation, to retail sales trainer, consultant's advisor, coach and association builder.

My first website did not communicate that I could be a client's security blanket, safety net or any other type of fortifying fabric to their life. Instead I had addressed so many niches of service that I just came off looking like that patchwork quilt—perhaps even like the random and mismatched pattern called a Crazy Quilt!

Fortunately the fix was quick. I simply arranged to have five websites built. Each site focused clearly on a specific service, a specific type of problem I could solve for a client. Gone were the multiple messages and the clutter. Now clients could see what I offered and how I was an obvious expert in the field in which they were seeking help.

Howard Shenson told me long ago: the best consultants are also in the business of developing information products that can help their clients solve problems. Do this on your website—or your websites. There will be no doubt that you are the obvious expert.

EE Jr.

Web-Savvy Strategies

Having a website and an email address are required today for almost any business. By showing that you're technologically savvy, you subtly ensure prospective clients that you're up-to-date in other areas as well, such as your consulting specialty. Beyond that, there is simply no better way to reach so many people, so easily, so quickly and for so little investment of your time.

A website lends a credibility to your practice that you cannot get from most other forms of marketing. Prospective clients can look up information about your consulting practice and your background without having to wait for you to send them a brochure. They can determine from your website what kinds of services you offer. They can privately 'scope you out,' allowing them to become familiar with you and your standards of service in a way that is comfortable for them.

The quality of your website can and should give potential clients an indication of the quality of your consulting work, such as your attention to detail or the importance you place on a professional image. A website can draw visitors from all over the world, which means you can receive business inquiries from people you've never met, who found your site by searching on the Internet.

Your email address, which is included on your website, gives potential clients a way to reach you without having to pick up the telephone or lick a stamp. They can email you anytime, day or night, which is good because some potential clients will contact you on impulse instead of making a note on their

Ten WebSITES!

I started with my first business card and website about four years ago. I now have at least ten sites that I maintain on a regular basis, monthly or quarterly. One site has evolved into the business I am now marketing, of providing branding for those in small businesses and non-profit organizations.

The price of a small one-page site is very low these days and having some professional assistance is wise. As your business grows you can add the link to your customer relations database for a system that pretty much runs itself.

CHRISTINA WELLMAN
http://www.consultingworks.org

calendars to call you (and then possibly forgetting to do it). Best of all, no one is ever in the wrong time zone to learn more about you and your services or to send you a communication, thanks to the Internet and email.

Consider these four different approaches to make your website work for you:

The **Business Card** or **Brochure** Website	Explains what you do and gives the reader your contact information
The **Information Exchange** Website	An interactive vehicle for gathering and disseminating facts and opinions about a topic related to your business
The **Retail Store** Website	Created soley to sell goods or services
The **Multi-Function** (not Multi-Focus) Website	A combination of any or all of the above.

Which of these four ways you use your website depends obviously, on what you are offering to your clients or customers. It also depends on how much time you can devote to maintaining your website.

In this chapter we focus on the second use: creating a website that is rich in information—content—that applies to your area of expertise and that is focused on one of your niches of service. This type of use is great to help establish your reputation as the obvious expert and to serve as a dynamic brochure to showcase your work. It can be a powerful vehicle to sell your products and services.

Testing The Waters

I'd heard that giving away free copies of my books is one of the best marketing tools I can use. But it gets expensive to ship free copies to every potential reader, talk show host, media contact, etc. So I decided to put one of my books online—an entire mystery novel. I was surprised by the results. More sales from online booksellers, more sales from libraries and more requests for interviews! Online chat hosts, such as for *AOL Books* and *Oprah's* online book community, get a feeling for my books quickly. The hosts' promotion of me and my books has been impressive —detailed interviewing that is a direct result from information easily gleaned at my website.

NATALIE THOMAS
http://www.independentmysteries.com

 The hardest challenge you have is to forget what you know and approach your subject from the point of view of someone who knows nothing.

Roger Parker

"Give up a brag-and-boast approach and instead focus your energies with answering on your website, the questions you are asked in person," advises Roger.

"In order to become an obvious expert, you have to adopt a persona and perspective of total naiveté and answer the questions. *What are the simple things that everyone takes for granted?*

"My books have succeeded in many cases because they explain the obvious that other books take for granted. The success of the 'Dummies' books is because they tell you how to turn on the computer. Everyone else assumes you know how to turn on the computer."

Getting Started

The first step in creating a content-rich website is to put together an outline. You'll need a home page, which is the first screen a visitor sees when that person clicks on your web address. From there, you'll need other screens or "pages" the visitor can reach by clicking on graphic "buttons" that lead to various sections of your website. You have to decide how you want the pages of the site to branch out from the home page before you can construct the site or ask someone else to build it for you.

Surf the Internet for a while and look at other professionals' sites. Determine what you do and don't like about them. You'll start to get an idea of the kinds of pages you'd like to include on your site. You might also get some design ideas.

In general, your site must include information about:

You

Your Business

Your Industry

Your Services and Products

Your Value to a Customer

Bring Them Back For More

Websites are too often used as online brochures. Do you read a promotional brochure that you have been given more than once? Probably not. Do you want your visitors to stop by your website only once? Probably not. To keep them coming back for more and to create an image of yourself as an expert in your field, you must provide free samples of your rock-solid content. I find the best way to demonstrate your expertise is to provide it in Video and Printable format. Video is great for short interactive content. Print allows your visitor to take content with them. Remember, just as in advertising, reach and frequency are everything!

TIM SPIELMAN
http://www.stragitek.com

Your information may not need to be in this order. The visitor must simply be able to quickly determine your value to him or her, or you risk that visitor losing interest or seeking a more user-friendly site.

Content

Kevin Hogan preeminent author of *The Psychology of Persuasion: How To Persuade Others to Your Way of Thinking,* recommends your website include three specific points of proof about your expertise. Also, he advises that it should give visitors many different reasons to return to your site—reasons that are beneficial to them, and not just about showcasing who you are.

Kevin has posted more than 900 pages of articles on his own website that visitors can download without charge. To help keep visitors coming back often, he adds new articles all the time. Visitors know they can go to his site as a resource for their own research.

Your website needs to show what makes you different from the competition.

Information That Kevin Hogan Recommends Should Be On Your Site:

A short biography. Your site could contain both your short bio and your long version. The short biography is a one-paragraph description that might appear next to your photo and is similar to or the same as one you would use in a brochure about your business. It explains who you are, what you do and why your business is unique.

Lengthier biographical information. The longer biography goes into detail without reading like your lifetime résumé. It should stick to benefits and results statements about your business that will appeal to clients. Underscoring the importance of the long bio, Kevin points out that on his website, it is the third most often clicked page.

"Always remember that your biography is only a sales tool," Kevin says. "It still has to be focused on the customer." You can create a client focused site by mentioning some of your clients by name along with the services you provided for them. Describing your real-world results makes a much better impression than simply listing where you went to school and which jobs you held before you became a consultant.

Testimonials from current and former clients.

Testimonials help potential clients who are visiting your website see exactly what you might be able to do for them.

Case studies about your business. Instead of writing "I'm the world's greatest consultant," you can sell yourself by telling a story about helping a specific client. Your website visitors will identify from these stories that you can help them in the same ways you have helped others.

Photographs of you from events. While you're speaking to those service clubs, ask a photographer (or someone who's good with a digital camera) to take your picture. Showing yourself as an authority delivering a speech paints a picture of you as the obvious expert. You also can post photographs of yourself talking with recognizable people, including community leaders or other experts in your field.

A list of related services and other consultants. Provide hyperlinks to other helpful websites. Define yourself as the go-to person for information.

Reminders of upcoming events. You're the expert, so you should know the details about the next convention in your industry. You should also include information about your upcoming seminars and speaking engagements. This section can even include follow-up comments about recent events.

A storefront or catalog. Create an ecommerce section where visitors can purchase products by using an order form. The form must have a way of accepting credit cards over the Internet and

Consulting Portal

When I've traveled outside the USA on business trips, I've found that business people, investment bankers and venture capitalists have all used my website to learn about me, my services, and—more than anything else—what areas of specialty I offer. I've found my personal website serves as probably the most effective consulting portal I could purchase, at any price. Any new or beginning consultant should establish a quality personal webpage. Don't forget to change it regularly. Update the content so that the material offered to the world stays fresh. I change newsletters, or surveys, or writings about management, regularly. And I continue to be surprised when clients comment to me about something I wrote online—sometimes even a year ago.

ALAN GUINN
www.theguinnconsultancygroup.com

The Secret Is Content–Content–Content!

I decided to build a website that would allow people to have FUN, laugh, understand they were NOT alone and show them they could make significant changes. The key was someone had to take the time to tell them not only what to do, but how to do it!

The end result was that my website continues to rank on a Top 20 List. It has created publicity for me in *Parenting Magazine, BH&G, Good Housekeeping* and as a resource in numerous books authored by other people.

TIPS Never fear giving away too much information. Get involved with other groups or listeners who need the expertise you have to offer. Create interactive areas for people to send comments to you: a guest book, request for service forms, website evaluation forms, registry area, bulletin boards where they can get YOUR expert advice, a chat room for you to host your own online consulting or workshops, and most of all update it regularly and notify your visitors.

JULIE SIGNORE
http://www.123sortit.com

must assure visitors that it is secure and that their personal information cannot be stolen.

The products you sell from your storefront section can be those you have created, including your books and reports, items you're licensed to sell, other products that pertain to your business, or just products you endorse, including other people's books.

Whatever your niche is, there are books, audiotapes and marketing materials that you can purchase yourself from wholesalers and publishers and then sell on your website. Doing this will give your stamp of authenticity to the products and will enhance your image as well.

Other Tips On Content

Try a digest approach. Gather the timely, relevant information in your field and present it on your webpage to your visitors in an easy-to-comprehend format.

"There's too much information out there, and the person who simplifies and helps website visitors separate the wheat from the chaff becomes incredibly valuable," Roger says.

He points to Jay Nelson, who publishes a newsletter called *Design Tools Monthly*. The newsletter focuses on anything that happened in the past month that graphic designers who use Macintosh® computers might need to know.

"There are twenty-five magazines you would have to read to be up to date," Roger says. "What he does is summarize in eight pages the most important articles from those twenty-five magazines."

Interpret trends, events, challenges and problems. Help your website visitors sort out what's important in your industry and simplify it. Tell them what you think about an issue, and it will help them determine their own thoughts on the subject.

"There are a lot of facts out there, but very few people know how to put them into context," Roger says. "People want your opinion . . . It takes knowledge to have an opinion."

Let the content reflect your style and personality. People don't want to be bored, and the tone of your website, when properly handled, can make you stand out from everyone else. Someone who writes with a glimmer of humor is better liked, and people will look forward to reading that person's work more than they would a monotone, rambling site.

Show evidence of your passion. People will be much more eager to hire you if they see you have a genuine enthusiasm for your clients and their businesses. If you appear bored, and your website appears tired, you won't inspire people to contact you.

"One of the highest compliments I ever got was a client telling me that outside of his wife, my opinion counted far more than anyone else's," Roger says. "He knew that I loved his business."

Consider publishing book reviews. You can provide a service for visitors to your website by helping them choose the best publications about your industry. By contacting publishers, you might be able to get on the list of people who review books before they are released to the public, and this can put you on the cutting edge. People will turn to your website to determine whether they should bother to buy a new book. Taking a stand, whether it's for or against, shows that you are expert enough to have an informed opinion.

Ask your readers or clients to submit their stories. If you are going to be in the information-selling business, you need raw materials. You need a constant flow of new ideas. You can get this by asking visitors to email you information that you can share on the website. For example, you can have a question-and-answer section where you publish readers' concerns along with your answers to their problems. This approach comes with a bonus: The information you collect is perfect fodder for your next book or marketing initiative.

Publish a short survey or quiz periodically. First publish

It's A Visual Medium

Internet users are NOT readers; they are viewers! If there has to be a special key to creating an engaging, content rich website, this is one to remember. There are varieties of learning and communication and personality style, and you can address the needs of each as the viewers scroll down through your site, providing minute details and data to those who desire it. But on the top layer, keep your information brief, engaging and easy-to-follow. The more 'high-tech' our communication becomes, the more 'high-touch' our approach should be. We are not a group of computers seeking information from other computers; we are people using computers to communicate effectively with other people. Relate to them personally.

CHRIS CAREY
http://www.ChrisCarey.com

LINK! LINK! LINK!

After every speech, seminar or consulting engagement, get your clients to link from their websites to your website. It will substantially increase the number of hits you get on your website, and it will also increase your product sales if you sell product on your website.

Before each engagement, upload onto your website your handouts, slides you use, any relevant articles, and special products that relate to that specific engagement. Put it all in a special folder or link specifically created for each client. It's not that much work, especially if you're using info that's already on your website. It's just reorganizing the material or setting up special links that lead each client and its employees to the info on your website. Many companies will keep the link to your website indefinitely, so you'll even draw employees who are new to the company. It also serves as a way to give you specific feedback about your program in terms of what they liked best/least. This helps you to adjust your future program content. It also makes it easy for clients to recommend you to others outside of their company.

TONY ALESSANDRA
http://www.alessandra.com

the quiz, and then publish the results. Make sure you offer a new survey or quiz every week or two. Keep readers coming back to see whether they 'won' or if their answers were the most popular. Quizzes also help you gather important information. You can ask visitors to rank the most influential people in your field, or to give their opinions about a timely issue. If you use multiple-choice answers, you can show the results in a pie chart so readers can see whether they fit in with the mainstream or if they are out there on their own.

Create several single-purpose websites stemming from your main address. Each branch website has its own name and is descriptive of a certain issue, but it actually functions as a sub-site of your main website. Nick Nichols says he uses this technique to attract visitors who are interested in a specific issue that is one of his specialties.

"I have several websites I use to target different types of audiences, depending on what I'm trying to get across," Nichols says. "I think this is extremely important to people who are beginning or trying to build their practice."

To accomplish this, all you need is one website, hosted by one company. You can create sub-areas of that website and direct visitors to the other site through a **cloaked URL.**

> *Although you might be a generalist in your field, people need to believe and perceive that you are a specialist in their area.*
>
> Nick Nichols

Don't give away the whole store. Your website should be used as a sales tool, just like your marketing collateral, suggests Lynn Stewart. In other words, your website should give potential clients a good idea of what you could offer them and entice them to contact you.

"I like a website to be a point of information," Lynn says. "It doesn't need to tell the whole story. If it has too much information, it allows the client to go to the website, review it and make a determination rather than ever getting back to you and giving you a chance to sell whatever you're selling."

Design And Construction Tips

- Make your website easy to read. Choose one or two fonts and stick with them instead of garbling the site with many different typestyles. Save the artistic fonts for wedding invitations or your personal home page. Keep text readable.
- Design the website so that it can be printed easily and will look good when it's printed. Many people don't think to test what their site looks like in print. People print web pages to peruse later or to pass along to someone in a board meeting, only to realize that some part has been cut off or they can't read the information.
- Don't put too many photos or graphic elements on your website. Too many graphics lengthen the time it takes a page to load from a visitor's browser. The visitor may get impatient or bored and will stop the process and move on to something else.
- Offer a service that people cannot get offline. Give them a price break for contacting you online, or forms they can fill out to request information or services without taking time to pick up the phone.

Trade links with related, non-competing websites in your niche. For example, if you're a computer consultant for small businesses in your local area, trade reciprocal website links with local CPAs, management consultants, electronics retailers and telephone installers. It's real simple. Just set up a page of links on your website and send out some invites to related local firms offering to trade equal space. Besides the free advertising and boost to your search engine rankings, these informal link

Skip The Flash

Site visitors want information and they want it fast! Three steps will drive readers to the content you have to offer:

1 Your site should load quickly—skip the flash, the music and the bells and whistles. If your site isn't up in 15 seconds using a phone connection, visitors will move on. Maximum page site is 45 KB.

2 Clearly articulate within 5 seconds, "What's in it for me, the site visitor?" Include your site's Unique Selling Proposition.

3 Have a consistent, primary navigation scheme with no more than nine choices. It should be the same on all pages and should run across the top or down the left side of each page.

These steps will draw people in to explore and fully utilize your site.

CORBIN BALL
http://www.corbinball.com

trades can also open the door to talking about other more lucrative offline networking opportunities.

Joshua Feinberg

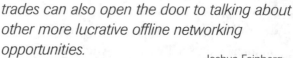

Drive Traffic To Your Site

You can have the greatest website in the world, but that won't matter if you don't have a way of drawing visitors or traffic, to the address. There are several effective ways of doing this.

Search engines. One easy way of bringing in more visitors is to register with search engines that seek sites such as yours through the use of keywords. Industry figures show more than half of all traffic directed to websites comes from search engines. People surfing the web type in specific words, such as "marketing consultant," and they see on their screens a list of sites that might pertain to their search request. For your website to appear on that list, and preferably near the top, you may want to pay a service to keep it there.

Links. Make a deal with all of your friends, clients and associates who have businesses that complement but do not compete with yours. They put a link to your site on their sites and vice versa. This is a good way of attracting a specific audience interested in your area of expertise. You might also check with groups such as Chambers of Commerce that run links to businesses on their website. Also, the websites of many organizations publish links to their members' sites, so check within your own network of organizations.

Advertising. You may want to purchase ads on websites your potential clients might visit while they are shopping online, researching or just browsing. Avoid ads on sites that are so broad or general they attract anyone and everyone, those visitors aren't necessarily your target audience. Numbers don't matter here—the quality of the visitor matters. To get the most for your money, narrow your choices to highly specialized sites that

Search Engine Ranking

I use web content to create "side door" pages that are optimized for search engine positioning. For instance, I have 120 mini-articles all optimized on one very specific keyword phrase. Having an entire website very specifically focussing on one keyword or keyword phrase gives you an enormous boost in search engine rankings because the search engine sees your site as a really great resource on the topic the searcher is looking for.

TOM ANTION
http://www.Public-Speaking.org

might not charge as much for advertising and can deliver you the highest number of potential new clients.

Word of mouth. Talk up your website wherever you go: at your next professional convention, in your workshops, at the local service club functions, in the stadium at a professional sports game. Print your web address on your business cards, letterhead, newsletters and other material, and attach it to your signature when you email anyone. You'll be amazed how many people will check out your website and pass it along to their friends and acquaintances.

Email And Electronic Incentives

Reprinted with permission from the International Guild of Professional Consultants Special Report, ©2002.

Email and electronic incentives provide the engine that "drives" the five-stage client relationship cycle. Understanding which of the five stages you are in with each client is important to identify how to respond to their specific needs.

The Five Stages of the Client Relationship Cycle:

AWARENESS
when prospects first become aware of you.

COMPARISON
when prospects about to make a buying decision, must make a choice between alternatives.

TRANSACTION
the moment when a prospect is converted into a client, or a repeat buyer.

REINFORCEMENT
Post-sales communications that confirm the buyer has made the right decision.

ADVOCACY
providing tools and motivation for clients to refer you to their friends, peers and co-workers.

Category-Killer Domain Names

I realized that the websites I visit most frequently have a constantly changing assortment of fascinating new articles. I decided to add such articles to my website. I also decided to add an eBook which visitors could download free of charge. My highly specialized website does not deal with all of my work or consulting but focuses on only one of my specializations: the domain names of $50 million to $5 billion products.

I have found that the use of these "category-killer" domain names can lead to high level placement in search engines and that is what this website is devoted to. I am now working on several other websites that are focused on my other areas of expertise. I have found it is much more effective to have a website devoted to one major topic of interest.

DONALD MOINE
http://www.DrMoine.com

Efficient Websites

To help you build your reputation and profit, your website should have lots of information that is relevant for your key visitors. That information should be easy to find and use.

1 Use your visitor's language.

2 Use a site-specific search engine to help folks find what they're looking for.

3 Forget fancy stuff that slows your site down. The entry pages on your site should load in ten seconds or less for a first-time user with a dialup connection.

4 Last, make sure your site is drenched with links and interactive devices, including ways to contact you. Use autoresponders and good email management to get back to folks fast.

WALLY BOCK
http://www.bockinfo.com

Once you have identified which stage you and your prospective client are in, use email and electronic incentives effectively to further your relationship.

Email permits you to communicate for free with clients and prospects. No more delays, postage costs and extra costs for color or extra pages.

Electronic incentives are, likewise, free. When you prepare an email newsletter or a 24-page Special Report demonstrating your competence and knowledge of a specialized area, you can deliver that credibility-building document for free. All you are out is the time you spent preparing and formatting the document (i.e., choosing an attractive combination of layout, colors, typefaces, type sizes and line spacing).

The speed with which visitors receive and can obtain your electronic incentives is equally important.

Autoresponders

Prospects have short memories. When you desire information you want it right now—not a week or ten days later. Yet, this usually happens when you circle a "Reader's Service" card in a magazine or—all too often—request information from a large firm's website.

Often, two or more weeks go by before the requested information arrives in the mail—often in a hand-addressed envelope!

This of course, is wrong because the Internet has trained us to expect immediate gratification. Since email is delivered within moments of sending out clients and prospects expect immediate responses.

That's where autoresponders come in. An autoresponder is an email program that automatically responds (hence the term) to email sent to a specific email address. Let's say you're offering visitors at the Awareness Stage (those who are encountering your advertising materials or website for the first time) a free *"Guide to Purchasing Consulting Services in the Financial Services Field."* when visitors enter their email address in the registration form and press the Submit button, two things happen:

- a return email is immediately sent containing the incentive, i.e., the Free Guide, as an attachment.

- an email is sent to you notifying you that another potential client has requested your Free Guide and (hopefully) has asked to be added to your email newsletter list.

Depending on how your website has been set up, visitors' email addresses may also be automatically added to a database permitting follow-up.

Follow-Up

What happens next is up to you. One option is to wait a day and follow-up with a second email. Your 'excuse' for this follow-up email is to thank visitors for requesting the electronic incentive and ask if he or she found it useful and/or ask if he has any further questions. Your goal at that point is to establish a dialog, not only finding out how well liked your incentive was, but what additional information the visitor may need.

As your email correspondence continues, you can then "raise the stakes" by qualifying their interest and—if appropriate— asking them for their mailing address so you can send them some further information. You might also ask them for their telephone number, so you can establish a personal communication.

It's important that you move slowly at this point. If you ask for too much information too early in the 'courtship,' you're likely to turn off your visitors. There is an inverse relationship between the number of people who request an electronic incentive and the amount of information they must provide to receive it.

Building Traffic

Having done all the things everyone advises, like having good meta tags, registering in all the search engines I could find, running a link to my web site campaign, creating discussion groups and newsletters, and much more, I decided I needed something new to increase traffic.

One of my eCommerce web sites which gets several thousand visitors daily and sells as high as $10,000 of product per week needed a boost. What additional content can I add that will help attract more visitors and sell more product?

Adding the opportunity to sell and buy items by auction seemed to be the answer. Not only does it attract more visitors but it adds to the revenue stream from my business tools product shopping cart eStore. Now not only do they have the chance to sell their items for a small fee, but they also can buy items at a discount and it gives us an opportunity to sell slow moving and older products.

Since we now show up as an auction, the bots that index for the search engines have us in a new category as well as the many others. So traffic is better because of the new content. And I'm not the only one adding content, my auction users are also.

CARL KLINE
http://www.4expertise.com

Less Is Usually More

In my several years of selling web services and consulting on web strategy, I am always surprised to find how many businesses miss opportunities to leverage the potential of their web sites. The following points are some general suggestions based on my experiences.

1 *Keep it fresh!* Update your content regularly. There is nothing more frustrating than visiting a calendar of "upcoming events" only to find a listing of 2001 tradeshows and seminars.

2 *Ditch the "under construction" signs.* If the page is not complete, don't post it to your site. Visitors won't return to check on it at a later date.

3 *Give and receive.* A web site is a great way to offer information, but it's also a fabulous tool for gathering essential marketing information. Web based forms and surveys can provide valuable user data and feedback.

4 *Less is usually more.* Don't force visitors to scroll through lengthy copy to find the information they need. Focus on key points, and offer detailed information as an option.

JENNIFER ZICK
http://www.reside.biz

But, if you allow your relationship to develop organically, instead of forcing yourself, and limit your questions to just those appropriate on the basis of prospect responses, you'll find that visitors will be increasingly willing to share contact and buying information. The more questions you ask via email and on the phone, the more you'll learn about the challenges your prospect is facing and the better able you will be to fine-tune your offerings to emphasize the solutions you offer that best match their problems.

For more information on creating a
Content-Based Website, visit:
www.obvious-expert.com/website

Relationship Marketing On The Internet

A SPECIAL CONTRIBUTION FROM
☙ Roger C. Parker ☙

Identifying Marketing Partners on the Internet

Your challenge as a consultant is to identify similar marketing partners, businesses with whom you can structure win-win marketing promotions; promotions which are of interest to your marketing partners because they introduce them to new clients who will continue to buy from them in the future.

E X E R C I S E

Ask yourself questions like:

1. Which firms could benefit from an introduction to my type of clients?

_____

_____

2. Who sells products that my clients need, but may be buying from competing suppliers?

_____

_____

3. Where are there opportunities for on-going purchases?

_____

_____

4. What types of products or services do your clients routinely purchase that you might be able to help them locate and obtain?

_____

_____

Doing this may be easier said than done, but it lies at the core of the success of your relationship marketing program.

If, for example, you are a marketing consultant, your marketing partners might include:

◆ **Commercial printers** firms need someone to print their brochures, letterheads, invoices, postcards and newsletters.

◆ **Sources of type, stock photographs or clip-art** strong brand identities are based on the careful use of distinct typefaces and artwork.

◆ **Commercial addressing and label firms** because firms that specialize in applying labels and separating mailings by Zip Code are far more efficient than in-house facilities.

◆ **Graphic designers** because marketing materials need to be good-looking.

◆ **List brokers** because your clients may want to purchase the mailing addresses of qualified prospects.

◆ **Book, magazine and newsletter publishers** interested in reaching the marketing community.

◆ **Premium and incentive firms** firms that distribute pens, inspirational plaques, and other products inscribed with the client's name.

◆ **Software publishers,** especially those who offer programs specially designed for niche markets.

◆ **Professional photographers** who can take custom photographs of people or products.

◆ **Conference, seminar and workshop promoters** who could also benefit from an introduction to your clients.

This list could go on and on. Although you may not be a marketing consultant, the above lists shows how many 'hidden' potential marketing partners there may be with whom you can structure effective promotions.

Your first step is to identify a similar list of suppliers that complement your consulting niche. Then contact their marketing representatives and develop joint incentive programs that will introduce them to your clients in a manner the paves the way for future business.

List of Potential Clients	Contact Date	Marketing Initiative Planned	Target Implementation Date

Your goal is to convince your marketing partners that offering a 50% discount on an executive portrait, for example, is a far less costly way to promote their business than increasing the size of their ad in the telephone book or buying an ad in a publication.

The thing to bear in mind is that you're doing your marketing partners as much of a favor as they are doing for you. You're not asking for something for free: you're introducing them to prospects who may turn into clients for life!

ROGER C. PARKER

Roger's Parting Thought:

> *The biggest problem that I see most consultants making is failure to differentiate between customer acquisition and customer retention. Many consultants see the web as simply a customer acquisition tool and focus all their efforts on trying to sell strangers on their competence. A much better alternative would be to focus equal, if not more, attention on customer retention, i.e. developing ways to better serve their current and previous customers.*
>
> *Often a first step is to develop an offline print program, i.e., postcards or word processor letters that will drive current and previous customers to your website, where the visitor can sign up to receive high-octane content or premium content information that prospects and casual visitors don't enjoy access to.*
>
> *It costs six to seven times as much to sell a new customer than a previous customer. That's known. What's unknown, for many, is how to use websites to better serve past customers.*

Join Up: The Real Value of Memberships and Certifications

WAR STORY #10 *After spending so much time on the lecture circuit myself, speaking to so many clubs and associations, I started to realize just how very valuable memberships were to their members. Howard and I began creating theories on how association memberships could best serve independent practitioners.*

He shared with me the story of an old friend of his who called him one day and lamented that he was working in a dead-end job in a dead-end company where he wasn't making enough money. He said he had no job leads in town and was wondering whether he should move to a new city where the opportunities might be better.

The man was extremely introverted and he wasn't networking the way one should when it's time to look for a new job. So Howard suggested the man join the local chapter of a professional organization for people in his field. But he cautioned the man not just to sign up and pay dues. Howard told him to get active; volunteer for one or two committees in the organization. Spend time working side by side with the other volunteers.

Within a few short months, the man had developed relationships within the organization that led to two major changes in his work life: 1) a new job at a company substantially increasing both his salary and his stature in his field; and 2) several part-time consultations that came from referrals within the professional organization, allowing him to earn more money on the side while he was working in his new full time job.

Oh yes, the shy and introverted man, who happened to also be a frequently-dateless bachelor in his early forties, made one other life change because of his involvements in service organizations— he met and happily married a former "Miss Kansas," who was then host of her own local television talk show.

There are countless stories confirming how participation in associations can boost one's consulting career and, more importantly, one's earnings. In addition, this single step adds greatly to a consultant's credibility as the obvious expert. Apparently, it can even improve your personal life, as well!

Because Howard and I both recognized the need for an association dedicated to helping new consultants connect with experienced consultants, we decided to launch a national association ourselves: The forerunner of The International Guild of Professional Consultants was born.

EE Jr.

Time Well Spent

When I was evaluating which organizations to spend my time, the non profit Minnesota Entrepreneurs, Inc. was at the top of my list. Within fifteen months, I'd worked my way up from board member to vice president and was recently elected president. Now when journalists in Minnesota and around the country want to speak with an entrepreneur whose ear is close to the ground, they call on me, the Obvious Expert!

ERIC P. STRAUSS
http://www.entrepreneursforhire.com

The Value of Memberships

No matter where you live, there are countless associations open to new members—that means you. Most of them hold membership drives and offer special perks to anyone who joins. They actively seek ways to recruit new people every year. It's not difficult to become a member, but to gain the full benefits of association membership, you should remember two important rules:

1   **You cannot simply join an association; you must actively participate in it, and**

2   **It takes membership in at least three organizations to build a strong consulting practice.**

Appropriate groups to join might include:

A professional organization within your industry. If you want to be perceived as one of the best consultants in your field, then your investment and involvement in an industry trade association is a must. It will signify to others that you are well grounded within your field and have a personal commitment to excellence. When you invest in this type of membership, the benefits are tremendous.

A professional organization of people in a cross-section of industries. In a group of this nature, such as a Chamber of Commerce, you can compare best practices with other professionals and pick up new ideas you can incorporate in your practice.

A civic service club, social club or religious organization. Instead of merely socializing in these organizations, make it a point to get to know the leaders in your community who are now your peer members. You never know where these connections will lead you or how they might help your business at some point while enriching your personal life.

Get Involved Instead Of Just Paying Dues

Join a committee in the group, work on a special project or take a seat on the board of directors. The more you put into your involvement, the more you'll get out of it. Working side by side with your peers in the group will give you opportunities to develop relationships that will help spread the word about you and what you do.

One of Lynn Stewart's clients was, at that time, the Associate Dean of Admissions at a top university in New York. The client had been a member of three different organizations in her industry for about fifteen years and wasn't sure of the benefit she was receiving from her membership. We suggested she join a

Stay Connected

No matter what industry you are involved in, keeping in contact with other individuals in your profession can only be a benefit. Everyone has different life experiences and we all benefit by associating with each other and sharing ideas. For this reason, I am actively involved in several associations. Also being certified has demonstrated to my clients that I am serious about my profession plus, it gave me more in-depth knowledge of the overall consulting industry.

ALAN ALPERT
http://smartofficesolutions.com

Education Is A Lifetime Process

Many people 'front-end load' their educations and think they have it covered. They believe that because ten, twenty or more years ago they went to college, or even to graduate school, that they have learned what they need to know about business. They could not be more off base!

Just as you do not try to cram all of your trips to the dentist or all of your exercise classes into the years between ages 18 and 22—why do people think you can do this with education?

Your 'degree in life' is an on-going process. It is comprised of your experiences, your relation-ships and the educational opportunities you deliberately build into every year—every month of your life.

Seek workshops, bootcamps and seminars to increase the breadth, depth and up-to-date-ness of your professional educa-tion. Earn certifications in your industry to keep you current, competitive and confident.

JASON TREMBLAY
http://www.sellnowmedia.com

committee in each organization. That simple act helped her see results almost immediately. There is something about peer level association that works for you with positive results.

"So many people overlook this step," Lynn tells us. "They think that just by showing up, they're going to get something out of membership. They think that's how you become known. This is not true. You actually have to work on developing your network within an organization."

Find the Right Organizations

Professional associations have the special advantage of giving you a chance to interact with people who have the same type of business as you have. You can get valuable insight when you sit around in a casual or perhaps business-type environment, round-table with several other people or one-on-one and talk about your challenges, your issues and your 'moments of truth.'

Other associations also can meet both your interests and your professional needs. There are all types of groups, including:

- Social and welfare associations

- Health and medical organizations

- Public affairs organizations

- Fraternities and sororities

- Nationality and ethnic-based organizations

- Religious organizations

- Veterans groups

- Heredity and patriotic organizations

- Sports participation groups

- Sporting fan organizations

- Parenting groups, such as Little League, PTAs, PTOs

- Scouting associations, such as the Boy or Girl Scouts

- Hobby groups

- Labor unions and associations

- Chambers of Commerce

- Trade and tourism associations

- Popular culture fan clubs

- Theater associations

- Volunteer groups for special events

One of the most important organizations you can join, Frank Candy says, is the International Guild of Professional Consultants. Frank, one of the group's founding members, says his investment of time, money and resources "has paid back many, many times over." Besides giving him opportunities to associate with people in his industry, the Guild offers a weekly ezine called, *Consultants in the News,* which publishes stories about consultants from print media outlets all over the nation.

Steven Haas, another long-time IGPC member, recommends you join not only the international group but also a local consultants network and a national consulting association. These groups foster public confidence in the profession as a whole, he says, because:

- They are committed to promoting and upholding high ethical and professional standards.

- They encourage interaction as well as foster and sponsor networking activities that bring consultants together.

- They allow consultants to share tools, techniques and best practices through a variety of educational venues.

- They provide academic insight and industry-specific guidance through their newsletters, websites and specialty publications.

Focused On Focus

My expertise is helping business people to see what is not so obvious, that is, their lack of focus. People who focus most of their time doing what they do best, prosper. Those who don't, struggle.

Our extensive research proves that most people, especially business leaders, struggle to achieve 50% focus! Here's an example of why we are the Obvious Focusing Experts:

One of our clients, Bob, is a commercial builder. He owns his own company. Using our coaching strategies, his level of focus jumped from 50% to 90%. His gross revenues soared from $8 million to $32 million. In addition, his confidence dramatically increased along with his time off for family and fun.

The Achievers Coaching program is a total focusing system that helps business people focus on their strengths while enjoying an excellent balance between work and family. Success is all about focus and follow-through.

LES HEWITT
http://www.achievers.com

Getting Involved

'I worked with you on the board of ____, and saw how effective you were at getting things done.' is a common statement I hear when a potential client calls me and asks to set up an appointment to consider working together. I learned early in life that getting involved in my community pays big dividends in two ways: it grows my business and it feeds my soul. Competition for client dollars is increasing daily. The old saying– "People buy from those they like and trust" is truer today than ever before. Visible, passionate involvement in activities in your community provides benefit in three ways: the organization will benefit from your expertise and leadership, potential clients translate that effectiveness into solving their professional issues and want to hire you and then perhaps best of all, you become a better, more complete person. What more could you want from a strategy?

SARALYN COLLINS
http://www.thetrainingbridge.com

Benefits Of Joining

Support from colleagues. When you work by yourself, or at the top of your own company, you may feel isolated or at least, insulated. You do not have colleague relationships in the way you would if you were in a corporate setting.

Being a member of an organization offers you a network of support from people who are your equal. You can go to them to brainstorm ideas that you cannot discuss with potential clients, your employees or your family members and friends.

"You can become overwhelmed when you think you're the only person doing this," Lynn reminds us. "You kind of waver between, 'If I ask somebody for help, I'm going to sound like I don't know what I'm doing' and if 'I don't ask, I'm not going to know.' You really need to get involved with other people—preferably other consultants, people who know the industry. Use them as referral sources before you decide to just take on the world."

Membership directories. Potential clients consult directories to find businesses that specialize in what the client needs. You want your name, along with your consulting specialty, to be listed. The Internet adds another dimension to member directories. The International Guild of Professional Consultants provides an online directory of its members, searchable geographically or by specialty.

Introductions. Networking can get your name circulating among the right people and pave the way for introductions that will help your business. Every time you meet someone new in your networking, you are expanding your contact circle to potentially include *his* or *her* contact circle.

Training and professional growth. Associations are good places to look for training and ideas that can continue your growth in your field of expertise.

Improved credentials. Listing your membership in professional organizations looks good on your letterhead, brochures, resume, website, newsletter and biographical information with published works.

Improved credibility. Your participation lends you the credibility of the association, even if you are unknown, William Cohen says in his book *How to Make it BIG as a Consultant* (©2001 AMACOM).

Visibility for your practice. Take a leadership role in an association. Your visibility as an individual and an expert will increase; marketing your practice will be easier and your business growth will be enhanced.

Insight into competition. In an organization you can size up the competition and see what other consultants are doing. Instead of treating your competitor relationships as adversarial, you should see other consultants as colleagues. One of them might someday pass along business to you, or you might be able to partner with them on special projects.

Research and market studies. Industry trade associations often conduct important research and market studies on trends and how they affect your business.

Exposure to key contacts. By attending events, seminars and conferences within your industry, you can gain access to industry leaders, government officials, potential mentors and other people who otherwise you might not have known.

Political opportunities. Through some organizations, you can become involved in lobbying activities that bring about industry-wide changes.

Discounts on goods and services. Many associations offer benefits including discounts on travel, lodging, office supplies, insurance, services and other items.

Move In The Right Direction

Sign up on every free directory that you can. The web has many business directories that will list you for free; I sign up on every one I find. There are services where an expert can provide free advice and I do. Each person I have helped has my name & contact information. Even the look-up-your-old-classmates web sites can be effective. If your child's school has a business/service directory, sign up! If not, start one.

STEPHANIE BACAK, CFP
http://www.powerfulpromoter.com

Discover The Value

One of my consulting clients regularly complains that his business does not grow. Another of my clients sends emails every month about how well his business regularly gets new clients.

The difference between Client A and Client B is that A refuses to 'waste' any money on membership fees and any time on getting involved with any associations. B has discovered the value of joining and participating in four different associations—and considers this a very valuable investment of his marketing time and dollars. B is the obvious expert.

RICHARD GERSON, PhD
http://www.richgerson.com

Professional certification

Professions of all types require their practitioners to be certified, including: finance, management, human resources and information technology. Becoming certified is more important these days than ever.

Society has become more global and more technologically advanced than it was even five years ago. A Bachelor's, Master's or even a Doctoral degree is no longer proof that a professional knows enough about a particular business to succeed in it. Technology is advancing so quickly that there's a giant gap between the foundation one receives in formal education and the technical competency that is required today.

Why Become Certified?

Phillip Barnhardt, author of *The Guide to National Professional Certification Programs* (©1997 CRC Press), describes the situation this way:

Three trends act together to make professional certification important to both the organization and the individual:

1 University degrees no longer solely represent, if they ever did, the measure of professional knowledge and capability.

2 The downsizing of corporations, coupled with teaming, outsourcing and temping, has forced professionals to take control of their own careers, independent of their employer.

3 The business environment requires almost constant training, development and professional involvement beyond one's particular job title.

Certification usually recognizes an individual's mastery of a profession by confirming proficiency, showing career involvement and assuring knowledge, Phillip tells us. But it also says much about the individual.

"The basic requirements for many programs require extensive

personal commitment. Individuals who show the motivation, time and expense (investment) necessary to pursue and maintain certification have made a commitment to their profession," Phillip explains.

A Certified Professional Consultant credential, for example, represents experience, capability and adherence to ethical and professional standards. In the consulting field, a comprehensive certification program should provide real life strategies in areas of marketing, promotion, negotiating, pricing services, proposal preparation, contracts and agreements, legal issues and others. Few university programs address the broad scope of the consulting profession.

Among the reasons to obtain certification as a consultant:

For your practice:

- Build your credibility.

- Earn a recognized credential.

- Increase your marketability.

- Gain recognition as one who has mastered the skills—and has the drive to learn new ones.

- Earn higher fees than if you were not certified.

- Experience a sense of personal achievement.

- Become known as a certified professional who believes in himself and what he does.

- Gain an important third-party endorsement to your knowledge and experience that will stand above your résumé and personal reference.

- Network with other professionals holding the same or similar certification as a unique group of particularly qualified individuals.

- Maximize opportunities to upgrade skills through

You Never Know Who Holds The Key

Networking is the key to promoting your business. Whether you provide seminars or you focus on building a business; people skills are essential. Positive communication is the key to people believing in you and your services. Confidence in yourself is essential for success. Even if you are new at the process, always remember there is someone to learn from and someone that can learn from you.

Relationship building is the key to a successful business. It takes time and effort to get to know people, but you never know who holds the key to a door! Keep focused on a friendly, open and upbeat attitude and you will magnetically draw people to you and your services.

DENIECE BOSSLER
http://www.totalperson.com

participation in continuing education programs.

- Enjoy a qualitative advantage in today's highly competitive market.

For your profession:

- Raise the image of consulting as a career.

- Promote the concept of lifelong learning for consultants.

- Broaden the teaching of consulting as a career through university systems and schools of continuing education.

- Raise the professional standards and stature of those engaged in consulting services.

- Assist clients in the selection of qualified consultants.

- Provide a catalyst for increasing the substantive body of knowledge in consulting.

When you're working as part of a corporation, it's easier to know when and how to take time for improving your skills or upgrading your knowledge. However when you work for yourself, it's not as easy to remember that this is important.

Success trainer Brian Tracy says you must adopt "The Self-Employed Attitude":

"As the president of your own personal services corporation, you're in charge of your own training department . . . You should have an ongoing personal and professional development program. Each month, each quarter, each year, you should have a plan for what you need to learn and how you are going to learn it.

"You should allocate a certain amount of money and a certain number of hours each day, each month, to learn what you need to learn so you can achieve the goals you want to achieve. . . You are paid in direct proportion to the value of your services, from the time you take your first job until the time you retire.

Credentials Matter

The most important thing I did in preparing to launch my books and my speaking career was to actively *LISTEN*. As a financial consultant for many years, I listened deeply to people's range of emotions in their money matters. I listened to consultants in both the psychology and financial professions. There were little or no resources available to people who wanted to understand and integrate the two.

Another key thing I did to become the expert was to earn credentials and experience in both professions, and then conduct workshops in professional associations, as well as consumer workshops. This gave me the research and credibility to write the educational materials needed and take it to the consumer and professional markets.

SUSAN ZIMMERMAN
http://www.zimmermanfinancial.com

"Harvard University studies on motivation some years ago found that the experience of personal growth is one of the best of all motivators. When you feel yourself learning and growing, and becoming more capable and confident, you get a natural high. You feel happy and exhilarated. You feel positive and excited about your life and your future.

"On the other hand, when people stop growing as a result of no longer learning new things, they begin to stagnate mentally. People who have stopped growing are far more prone to negativity, pessimism, fears, doubt and anxiety; and you can throw these all off by deciding what it is you need to learn, and by putting your whole heart into learning those things you need in a rapid and enjoyable way."

Choosing A Program

Phillip Barnhardt suggests you look at these elements in assessing what makes a good certification course:

Title or designation. What title you will receive once you have completed the certification process.

Sponsoring organization. Whether the certifying body is recognized or supported by a leading professional or industry organization. "These certifications are not membership benefits or fundraising ventures," Phillip says. "Most are serious attempts to define a specific profession. By providing standards for the profession, certifying organizations encourage acceptance of the profession."

Ethics and conduct. Whether the certifying body upholds its own credibility by regulating the conduct of its professionals.

Faculty. Whether the program is taught by professionals who are active leaders in the field. They should have experience doing what they are teaching.

Professional education. Determine whether the program is

You Have To Let Others Know

As a member of several business and professional organizations, including National Association of Women Business Owners, I have found my memberships an invaluable tool to let other businesswomen know about *mzbiz*. I know the key to my success is getting my magazine in front of businesswomen, so I attend every networking event I can to meet potential writers, subscribers and advertisers. Members of professional organizations support each other and this network of advice and support is a wonderful opportunity for business start-ups. If you don't let others know about your business, you might as well not have one, and professional organizations are the perfect way to let others know about your business.

JENNIFER DICKS
http://www.mzbiz.net

Spokes In Your Wheel

The best advice I can give, no matter what your field of expertise, is to build what I call a 'Practice Wheel'. It fits in any field, from being a stay-at-home parent to a CEO of a Fortune 500 company. There is obviously the general field in which you are an expert; there are also subcategories that relate to your field. For example, I am a chiropractor but there are sub-specialties in my field.

Imagine your life as a wheel. Each time you become an expert in a subcategory of your chosen field, you add a spoke to your wheel. The more spokes you have in your wheel, the stronger your wheel is, thus the stronger you are in your chosen field. I have 23 certifications in the natural health field (23 spokes, plus my other degrees.) You don't necessarily have to get college degrees, just keep building more spokes and your wheel will be invincible.

Dr. Joe Esposito
http://www.drjoeesposito.com

relevant to the challenges faced by professionals.

Professional contributions/recertification. Find out if the program has some way of making sure your certification credentials stay current. This proves to potential clients that your certification means you are up-to-date in your profession. It also ensures that people remain active in local, regional and national organizations that provide the certification.

Examination. Certification should be applied to gauge a professional's abilities.

Special requirements. What else you need to do to become and remain certified.

Fees/Costs. How much you will have to pay initially and anytime you become recertified.

Using Your Certification

The public perceives professional certification as equal to competency, and that adds up to dollars in the marketplace. When potential clients see that you are certified as a professional in your field, it shows you have devoted time, money and energy to become proficient in your practice. It demonstrates that you have something the average person does not possess, says Richard Johnson. It proves your commitment to the subject matter and your industry.

People who hire you as a consultant are concerned about return on their investment. They want to know whether you can do it right the first time, and whether you're dependable and reliable.

When potential clients are seeking expertise from someone like you, they are looking for training, education and experience. Wil Horton says, "Experience is hard to judge. People can tell you about their experience, but you don't know how recent it is or whether it's relevant. So one of the things we've turned to as a culture is certification. We know our doctors and lawyers are board certified. Our mechanics are certified.

"It's not a new phenomenon," Wil adds "But I think it's reached a point where a lot of the public will not take you seriously unless you can show you're certified by some outside organization other than yourself. Even in non-licensed fields, where legally it doesn't matter whether you're certified, perception is reality. People want to see that certification, or who you're certified by. It lends you credibility that you can't just give yourself. It just keeps pointing to one thing: expertise."

A fisherman's motto is: fish where the fish are–but where other fishermen aren't. The same can be said of small business marketing and client prospecting. Instead of just joining your industry groups, join tangentially related organizations. Attend the meetings first to gauge their worth. Joining later shows commitment. Mingling with your peers often places you amongst competition. Meeting with those in related, complementary fields among people who can use your services makes you unique, and positions you as an expert in a field they need.

Jeff Zbar

The Value Of Memberships

I hooked up with a professional organization back in 1985. I started going to meetings and then joined in 1986. Now—to put it succinctly—the financial difference to my business as a result of my membership has been worth at least a half million dollars. The reason I have gotten this out of it is because of the opportunity to network with everybody, to get involved with other people and for me, to improve my professional skills.

A friend of mine helped encourage my focus here when she said, "I think I can make more money by coming here to meetings and talking to people than if I stayed home and watched TV."

JOHN HEDTKE
http://www.hedtke.com

A SPECIAL CONTRIBUTION FROM
Steven P. Haas, CPC, CPMC

First Help Clients Make Money

Most consultants are 'soft'. Early in my career, I put together for a client, a mission statement, an organizational chart, a business plan and a sales and marketing plan. He said to me, "I have a 2-inch-thick stack of papers, but I haven't made any more money."

Because of this, I have since specialized in being a 'hard' consultant. I always first look for fast, easy-to-implement ideas that will immediately build profits. The radical concept here is to make money for your clients first and foremost, with everything else being secondary.

R. WAYNE EISENHART, PHD
http://www.entrepreneurial
development.com

From Wonder to Thunder: the Elsom Eldridge, Jr. Way

After honing my marketing and merchandising skills in Corporate America for more than eight years, I decided one day to "fire the boss" forever. I left the large grocery chain that had been my employer and moved from my native Iowa, where I had grown up the second son in a family of five.

In Colorado, I had an opportunity to own and operate a restaurant that I would grow over time, with the help of a partner, into a popular chain of eateries throughout several of Colorado's ski resorts.

My career was good. My family life was good. Then came Christmas Eve of 1991, when I was told I had a brain tumor. The doctors gave me two weeks to live—quite a wake-up call. I went off to buy the last Christmas gifts that I would ever give to my daughter, and I remember looking for things that would last forever.

My actual Christmas came about a week later when I emerged from surgery and realized the doctors had removed the tumor. They were confident it would not come back. However, the surgery was so invasive that it caused long-term brain damage. I had to learn how to speak and read and write all over again.

My recovery was a very long haul—about six months after surgery, I felt I'd achieved an incredible victory when my family gave me permission to walk around the block all by myself again.

I was initially designated as Level III Disability and was never expected to work again, but I moved to Minnesota, where a state rehabilitation agency agreed to work with me. Workers at the agency encouraged me to interview for jobs where, if I were lucky,

I'd be able to drive a forklift for the rest of my life.

I didn't listen to them. I knew I wanted something else, but I still didn't have a clue what the future would hold for me—until my father helped me crack the code. I remember he told me one day, "You can't do what you used to do, but you can certainly teach others how you did it."

The rehabilitation workers humored me and allowed me to start a home-based consulting practice. Let me tell you, it did not go well. My practice was not earning enough money for me to support myself, much less my family.

I was still on disability insurance when I received a phone call one day following up on my request for information from The International Guild of Professional Consultants near Orlando, Florida. A very kind woman listened to me, believed in me and invited me to come to a consulting orientation class. I decided to invest my time in it—after all, I had nothing to lose.

I drove to St. Paul, Minnesota, and spent the morning at a seminar, where the speaker shared with us the story of a man who had once also had a struggling consulting practice. The speaker told us about the strategies this man had implemented to jumpstart his practice, really separate himself from his competitors and get the attention of new and prospective clients. The man was Elsom Eldridge Jr.

I went back home and implemented those strategies. My practice started to move in the right direction, but I still had a long way to go. About six months later, I had the opportunity to meet Mr. Eldridge when he came to Chicago on a meeting.

That's all it took—I was on a plane. I met Mr. Eldridge on his birthday, but in many ways, I was the one reborn that day. Little did I realize then just how much he would change my life forever.

By the time I finished the Certified Professional Consultant certification program I knew exactly who I was, what I did for a living, what it was that made me different, and how to articulate those unique differences to the people that I'd meet. I went back

Just The Facts

In my thirty-eight years of being a Management Consultant to some of the top 599 companies, I have found that the most important aspect of my job is to be honest with my client—no BS—just the facts on the project. Always underestimate your result to the client, even if you know that the results will be greater; if you give more than you say, they will refer you to everyone.

A very important factor is communication with the client. Inform them of just what you are doing. Do not set up deadlines that you cannot meet. Always give yourself extra time. I established a network of over 367 alliances around the world that just love when I call them with a project and we work out a deal and they become my sub-contractor.

I do not advertise; I work all by word of mouth and referrals. I keep a low overhead in using services that fit my needs in everyday operations.

Your client is not interested in your office and all the bodies running around; I have been there and done that. They are only interested in results and that is the true road to Business Success.

PATRICK WALTERS
http://www.waiusa.com

Join Up And Stand Up

Joining an organization is easy, but participating is what makes the difference. I'd been an active member of the National Guild of Hypnotists and several other professional organizations for many years. When hypnosis became a current topic in State politics, I immediately volunteered to the President of the Guild and the NGH Legislative Officer, to do whatever was needed on behalf of hypnotists in my State. This volunteer role took considerable amounts of (unpaid) time and effort over a few years while we fought proposals of restrictive legislation. However, it also allowed me to work closely with some of the most well-known hypnotists and professional hypnosis organizations in the State, and with the members of my State Legislature. This background has helped establish me as an obvious expert both to my colleagues and my clients.

LISA HALPIN
http://www.hypnosisdoctor.com

home and implemented the new strategies, and my practice really started to move. I got off disability forever and was happy to become a taxpayer again.

But I wanted more. So I contacted the IGPC offices again to enroll in the *Certified Professional Marketing Consultant* certification program. There I learned how to build traffic in my practice, increase my closing percentages, increase my average client order and extract over time, more total client value from the relationship. I went home and implemented those strategies in my practice. It worked so well that I was soon able to purchase a portion of an accounting firm.

I put my newfound consulting knowledge to work in the accounting practice and things really took off. I had so much business coming in that I decided to design and develop a series of entrepreneurial boot camps that would allow me to serve many clients at the same time.

This was 'paid prospecting' for me. I was actually getting paid, in the form of boot camp tuitions, while being able to pick and choose which clients I wanted to continue to work for on an ongoing basis.

With my business evolving so quickly, I decided to improve my competitive position and differentiate myself once again. Today I serve as a *Virtual Vice President* to a variety of companies, and Elsom Eldridge and I are the best of friends.

Along the way, he has taught me that consulting and service marketing are nothing more than a big popularity contest, a contest in which all of your training, your experience, your competence and your excellence only serve as the entry fee. From there, you need to set yourself apart from your competitors and get noticed.

There are approximately 2 million consultants in North America. About 10 percent, or 200,000, are real. Many of the rest are in between jobs and are better known as 'transitional' consultants.

If you're really committed to developing your independent

consulting practice and don't want to be a transitional consultant, then you have been reading the right book. Elsom Eldridge loves to help consultants and practitioners package their personal wisdom and take it to market.

This book provides you powerful strategies—the same strategies I implemented in my own practice; the same strategies that moved me from wonder to thunder. Strategies that will work for you, if implemented properly. Strategies that will help you package and position yourself to magnetically attract new clients and new prospects to your firm.

Take these strategies and implement them in your own practice—build a practice and a lifestyle that allow you to sing in whatever you do.

After all, that is why you fired the boss, isn't it?

STEVEN HAAS, CPC, CPMC

For more information on
Memberships and Certifications, visit:
www.obvious-expert.com/memberships

Showcase Your Talents

Once you've identified your niche market, concentrate on those organizations. Don't just join, however. Offer to be on a working committee. Volunteer for projects, which showcase your talents. Then, when something comes up within the organization, people will turn to you as the Obvious Expert. Do a bang-up job. Even though this work is done pro bono, you will make a memorable, positive impression. When other committee members go back to their place of business and something occurs, your name could easily be at the top of the list of those they contact for a paid business opportunity.

JUDY HOFFMAN
http://www.judyhoffman.com

Memberships and Certifications Prove (And Improve) Your Expertise

Where Do You Fit In?

> " Every man owes part of his time and money to the business or industry to which he is engaged. No man has a moral right to withhold his support from an organization that is striving to improve conditions within his sphere.
>
> Theodore Roosevelt "

Each of us needs more than our jobs and our home lives. We need fellowship and to share time with others with whom we feel connected. We also benefit directly and indirectly in our business lives, through all types of clubs and association memberships.

Seek involvement in organizations as a way to feed the neglected or undernourished areas of your life. If your job and your parenting responsibilities seem to require all of your time, then yes, be a member of professional organizations in your field, and yes, become involved in organizations affiliated with the needs and interests of your children, but most importantly, become involved in groups that you simply enjoy and which allow you outlets and stimulus beyond your other roles.

Your return from memberships and participation can vary based on the group you join and if it is the right group for you. Organization involvements can give you a headstart or just a headache. They can bring you lots of opportunities or burn up lots of time. And most distinctively, they can help you or they can simply expect you to help them.

Before you commit one hour of your valuable time to organization membership, put the group to the test and make sure you will both enjoy and benefit from the time and money you will need to invest. Find the right group, then expand your horizons and enrich your life.

Ask yourself:

◆ Do I know what this group stands for? Are their philosophies in keeping with my own?

◆ Does this group platform for political change within sectors that are important to me either personally or within my career field?

◆ Do I genuinely like many of the current members I have met?

◆ Will I benefit spiritually, personally, financially, intellectually, academically or vocationally because of my membership in this group?

◆ Will attending the meetings and events be a delight, a bore or just a chore?

EXERCISE

List three things that seem to be missing in your life. Perhaps your answers will be things like physical exercise, intellectual stimulation or personal growth opportunities. Whatever matters most to you, put it on your list.

_____

_____

_____

Next give yourself a time limit; somewhere between three hours and three days. Find at least one club or group that focuses on the area of your life that you have been neglecting. Now rework your schedule and get to the next meeting. Make a commitment to join and participate in at least one organization that will help nurture the neglected aspects of your life.

EXERCISE

Connect in cyberspace. Use your favorite search engine and track down online organizations, groups, classes or certification programs which focus on areas that you see as overlooked or under stimulated in your life. Get involved with a group through chats, online lectures and information boards or lists. Such memberships can give you valuable information on topics you seek, new training and certifications, and the convenience of being involved in a group who will be geographically diverse, non-judgmental and hold their meeting in a place you can almost always get to—your keyboard and monitor. Best of all, they won't even mind if you show up for class or meetings wearing your favorite old sweat pants or your flannel pajamas! Now cast your net into cyberspace and take advantage of the opportunities for personal growth.

Dynamic Networking

CHAPTER 11

While I was studying for my Master's Degree at Harvard, I volunteered to develop the first annual Educational Arts Association Conference. The conference for educators in June 1974 was to include more than one hundred seminar sessions by guest speakers from all over the world. I did not know where to begin. Even though I was older than the average student, I did not associate with people who were lofty enough to be guest speakers.

So I made a list of titles of seminars I'd like to see at the conference, and then I headed to the library. I looked up the authors who were the most versed at each topic and then got on the phone. I started calling everyone I could think of, all over the United States and Europe, to find educational gurus to speak at this first-time conference. Each person I spoke with would recommend someone else, who would recommend someone else. These people allowed me to tap into their network.

In just twenty-one days, I wound up with sixty-nine experts to teach one hundred sessions. Four of the experts were flying in from England.

The conference was so popular that the next conference was much easier to put together. Again, I tapped into the network of people who shared an interest in this subject and in education in general. Attendance at the second conference doubled. I was thrilled. To me, it meant I knew what I was doing as a conference organizer and a networker.

Get Visible

I believe the keys to networking are to become visible and to be remembered. Simply said, people conduct business with people they know.

I always ask people that I meet what is "unique" about them or their business. This creates a bond to use when following-up and also provides a foundation to build a professional friendship.

MARTHA LANIER
http://marthalanier.com

So you can imagine how puffed-up I was when one of the speakers that second year extended the offer for the third conference to be held clear across the continent in Seattle. Of course I accepted.

I had overlooked one thing: The loyal following of attendees the conference had built during its first two years was centered in the northeastern U.S. Teachers from schools and colleges all over New England had attended the first two conferences with a burning enthusiasm.

The third conference fell in the same year the state of Washington cut back its education funding. Principals told teachers that if they wanted to attend the conference in Seattle, they would have to pay out of their own pockets. And just to drive the final nail in conference attendance, the Washington State Department of Education announced that one-third of its teachers would soon be receiving pink slips.

Attendance dwindled. That third conference ran seriously in the red. I had learned a very important lesson about networking. Whatever you are doing, whether it is organizing conventions or planning seminars, build out. Don't leap from one side of the continent to another. Remember that a network is exactly like branches stemming outward from the trunk of a strong tree, or concentric circles made by your first big splash. Gradually establish yourself in neighboring areas so you do not abandon the people who helped bring success to your original cause. Tie it all together.

Build your network so you do not leave behind the first people whose cards you put into your Rolodex or whose names you entered in your Contacts folder. Lastly, and most importantly, tie all of your business contacts together whenever you can, introducing one person in your network to another. Your network will become finitely more valuable to you; you will have created your own special business tool.

EE Jr.

Maximized Networking

As consultants, we are always networking. Our job is to shake as many hands as we can in our quest for the next big client. We find ways 'accidentally' to bump into people who are prime candidates for our service. We ask our friends for introductions. We ask our friends' friends for introductions.

Oddly enough, we find that the new people we meet often know some of the same people we have met before—people who are seemingly not connected to one another by geography, profession, interest or other logical factors. Thanks to Walt Disney, we have a perfect way of summing up the situation: "It's a small world after all!"

Psychologist Stanley Milgram actually studied this phenomenon in the late 1960s and came up with a theory called the "six degrees of separation." Stanley determined that every person is six steps or fewer away from any other person. In other words, if you wanted to meet a particular person—say, a movie star—you could start checking with people you know, and one of them would know someone who would know someone and eventually, you would meet your movie star.

Journalist Malcolm Gladwell wrote in his book, *The Tipping Point: How Little Things Can Make a Big Difference* (©2000 Little, Brown and Co.) about *"The Law of the Few."* His contention is that in the six degrees of separation, not all degrees are equal.

There are certain people who seem to know a lot more people than others. Those people are known as Connectors, and they have an extraordinary knack for making friends and acquaintances. In other words, they're master networkers.

But truly masterful Connectors don't just network. They take it a step beyond. Instead of cultivating relationships to further their own interests, these people play a sort of professional matchmaker service, connecting people who might be able to do business with one another.

Walk The Walk
Talk The Talk

I'm a devout advocate of networking. It's how I've been able to build a primarily repeat and referral business. It's a matter of understanding that everyone you come into contact with has the potential to help you build your business.

Therefore I always travel looking professional, always carry my business cards, and always initiate conversations with strangers to find out more about them.

Here are four pointers:

- Initiate conversation.

- Be interested in others.

- Get their business cards.

- Follow through with something of value to them (an article of interest, reference to something they talked about, etc.).

Continually look to meet people. Help them and then stay in touch on a regular basis.

MARJORIE BRODY
http://www.MarjorieBrody.com

Like Networking On Steroids

Building business alliances has been the best thing I have done to build my business and my expertise. It is like networking on steroids! Never throwing business away—throw it to someone else and tell them to mention your name. This makes you a walking, talking Rolodex, an expert not only at what you do, but also at referrals and testimonials. Everyone loves referral business and testimonials!

You should even throw business to your competition. Yes, to your competition! Believe me you will get back more than you give because this concept shocks people. You keep your name out front and help other people build their business as well. Many of my referrals come from my direct competition.

It's great because I get my foot in a new door with each referral. My competitors even promote me to their clients, and I do the same for them. It is a win-win for everyone—you, the client and even your competitor!

DEBBIE ALLEN
http://www.DebbieAllen.com

> " Networking is more about farming than it is about hunting. It's about cultivating relationships with other business professionals. . . it is not what you know -or- who you know. It's how well you know them that counts.
>
> Ivan Misner "

A great example of ultimate networking is found in the members of BNI (Business Network International) that was founded by Dr. Ivan Misner in 1985 as a way for business people to generate referrals in a structured, professional environment. They define their philosophy as simply, "Givers gain," and believe that if you give business to people, you will get business from them.

What might be at work at BNI, and with other professionals who have discovered the value of 'network-giving,' is what author Kevin Hogan calls "The Law of Reciprocity." In his book, *The Psychology of Persuasion: How to Persuade Others to Your Way of Thinking* (©1996 Pelican Publishing), Hogan says that when someone gives you something of perceived value, you immediately respond with the desire to give something back.

This does not mean that you immediately give something back, but rather, you start thinking right away of what you can give. One of the biggest examples of the way this law works is illustrated by Christmas presents.

When you do something for a person in your network—refer a client, hook up that person with a potential business partner or help kick off a new product or service—that person feels a certain loyalty toward you. That person will do everything in his or her power to make sure you know about that loyalty: speaking highly of you to others, referring you as a consultant, offering you assistance in some way.

Taking networking to that next level can be an invaluable resource for a consultant. The more people you have in your corner, the more business will find you instead of you having to find business. Successful networking helps you:

- Gain new clients through referrals.

- Serve your current and former clients.

- Gain recognition from influential people who can help your business.

- Feel a sense of accomplishment for making a difference in other people's lives or in your industry.

- Keep track of what other people in your network are doing.

- Establish yourself as a go-to person for any problem or need.

- Become known as the obvious expert.

Get Started

Fantastic Rolodexes are built one card at a time. Make it a point to meet people whose work might dovetail nicely with yours. When you get business cards from these folks, make a note of where, when and how you met them, along with any information they might have told you about themselves and their business.

Some consultants use business cards and physical Rolodexes. Others use computer contact management systems, such as Act. Today, personal digital assistants are popular because they fit into your pocket and can swap information with your computer.

'Who' To Get It Done

You never know how a good deed will return to you. Once, when working on a task force, someone remarked about me, "Your first name should be 'Who' not Deb. In fact we should call you 'Who-Howe!' (my former last name)" "Why would you want to do that?" I queried. "Because," they continued, "if you don't know 'how' to do something, you know 'who' to go to get it done!"

That statement reminded me that it is always good to be viewed as a resource—if people can come to you for good leads to other people, then they will also come to you when they need your services!

DEB HAGGERTY
http://www.DebHaggerty.com

Optimize your network to improve your net worth!—Build relationships first and the referrals will follow.

Roberta Shaler

Utilize Your Opportunities

The biggest mistake people make with networking is that they see it as something they do, rather than something they live. Thousands of dollars are lost by people going to Chambers of Commerce, month after month because attendees never follow-up with people that they meet, or they speak only to people they already know. They never move out of their comfort zones.

Seeing networking as a life skill means that when I receive an invitation to a networking function, I ask myself: If I did attend this event, what would I want to achieve? Can I plan to arrive early to this event and leave late to really maximize my attendance? How will I follow-up with anyone I meet at this function?

1 prepare for anticipated outcomes before you arrive at the event.

2 at the event, talk to strangers; force yourself to move out of your comfort zone.

3 always follow-up and do what you say you are going to do. Be consistent, be professional and most of all, earn the right to ask a favor of someone by first doing something for them.

ROBYN HENDERSON
http://www.networkingtowin.com.au

It does not matter which method you use. The object is to expand your network—and then to let the people in your network help you expand it some more.

Keep In Touch

We recommend a follow-up system that works well for your clients and your networking contacts alike. It calls for you to make contact with each person at least twelve to twenty-four times a year. Your goal is to put yourself into the position of being in the right place at the right time through your marketing. The reasons for contacting each person are limitless. But here are some suggestions:

An article with your name in it. Anytime you have written an article or are written about in a newspaper, magazine, newsletter or other publication, copy it and send it to the people in your network. Email makes this especially easy today because it costs no money to send it electronically. Whether you send a physical copy or an electronic one, be sure to include a note— even something simple such as "I thought you'd be interested in seeing this."

An article with the other person's name in it. If you see a story or photograph of the other person in a newspaper or magazine, clip it out and send it along with a note saying, "Congratulations, and I thought you might want this extra copy."

A transcript of your latest speech or seminar. Because you might sell these as products, the people in your network will realize you are generously giving them something of value if you send them a copy. You might include a note that reads, "I thought this might be informative for you."

An article of interest to the other person. Clipping this out and sending it to the other person can accomplish three things: It will show you are thinking of the other person, that you keep up with the latest news and trends and that you are aware of the other person's interests.

News of your latest book, tape, seminar, new product or new service. The accompanying note could say, "I wanted to let you know about this in case you know anyone who could use it."

Holiday greetings Acknowledge holidays, making sure you handle religious holidays in a culturally appropriate way. The contact's birthday, anniversary or other significant personal events are also good reasons to send greeting cards or personalized emails.

Thank-you notes. Personal, handwritten thank-you cards work in many situations: after someone has sent you a referral, added a name to your network, sent you a response to a query, purchased a product or attended a seminar or speech.

Invitations. Whether you are inviting them to your business holiday party, proposing a round of golf or asking them to attend your next speech or seminar, you are showing your contacts you are thinking about them in a positive way.

Surveys and questionnaires. By creating a survey about a topic of interest to the people in your network, you can accomplish several things besides staying in touch with people: gathering new material for your speeches, seminars, newsletter or news articles; compiling a report showing the results and sending it out to the same people who took the survey; and showing your contacts that you are on the cutting edge.

Your newsletter This takes care of several contacts a year, depending on whether you publish monthly or quarterly. It also lets your contacts see what you are doing and reminds them that you are available to do business with them.

Meeting The Right People

Successful networking is much more than meeting people or collecting business cards. It is about meeting the right people and developing relationships with them. Successful networkers realize that their contacts can help in a number of ways.

For example: they become your personal sales force—without the payroll costs; they can be an early warning system and provide you with competitive intelligence; they are a sounding board where you can practice your sales pitch; and they can open doors and introduce you to a whole new world of potential clients.

Networking is not an option; it is a necessity. It requires the casting of a wide net, and it requires work (net + work), but the benefits are limitless.

EDWARD HENDRICKS
http://www.ignitespirit.com

Humor. Some consultants cut out cartoons, funny quotes and jokes about their particular area of expertise and they fax them or email them to their networking contacts. One word of warning, however: Don't forward a lot of Internet junk mail to your contacts. Items such as chain letters, petitions and inappropriate humor can do more to harm your reputation than help it.

> *Set a goal to pass out at least 6 business cards a day; in 6 months you will have passed out 1000 cards. If 10% of the people respond, you will have 100 new clients. That will be 1000 new clients in five years.*
>
> Jerry Shea

Your Executive Advisory Board

At the core of your network should be a team of people you trust—people who are there for you when you run into certain kinds of situations and need advice, or an opinion, or a reality check or accountability to stay on course. These people make up your Executive Advisory Board.

Some consultants have had success by actually appointing people to be on their board for a certain period of time, such as one to three years. Ask potential Board members in your preferred way of contact—by phone, letter, fax or email, or over lunch—whether you can send them information from time to time about a challenge you are facing, along with some potential solutions. Tell them you would like them to read these challenges when they get them and give you their opinion.

Make sure they understand that it is an advisory position. Most people are already busy and need to know that you are not asking them to assume any responsibility, nor any fiduciary responsibility. They are simply there to advise you, and share

The End Result

We should change the word networking to simply relationship-building. I can trace most of my largest contracts to a word-of-mouth referral from someone I'd built a relationship with, either in the work environment or in a service or professional association.

I come from a family known for sending each other article clippings and book referrals. I carry that habit over into my work life. I simply enjoy providing contacts, ideas and resources to people I meet. I love brainstorming ways for others to reach their goals. I don't do it to keep my name in their awareness, but that is the end result. "Give and you will receive" really does work. The key is to not expect anything when you give.

KATHIE HIGHTOWER
http://www.jumpintolife.net

their opinion, issues and challenges of the day and moment.

Approach them by simply saying, 'I am in the process of forming an Advisory Board. Here is how it works. What I would expect you to do for me is share your wisdom and opinions. In turn, you should know I believe it is a two-way street and I would to be there to help you'.

If you happen to already know ways that you can assist them, then offer indeed to do that. People rarely turn down the offer.

Choose people who have more experience and wisdom in business than you have. We have gone to some of leaders of industry and asked them to be on Advisory Boards, and they rarely said 'No, thank you.' They almost always are very gracious, very grateful, and very giving of their time and knowledge and occasionally their resources.

Consultants who have tried this often lament that looking back on their careers, they only wish they had done it sooner.

Aim High

Do not make the mistake of assuming some people are too "big" to associate with you. As Roger Parker points out, the greatest people are often very lonely because of their greatness. Sometimes people who are well known in their fields welcome one-on-one relationships with what Roger calls their "appreciators."

Roger shares that he and a friend frequented nightclubs in the 1960s to hear Chicago Blues artists Muddy Waters and his half-brother, Otis Stan. Roger and his friend would go back to Roger's apartment, and his friend would say, "Gee, wouldn't it be great to have the guys with us?" But then he would add, "No, they wouldn't want to be with us. They are far too famous."

Otis Stan died at a young age, and an article about him in *Rolling Stone* mentioned that he had typically finished his shows and gone back to his hotel room to drink himself into oblivion because no one ever invited him out.

"It just blew me away because we could have had some great

Survey The Crowd

When I first arrive at an event, I take some time to meander around the room, checking out nametags, and making a mental list of who I'd like to meet during the event. Then, I scope out those people I already know. Later, when someone I know is in a conversation with someone I'd like to meet, I approach my contact to say hello. I am able to reconnect with existing contacts, while making new contacts at the same time. With this strategy, I easily double my contacts at each event!

JENNIFER ZICK
http://www.reside.biz

times as equals," Roger says. "We could have listened to some records. Gone out for an early breakfast—and it could have been a wonderful, memorable night—only I was afraid to make the move and I never made it, and then he died."

Since then, Roger has made a conscious effort to approach people who have had a significant influence on him. "There are only two possible reactions they can give you," he said.

"They can say, 'You're a fool. Go away. I'm busy' or 'Hey, that sounds like fun. Let's do it.'

Expand Your Net

Successful networking is more than just shaking hands with people at events. It's sitting down with people in your network to brainstorm about one of their projects. It's making a phone call to one person in your network to get advice for someone else in your network. It's following up to ask two people in your network how they enjoyed the meeting you set up between them.

Dawn Gay, who has built up a considerable business network over the past thirty years, says one of her secrets is not to contact people only when she needs something.

>
> When you build your network, you're building relationships. You've heard the saying that in life, you meet people for a reason, a season or a lifetime. When people cross your path, there is a reason. Your job is to find out what it is and how you can best serve them. You don't worry how it will come out.
>
> Dawn Gay

"As a consultant, it is in your best interest to teach everyone you know how to be a networker. After all, you will benefit from it as well. They will tell people where they learned this great skill, and those people will tell the people they teach, and your network will continue to expand, effortlessly, for you.

Four Magic Words

When I started my business, I couldn't afford a public relations agency. So I called the president of the best firm in town and asked if I could spend a few minutes to learn how to get reporters to write articles about us. At our meeting, she surreptitiously passed me a crumbled piece of paper. She said it held the "four magic words of PR" and she offered it providing I opened the paper in private and that I never told anyone what was on it. Of course I agreed, pocketed the scrap and counted the minutes until I could learn the mystery. When I finally opened the note, her four word, hand-scrawled secret said: "Take Them To Lunch."

BRUCE TURKEL
http://www.turkel.info

"As your network grows, so does your influence. People look to you to be an information resource in all kinds of situations. When you are at the hub of a network of information, it is easy for anyone to see that you are the obvious expert," Dawn reminds us.

Giving, sharing, networking and connecting with your peers, your industry, your clients and potential clients are all acts of unselfishness. Yet none of us is capable of living an unselfish life at all times. So accept the fact that it is "okay" if sometimes we act unselfishly for selfish reasons—reasons that may include the desire to grow personally and to live a more meaningful life. Remember the instructions you receive when you are flying on a commercial plane and you are accompanied by a child? Sometimes the very best plan of unselfishness is to 'selfishly' put the oxygen mask on your own face first, so that you remain clearheaded, functional and capable of helping others get their masks on, too.

> " . . . A healthy self-interest way. . . as my father used to say in one of his sermons. . . it is the importance of healthy self-interest as opposed to selfishness; healthy self-interest helps to enrich our spirit
>
> Dexter Scott King
>
> (son of Dr. Martin Luther King Jr.) © 2003 BookTV "

A SPECIAL CONTRIBUTION FROM
Ed Brown

Obvious Expert **Ed Brown,** like many other consultants did not take a direct path into his role as Founder and Program Manager for The Core Edge Image and Charisma Institute. Instead, he started with a degree from Howard University and eight years on the City of Atlanta Police force before he decided to follow his

Word Of Mouth

Networking is a very important tool for getting your business on the map. I have experienced this using the "Word of Mouth" plan. I worked as a nutritionist research consultant. My clients spread the word of how productive my program is to nurses and staff at nearby clinics. Word of Mouth has helped me gain a new contract every month.

DENINE ROGERS
mydenine@yahoo.com

passion of helping others increase their confidence and improve their careers through personal image building.

Ed has recently finished writing his sixth book, *Image, Power and Charisma,* and currently teaches individuals and management teams how to build personal charisma for greater wealth, power and business success. Except when he is pursuing his love of world travel, Ed is so focused on the Charisma Institute that, in his own words, he lives alone without even a pet or a houseplant! We're just glad he took a few minutes to share the following with us:

Selfless Unselfishness

This might be the first and only time you ever read about selfishness being exalted. Before you turn off, wait a minute! The mantra among human beings are quotes such as," Do unto others as you would have them do onto you." And "what goes around comes around." All of these statements are true and words to live by. However, there underlies a reason they exist.

They are more than mere reminders, but instructions on how to live. Why? Because without a concerted campaign teaching us how to be selfless, human beings naturally would be barbaric and chaotic. While the first human is believed to have emerged some 3-4 million years ago, civilization based on permanent settlements in which human culture and biological evolution is linked has existed approximately 12,000 years. Consequently, the notion of civilization has not been in existence that long. For protection and survival, humans are inherently selfish and had to be conditioned to live among others without causing harm or death. This conditioning continues to go on in contemporary society with laws, government and religion as the catalyst for keeping humans "civil." As such, the notion of charisma is also a fairly new phenomenon and should be viewed also within the context of human engineering.

Be A Credible Consultant

I built two businesses (and got two key corporate jobs) primarily on word-of-mouth, and so can you! Learn to network strategically versus just network. Plan ahead and attend events where people can hire you or know people who can. Have a powerful, benefit-laden verbal business card that intrigues while it informs. Avoid titles and features. Carefully plan to gain top-of-the-mind positioning so people immediately recognize you as the obvious expert in your field. Ensure all your marketing efforts (business cards, collateral materials, press and electronic publicity, speaking engagements) point people in one direction: to you as the expert in your field. Get published in newsletters, magazines, on the Internet and write a book. Authors immediately gain credibility in their field.

LILLIAN BJORSETH
http://www.duoforce.com

The Art of Selfishness entails:

1 Conditioning yourself to give as much as you take.

If someone tells you that they only want the best for you without a personal agenda attached within the proposal, walk in the other direction. Generally, people look into most situations with a "What's in it for me" mentality. Whether it's love, family or job, people want to gain from the situations they experience. The object for achieving success is not to take so much so as to hurt the next person. It is understood that we will take what we need, but we must give and leave enough for the other party or risk creating an enemy.

2 Realizing that you are the center of your universe.

You see the world and everything in it from your vantage point! Consequently, your world revolves around your viewpoints and perspectives. Your experiences, beliefs and environment help define your reality. Since your world can only change by expanding your level of awareness, it behooves you to do so. By reading, traveling and living through others' experiences, your universe expands, so as not to be totally consumed by your individual "small" world. By expanding for yourself, the residual effect extends to the world.

3 Being accountable to your commitments.

Whether you are entering a marital or business contract, you can never be truly "one" with the contractee. In the agreement, you still bring your world view as the other party brings theirs. As such, you may agree on the terms in the hopes that all parties will abide by their commitments, but nothing is guaranteed with people naturally acting in their own interest. At best, we must compose all the facts insuring that it "feels" right with our sensibilities in upholding our agreements. The best deal is one where both parties feel that their interests were served!

For more information on
Networking Success, visit:

www.obvious-expert.com/networking

Givers Gain

When participating in networking organizations, you need to be prepared to introduce yourself. You will have limited time to deliver a message that is not only heard by others, but also remembered. You need to take the time to Prepare, Refine and Rehearse. *Prepare your message.* Do not try and just say something off the cuff. The Refining process entails practicing the message with a colleague or a friend and having them critique it and modify it. Rehearse your lines until they become completely natural.

To quote Ivan Misner, author of *The World's Best Known Marketing Secret,* "If you take the time to develop good presentations, people will take notice. If you don't, you are losing a great opportunity to someone else who will."

Once you know the range of skills, knowledge and resources around you, you can work out ways to help achieve each other's goals. This philosophy is the basis for "Giver's Gain." You listen. Hear what they say about their business, their techniques, their preferences, their goals and especially their needs. Listen for things you have in common, key issues, problems, directions, goals. Dig deeper, learn how you can work together to help each other.

JERRY SCHWARTZ
http://www.bnimaryland.com

Your doorbell rings. You are very busy and you consider ignoring it, but then decide to go ahead and open the door.

"Oh hello," you say, as you realize it is Evelyn standing on your front porch.

Evelyn is wearing a particularly attractive business suit. It crosses your mind that it might be Chanel® and her shoes and bag are definitely Prada®. She is holding what appears to be a stack of assorted business cards.

Evelyn smiles and extends her hand. As always, she is friendly and gracious, "Hello, how are you?" she asks, but without waiting for your answer she starts to speak.

"I am Evelyn Meyers with A. Acme Business Solutions. We are the only company in the tri-state area who take business payroll systems and automates them so that federal and state tax law changes are electronically updated. No effort, no action required on our client's part. With our software, clients know they are always in compliance with government mandates and that their risk of incurring tax penalties virtually disappears. Best of all, most of our clients typically save 21% through reduced administrative costs."

"Wow, that's impressive. Tell me more," you say. Although you have heard it all before, Evelyn does such a bang-up job of stating what she does and how her service really helps people, that you always find yourself asking her to continue. After a few more minutes of conversation, Evelyn gives you her business card and you go inside and get one of your own to give to her. "Great to see you," Evelyn says as she starts to leave. "I plan to be here next month, and I'll look for you again."

You close the door feeling as if you have just spent time with a very personable business woman, who seems to be an expert in her field. You really enjoyed your little chat; what a shame that you have absolutely no need for Evelyn's service nor do you know anyone who does.

"Was that someone at the door?" your spouse calls from the kitchen.

"Oh, it was only Evelyn, it's the second Tuesday of the month, so she's out networking again."

◆ **Do your networking efforts consist of walking the walk and talking the talk, but always with the same people at the same places?**

◆ **Do you, like Evelyn, fail to ask the person you are speaking with if they need what it is you do, or if they know anyone who does?**

◆ **Do you forget to ask for business or referrals?**

And, like Evelyn, do you just show up at the same events, on the scheduled date and exchange pleasantries and business cards with the same circle of people, week after week, month after month?

EXERCISE

Select randomly from your index file, the business cards of four consultants who work in businesses that are not competitive to yours.

For Consultant #1: Write down the name of one of your clients who would benefit from the services offered by #1.

_____

_____

For Consultant #2: Write down the name of another consultant you know who would benefit by meeting #2.

_____

_____

For Consultant #3: Write down the name of a prospective client you hope to gain (but haven't), who would benefit by meeting #3.

_____

_____

For Consultant #4: Write down the name of someone you know socially or through business who might or might not benefit by knowing this consultant, but who would really enjoy the consultant's company.

_____

_____

Now schedule lunches, a golf outing, or courtside seats at a basketball game for you and each of the "pairs" of people you plan to introduce.

The consultants will appreciate meeting a new contact. The clients and potential clients will appreciate that you are helping them solve problems, without concern for whether it results directly in business for you or not. And consultant #4 and the person to whom you introduce him or her, could develop a business relationship that you would never have been able to predict.

Whatever the results, all of the people involved will understand that you are the person who facilitated their meeting. The return on your invested time and effort will come back to you tomorrow or at some unforeseen date in the future, but it will come back to you. You made the effort to knit your net together more securely, and the result will always be stronger business and tighter business relationships.

CHAPTER 12

In The End, You Get What You Give (And Then Some!)

Peter Lowe, a nationally known inspirational and motivational speaker, shares with his audiences, five levels of success that he identifies as: **Survival, Security, Significance, Satisfaction** and **Surplus.**

Think about this list more closely. At the beginning of your career, perhaps you are concerned only with bringing in enough business and enough money to survive. Days, sometimes months and unfortunately, even years of one's life can grind by with survival and security as the alpha and omega focus.

For a large number of people, fulfilling the basics for surviving today and security to survive tomorrow, defines every day of their lives. For absolutely everyone, addressing these needs accounts for at least some of their days.

Yet after awhile (and after the application of effective business techniques) perhaps you begin to earn enough money to feel somewhat secure. When this happens, you may realize there is something missing; you will then set about examining your goals to make sure the work you are doing is significant in the larger scheme of life.

When you realize that you are truly working for the pleasure of what you do, and that you would do it for free if you weren't getting paid (but you don't tell anyone that) then you have reached the success-stage of satisfaction. Sooner or later, you then come to realize that

Giving = Receiving

When my Internet business started taking off with the resulting popularity, I made a vow that I would do my very best to help anyone who felt I could help, and asked me for the help. To me, it's not only an honor and a privilege, but a duty.

To this day, I believe I have lived up to that pledge (and much to the once-in-a-while dismay of my family members who understandably grumble about the endless hours I spend answering email:-) I can tell you in no uncertain terms that this philosophy is largely responsible for the success I have enjoyed for the past 4 years, while so many are struggling or have failed on the Internet.

Giving = Receiving is really one of the great laws of this wonderful universe! My advice is simple, but not always easy to follow-through on. If you find yourself in the fortunate position where people think enough about what you have to offer that they will ask you for help, then make the same vow I did. Help them. Every last one of them!

In cyber-terms, Sell a MEG but Give a GIG. It will surely help others, but in the end, it will help YOU even more!

RICK BENETEAU
http://www.interniche.net

your life is so full, it is time to share your good fortune with others; you have surplus.

Choose Your Cause

Steven Haas who has personally implemented each of our obvious expert strategies and thrived personally and professionally because of it says, "If you've implemented only half of the strategies in this book and they have worked only half as well as expected, that should be more than enough to jump-start your practice dramatically, and by now you should have quite a surplus."

Assuming your business is like most, you receive frequent requests for contributions of time, merchandise or even money to a variety of community efforts. You may have problems determining which causes are most worthy of your support, and even more difficulty in saying no to those that aren't. After all, each of these causes is the most important thing in the world to the people behind them.

In most cases, community activities are a positive use of your resources. However, if you decide to get involved, look for ways that your efforts will benefit your business as well as those of the community. As a starting point, strive to identify organizations that have values consistent with yours. Keep in mind that it is also important to select a project of which your customers would approve.

Your ultimate question should be, "Do we want our company to be associated with this specific organization?" With that question in mind, Steve has developed the following guidelines to assist you in selecting causes that may be the best fit for your own organization:

● **Start small.** In the initial stages of your community involvement effort, make a commitment your company can live with. Concentrate on simple projects that do not require a huge outlay of capital.

- **Keep things risk-free.** Slowly acquaint your organization with time and planning requirements until you fully understand the scope of the entire project. Expand your organization's involvement cautiously, and do not let it conflict with the work that pays the bills. It is very easy for an important cause to invade your work or even your family time. Remember–moderation in all things!

- **Establish principles.** Determine how your community involvement will fit with your organization's strategic plan and goals. This may be as general as affirming your support of the community or as complex as gaining new exposure, improving your public image or attempting to establish a new sense of service among your workforce. You must fully understand your purpose in getting involved in community efforts.

- **Create a process for decision making.** This helps review your company's charitable requests. This process can be as simple as the business owner making the decision alone or it can be a more intensive process involving a screening committee with a set criteria to reinforce the selection process.

- **Build a consensus.** Remember, you will need to be able to justify your decisions to both the requesting organization as well as those within your own company who will be participating in the projects that have been selected.

Everyone within your organization who will be affected by a chosen project should be both comfortable and excited about it. All must be prepared to handle an increase in their daily activities, including telephone calls, correspondence and many other surprises, depending on the scope of the project.

Defining Your Corporate Identity

Back in 1994, when online marketing was in its infancy, few people believed in its potential. We created the Tenagra Awards for Internet Marketing Excellence to showcase innovative online marketing strategies. But more than that, by recognizing and awarding excellence, the awards program established Tenagra as a leader within its industry and community, bringing the company continued recognition and clients.

CLIFF KURTZMAN
http://www.adastro.com

Followership

I wrote *The Courageous Follower* because I cared passionately about helping leaders use power well and not abuse it. I had no thought of monetary gain. I didn't realize then that publishing a book is the beginning, not the end of a journey. Since the book first appeared it has been cited, quoted and studied in every arena: the military, police, churches, educational institutions, non-profits, corporations and agencies. I have been asked to speak, write, conduct workshops and coach executives. So many people recognized how little attention this subject got and how much was needed. I became one of the few experts on followership and have helped numerous individuals and organizations on this subject while being generously compensated.

IRA CHALEFF
http://www.exe-coach.com

Cause-Related Marketing

If you are at the surplus stage and you are ready to give back, you probably have already assembled a professional team that includes an attorney(s), an accountant, and both tax and financial planning professionals to help you guard and grow that surplus.

"A good accountant and your financial planner can also help you avoid paying unnecessary taxes by showing you some legal strategies that reside within the federal tax code," Steve says. "One of these is strategic contributions to charitable organizations, which falls into an interesting category that I call cause-related marketing."

No one truly knows how to measure the impact of an effective cause-related marketing campaign. It is, however, a well known fact that this method of marketing can prove to be quite substantial in creating long term results. In fact, many companies recognize this type of marketing as the most effective method in existence.

Community involvement builds employee satisfaction and improves a company's public image. When employees feel good about what they have done for the community, they feel good about themselves. They work harder for you and your bottom line reflects it.

Tax Issues

You need to understand how much of your philanthropic activity is tax deductible. Bob Corallino, my New Hampshire-based accountant, gives this advice, "The rule of thumb for deductibility is that mileage and out-of-pocket expenses for goods are deductible, but donated time is not."

Two Important Tax Reminders

> As a company owner, you cannot deduct the value of your own donated time, and you have already deducted the salaries of any employees you have assigned to the project.

> You can deduct materials and goods essential to the function. However, you cannot deduct these items if you have already deducted them as a business expense. Just keep in mind, you cannot double-deduct any expenses.

"Community re-investment makes the world go around," Corallino says. "For some, it's a moral imperative that gives them a warm and comfortable feeling. For others, it's just good business. Give strategically so you can continue to give and then feel good about it . . . When it's done properly, you can help a lot of people and it comes back indirectly to your company in the form of new business, providing positive impact to your bottom line."

Saralyn Collins says the phenomenon of giving has a simple explanation. When potential clients see that you have taken on a major project just to help the community, they take notice. "And they'll automatically assume that if I'm serious about giving that I will donate my time, my energy, my effort, then how much more serious am I about my business? How much more dedicated am I going to be in business, when I'm getting paid for my work?"

Ways To Give

Community involvement helps your company by helping the community in which you conduct business. Involvement can be accomplished in a variety of ways.

- Colin Keogh of Smart Biometrics, an Orlando-based company, has found over the last twenty years, that his best source of business is the contacts he makes as he donates time and products to help people within his community. Whether it is cooking ribs for a local school

Win/Win Giving

Giving back to your community is a win/win situation. Remember, what goes around comes around.

1 Sit on the board. Be on a committee.

2 Volunteer to work the events and get to know the members.

3 Sponsor or support the events with services if money is not an option. This enhances your recognition level.

4 Attend meetings and participation to help boost belonging.

5 Donate your goods and services to the raffle or door prize. This is a tangible way to show them what you have to offer.

While participating, you are also building intimacy and loyalty. Loyalty is often rewarded with business.

RALEIGH PINSKEY
http://www.promoteyourself.com

to raise money or using local businesses to manufacture the majority of his products, the benefits far outweigh the costs.

Colin manufactures a product to help save children's lives. While designing the unit and preparing it for manufacture, he approached local businesses about the need to keep the manufacturing in the area. He assembled a team of local small manufacturers and developed the product. During the process the other businesses gave him hundreds of hours of engineering and help—all because they wanted to see the product built locally, and the money circulating within the community instead of elsewhere. While the product costs 3% more to manufacture locally, the savings created through the relationships he formed cannot be measured and far outweigh the additional cost.

- Russ Sinkler of the Clarity Group, a Minneapolis-based consulting firm, donates a substantial amount of his company's human resources to a variety of causes. The firm's work includes training and counseling for the Service Corps of Retired Executives (SCORE), campaign work for the American Lung Association® and behind-the-scenes assistance to friends, family members and associates within their own specific projects. "We are always interested in advancing those causes in which our resources will provide a positive impact," Sinkler says. "I guess with us, proper alignment is key. Always be certain everyone involved in your organization views the project as appropriate, and make sure you have the resources to get the job done well."

- One of Mark Eldridge's most rewarding opportunities to give, came when he multiplied his efforts by motivating others to join him in 'giving back'. During the time a few years ago when every day's headlines brought more

They'll Know You Are Good When You Are Famous In The Yukon

Donate your time or service to a charity or community group. On a business trip to the Yukon, Canada, I offered my consulting services to local entrepreneurs and donated all the proceeds to the local literacy foundation. Because I had traveled across the continent to get there I must have been an expert. And, because I offered to help local entrepreneurs while donating the money to charity—that got the attention of the local paper. The result was a full-page article, with my photo, in the Yukon News. Most of my clients don't live in the Yukon so I sent copies of that article to them. Their impression—he must be good if he made the news in the Yukon.

GEORGE TOROK
http://www.Torok.com

stories of school violence and shootings, Mark felt compelled to take a pro-active position. He recognized that lack of parental involvement both at home and at school might be contributing to the problems burdening our country's school-age children. With many parents too hard at work struggling to make ends meet, to spend enough time with their children, and others simply not knowing how to best get involved, Mark started a Dad's Club at his children's San Diego school.

With the support of the PTA and the principal, Mark was able to get 120 to 130 Dads, plus some moms and grandparents actively participating in school activities. The program was a major hit with the faculty, parents and especially the kids. It really made a difference, which is precisely what giving back is all about.

Idea Tithing

Mark Victor Hansen, #1 New York Times and USA Today best-selling co-author of *Chicken Soup for the Soul*®, who has dedicated his life to enhancing the personal and professional development of others, has a wonderful suggestion about giving back to the community, that he calls, idea tithing. The premise behind idea tithing is the same concept many traditional religions draw from Old Testament teachings about giving back of ten percent of one's earthly blessings, or the tithe.

Mark suggests that all people tithe their intellectual and creative efforts to the benefit of others. "It costs us nothing to share ideas," he reminds us. "My vision is that everyone—6+ billion of us—start to idea tithe. Together, we can make the world work for 100% of humanity! It can move their (the giver's) lives and the world forward…it can literally make the world work."

Stay True To Your Values

Even when you're giving back in the form of information—for

Giving Gets Results

Volunteering, extremely rewarding in itself, can also help (discreetly) to boost your business. You're the expert; you're the entrepreneur. And, there are non-profit organizations out there who want and need your talent; most groups struggle to find volunteers with common sense and solid leadership skills. You can offer that, so why not?

Busy successful people can always find time to help and mentor. Besides, when you help out you will find that your name starts to get mentioned in newsletters, magazines, newspapers, and sometimes, you may even win an award. Don't get me wrong, don't give back expecting anything in return, but I think you'll be pleasantly surprised by the experience and the results.

ROCHELLE BALCH
http://www.rochellebalch.com

instance, writing a magazine article that allows people to benefit from your experience without paying for your services—your work should align with your values.

"You have to speak from your heart," says Dawn Gay "You've got to be honest in what you're going to share and really look at the value of what you can bring to other people, rather than look at something from a self-serving prospective. I've learned over the past eight years of being in business that you have to look at everything from a giving perspective, and it will come back ten-fold."

Become a Resource

I have a personal mission related to serving solo entrepreneurs; that's why I got into this business in the first place.

My primary goal in every phone call, email, or speaking engagement is to serve as a resource. If I can't answer a question on the spot, I look up the answer and contact the person later. Every time I give a talk or workshop, I make an offer of "free questions forever." People ask how I can do that, but for me the real question is, why wouldn't I? I am serving my mission, and at the same time doing something that is good business. If people know they can contact you without obligation, they will.

C.J. HAYDEN
http://www.getclientsnow.com

> " *The world is filled with people who have suffered from one misfortune or another. The only thing that sets one apart from the rest is the desire and the attempt to help others. People who reach out beyond their pain, out into the world in a trusting way–they are the ones who make a difference. Nietzsche said, He who has a why to live for can bear with almost any how.*
>
> Kirk Douglas
> *My Stroke of Luck*
> © 2002 William Morrow & Company "

Can You Live The Giver's Life?

WAR STORY #12 "The age-old art of magic has a teenage apprentice and a generous one in Elsom Eldridge Jr. of 8 Abbot Street.

The 15-year old conjurer, son of Rev. and Mrs. Elsom Eldridge, and a graduate last week at Junior High school, as his contribution to the city's centennial celebration this week is giving shows at the King's Daughters Home, St. Joseph's and Nashua Protestant orphanages, as well as the Nashua Protestant Home for Aged Women and the Hunt Homes."

From the Nashua Telegraph, dateline: June 1953

My entire life, whether I intended it to or not, has included giving. As a child, I watched my father in the ministry, his life dedicated to both giving to God and to giving to his fellow man.

Since my childhood, I have been performing magic tricks for audiences, at times for a fee and many times without charge. Over the years, I have taught piano and organ classes, sometimes for both pleasure and profit, but often just for the pleasure of sharing music with others.

I spent years as a college instructor, which in itself calls for a kind of magic and a great deal of patient giving. My classroom instruction was always underpinned by long hours spent off the clock, tutoring, coaching and advising my students. As a professional consultant, I have given away more hours counseling and mentoring others in their moments of need—the very thing that I am supposed to be charging for—than I have ever billed to clients.

Does this make me a big hearted humanitarian? A foolish chump? Neither, although sometimes I can be a bit of both. You see, all of my efforts, both big hearted and foolish, have led me to where I am today: author, keynote speaker, consultant's consultant and seminar conductor who teaches people how to be better at what they do.

Giving to others has given back to me, and shaped my life in wonderful ways that I would have missed, had I somewhere along the way, chosen to live a different kind of life. The paths I have followed have reinforced for me the true rewards of living "the Giver's Life."

Inside of you, there is a special God-given talent that you have to offer to the world. Mine is teaching, but yours might be financial planning, understanding complex legal issues or perhaps the wordsmithing of language. If you are one of the lucky ones, you have already figured out a way to build your consulting practice around your talent and to profit from it. You hear it said so often that it has become cliché, nevertheless the statement remains

Matthew 25:40
The Holy Bible (NIVB)

"The King will reply, 'I tell you the truth, whatever you did for one of the least of these brothers of mine, you did for me.' "

quite true: *Do what you love and the money will follow.* My own addition to this philosophy is: *Do what you love–share what you love–and the blessings you receive will greatly overshadow the money that will, in fact, follow.*

Cause or community-based marketing is powerful, and beneficial to the recipient and the giver and will reward your business in ways you will not even be able to imagine at the time you make the effort. But I challenge you personally and professionally to take this concept of giving to an even higher level. I challenge you to apply the principles of, and begin to live the Giver's Life, for reasons that have nothing to do with the business rewards you will achieve.

Try following this simple three-step plan for leading the Giver's Life:

1   Write both long-term and short-term plans for giving. Approach this in much the same way as you create your personal plan for savings or investing. Use the mindset of, "pay yourself first." Write your intended charitable donations of time, talent and money into your business and your personal budgets and then pay them out before you pay anything else. Seek to accomplish long-term giving goals. At the same time, try to never go to bed at night until you have accomplished a daily goal of giving, as well.

2   Give without expectation. Not all of your sales calls or networking efforts yield results. Stop expecting your giving goals to always yield outcomes you can see or measure either. Trust God, who has directed us to be charitable, that your reward is being tallied, whether or not you recognize it at the time. Give wisely, but do not always require that you must know who or how you have helped.

3   Give when you believe you have nothing to give. Share not just what you would like to be able to share, but share what you have, whatever that may be. If your needs are being met

Hebrews 13:2
The Holy Bible (NIV)

"Do not forget to entertain strangers, for by so doing some people have entertained angels without knowing it."

today, then you have been blessed with enough to share with someone else.

If the Giver's Life is new to you, expect it to feel uncomfortable at first. Presume that your 'giving muscles' are in a training and conditioning mode, in preparation for the fit, powerful and rewarding marathon of life you have just begun to run. Keep moving forward toward your goals. I did not say it was easy at first; I only said it was profoundly rewarding, but don't just take my word on it.

I leave you with the following quotes from The Obvious Expert, who, by the way, wrote quite a book on the subject of giving:

On The Subject of Giving

We ourselves feel that what we are doing is just a drop in an ocean. But the ocean would be less because of that missing drop.

MOTHER THERESA OF CALCUTTA

"Give, and it will be given to you. A good measure, pressed down, shaken together and running over, will be poured into your lap. For with the measure you use, it will be measured to you."

Luke 6:38

"But just as you excel in everything—in faith, in speech, in knowledge, in complete earnestness and in your love for us—see that you also excel in this grace of giving."

2 Corinthians 8:7

EE Jr.

For more information on
Giving, visit:

www.obvious-expert.com/giving

True To Your Heart

Paul J. Meyer, successful businessman and philanthropist, lives a life mission of giving and sharing the blessings of giving with others. Author John Edmund Haggai, in his book, *Paul J. Meyer and the Art of Giving* (©1994, John Edmund Haggai, Kobrey Press) outlines a powerful challenge designed to motivate and teach others to live a giver's life and reap the resulting blessings. He uses Meyer's exemplary life as a role model.

Haggai identifies that, "time, influence, energy and abilities," are valid and worthwhile avenues for giving. Yet, it is the giving of money—the subject of his book—which Haggai explains is both, "crucial, and an essential ingredient of success."

Meyer teaches us to analyze our lives in terms of our needs and goals in the areas of:

Finance

Information

Relationships

Spirit

Time and Energy

Meyer says, "Reflect on your dreams. How are they distributed within this fivefold division?" One of the key ingredients to living the giver's life, Meyer advises; "See what will be, not what is."

Try living just one week of your life with the commitment to give in each of the five ways listed above. Assess and plan a way that you can give of your finances every single day during your target week. Perhaps you can only afford to buy a sandwich for someone who needs a meal; perhaps you can do more. Whatever your contribution, discipline yourself to make it happen each day for seven days.

In addition to sharing your wealth, share your knowledge, share your kindness, friendship and compassion, share your spiritual beliefs, and share your time and energy.

On this page is a chart to help you record what you have accomplished in each area of giving. If you miss an area or miss a day, don't worry. Just start counting your seven days all over again. Your goal is seven consecutive days of living a giver's life.

As you go through the week, unforeseen opportunities for giving will present themselves to you; be open to respond to them. Use the worksheet to log your progress as you begin to walk the life-pathway of a giver.

We believe you will find that the time and energy needed to accomplish your Seven Days of Giving will be far less than you might expect, and the benefits will be far greater than you can imagine. Give, not for the results of today, but for "what will be."

When you complete your week, don't stop. Make a life plan to live the giver's life as consistently as you can. Try it one week each month, try it for one entire month, try it for a lifetime!

SEVEN DAYS OF GIVING

	Monday	Tuesday	Wednesday	Thursday	Friday	Saturday	Sunday
Giving of Money							
Giving of Knowledge							
Giving of Self							
Giving of Spirit							
Giving of Time or Energy							

Any commitment to a disciplined effort may sometimes falter. You probably already know this from a personal experience trying to kick a bad habit, or to reshape your life with a good habit. There will be days when you do not or cannot live up to your goals.

These days are dangerous! Their threat lies not in the fact that you have failed for one moment, one hour or even one month. The danger is that 'falling off the wagon' with any commitment becomes a strangely opened door, before which we tend to stand, rationalize and then stumble through. It happens in the form of rationalizations like, "I've already blown my diet, I might as well eat that other cookie (or half box of cookies)," or "I haven't touched base with that client in months, there is no point in trying to start something now."

Give yourself permission to 'not be perfect'. Approach your commitment to living the giver's life expecting that you will succeed. If you falter, simply brush it off. Get up the next morning and set about to meet your daily commitment to give in each of the five ways. Add to one day of accomplished goals, another day of accomplished goals. String your days of success together like pearls, striving first for seven in a row, then for more, until you can drape them around your neck in the quiet, personal satisfaction of knowing that you are passing through this life sharing all that you can, giving far more than you take and thriving in the blessings and rewards that are intrinsic to living the giver's life.

> " *Your life does not get better by chance; it gets better by change.*
> Jim Rohn
> "

Obvious Expert **Jeremy Allen,** says this of his mentor, Jim Rohn:

"Never underestimate the power of influence. Jim encouraged me to constantly ask myself these questions: Who am I around? What are they doing to me? What have they got me reading? What have they got me saying? Where do they have me going? What do they have me thinking? And most importantly, what do they have me becoming? Finally, he taught me to ask myself the BIG question: Is it okay?"

◆ **Whose life are you influencing?**

◆ **Who is influencing you?**

◆ **Are you running your life by chance or by change?**

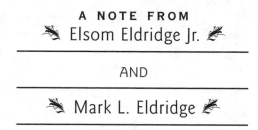

A NOTE FROM
✎ Elsom Eldridge Jr. ✎

AND

✎ Mark L. Eldridge ✎

Dear Reader,

We wanted to thank you for your interest in this book, our thoughts and those of the many wonderful people who contributed to this collection of wisdom and insights. We hope you have found it meaningful in your professional life and perhaps in your personal life as well. We truly believe the actions you take that are of genuine benefit to one always ultimately benefit the other.

As a consultant, you have chosen a very special career path. Through your efforts, every day you have the opportunity to enhance the businesses, finances and fame of others. In the process, you will enhance your own; you will start a momentous up-cycle within your life.

As we prepared to go to press with How To Position Yourself As The Obvious Expert we knew we had left many inspiring stories untold. That's one of the reasons that we are already hard at work on our next three books:

◆ **Everything You Always Wanted to Know About a Capability Brochure That Will Close Sales**

◆ **Build Your Competitive Advantage**

◆ **Get Your Book Published NOW!**

All of which will also include information from The Obvious Expert Advisors. If you have a story of learning, success or insight about your consulting business, we invite you to share it with us. And if you want to learn more about our teaching programs and those of the International Guild of Professional Consultants (IGPC) visit: **www.igpc.org/seminars**

Elsom Eldridge Jr. and Mark L. Eldridge

P.S. Your password to access website online support is: **EXPERT**

LOOKING BACK

The forerunner of the International Guild of Professional Consultants was founded in 1985, by Howard Shenson and Elsom Eldridge Jr.

In 1996, the IGPC, as it is recognized today was established to support and enhance the professional growth of consultants and the consulting industry. The IGPC exists to assist you in achieving success in your personal and professional goals. It is the only professional consultant's association that provides you a wide variety of resources, tailored to the diversified needs of today's consultant.

The IGPC is a non-profit professional and educational association that promotes professional interests, advancement of knowledge and enhancement of communication among professional consultants. The IGPC is as an international, interdisciplinary organization, serving professional consultants in all areas of specialization.

Today, as the pace, scope and ramifications of change increase, your need is for a resource that helps you both keep up with and influence change; this need is greater than ever. The IGPC is that resource. Our goal is to help members enhance their success by providing a bank of knowledge, training and encouragement.

AND MOVING

CPC and CPMC Certification Programs

When you see these initials following a consultant's name, it means that he or she is a Certified Professional Consultant, or a Certified Professional Marketing Consultant and has met the certification requirements of the Certified Professional Consultant Board of Standards. The IGPC administers these certification requirements, which boost the professionalism of the individual participants and the profession as a whole. With any of these designations, you will join the ranks of those who have demonstrated the highest standards of excellence in our profession.

FORWARD

Seminars and Workshops

Throughout the year, the IGPC hosts seminars and workshops around the country and members are invited to enroll at a special discounted price. Improve your professional consulting skills and expertise in these intensive one and two day workshops. Conducted by active, experienced consultants/professionals, these workshops feature: customized coursework, case studies and interactive hands-on sessions, all in formats that combine formal presentations with practical applications and provide dynamic discussion opportunities. The IGPC seminars and workshops excel at delivering workable, practical information to keep you on top of the newest trends, techniques, and technologies. The IGPC gives your business a competitive boost!

We invite you to call or visit us online to learn more about the opportunities the IGPC offers you.

WWW.IGPC.ORG

QUICK ORDER FORM

Telephone Orders Call 321-356-4374
and have your credit card ready.

Postal Orders

MasterMind Publishing, LLC
93 Colrain Stage Road • Heath, MA 01346

orders@obvious-expert.com

Please send the following:

❑ *How To Position Yourself As The Obvious Expert,* by Elsom Eldridge, Jr.
and Mark L. Eldridge $24.95

❑ *The Ultimate Home Study Course for Maximum Success in the Consulting
Business* All The Information, Knowledge, Direction, Guidance and Strategies You Need To Earn At
Least $100,000 A Year As A Consultant by Dan S. Kennedy and Elsom Eldridge, Jr.
Complete Course Plus 12 Audiocassettes $497.00

❑ *The Seminar On How To Create Profitable and Client-Building Seminars,*
by Elsom Eldridge, Jr. **Audio Program with Workbook** $147.00

❑ *Successful Proposal Writing,* by Elsom Eldridge, Jr.
Audio Program with Workbook $147.00

(All prices include Shipping & Handling.)

Please send more FREE information on:

❑ Other books   ❑ Speaking/Seminars   ❑ IGPC   ❑ Consulting

or visit *www.obvious-expert.com*

Name _____

Address _____

City _____ State _____ Zip _____

Telephone _____ email address _____

Payment:
❑ CHECK   ❑ MasterCard   ❑ AMERICAN EXPRESS   ❑ VISA   ❑ DISCOVER

Account Number _____ Expiration Date _____

Cardholder's Name _____ Cardholder's Signature _____

This material*, How To Position Yourself As The Obvious Expert, *can be presented in half day, full day or weekend workshops.

Other business presentations and motivational presentations are available as well.

For Further Information Contact:

    Elsom Eldridge Jr.

    The Eldridge Group

    5703 Red Bug Lake Road, #403

    Winter Springs, Florida 32708

    321-356-4374

    407-678-8173

Direct email inquiries to: **elsom@obvious-expert.com**

Books authored by Howard Shenson are available at

www.obvious-expert.com/shensonbooks

Linda Mackenzie 156
Creative Health & Spirit
Manhattan Beach, California
http://www.healthylife.net

Jacqueline Marcell 35
Impressive Press
Irvine, California
http://www.ElderRage.com
J.Marcell@ecox.net

Sherry Maysonave 157
Empowerment Enterprises LLC
Austin, Texas
http://www.casualpower.com
sherry@casualpower.com

Kevin W. McCarthy 3
The On-Purpose School for Leaders
Winter Park, Florida
http://www.on-purpose.com
kwmccarthy@on-purpose.com

Chris McClean 114
Pertinent Information Ltd
Victoria, British Columbia, CANADA
http://www.7lessoncourses.com
chris@pertinent.com

Leslie McClure 162
411 Video Information
Pebble Beach, California
http://www.411videoinfo.com
Leslie@411videoinfo.com

Lynne McClure 93
McClure Associates, Inc.
Mesa, Arizona
http://www.McClureAssociates.com
LMcClure@McClureAssociates.com

Robert Menard, II 66
Vinca Corporation/SPEECH2
Flower Mound, Texas
http://www.RobertMenard.com
RobertMenard@RobertMenard.com

Paul J. Meyer 244
Waco, Texas
http://www.pauljmeyer.com
info@attitudesrus.com

Robert Middleton 58
Action Plan Marketing
Palo Alto, California
http://www.actionplan.com

Barry Minkin 155
Minkin Affiliates
San Jose, California
http://www.minkinaffiliates.com
barryminkin@earthlink.net

Ivan Misner 220
BNI
San Dismas, California
http://www.bni.com
misner@bni.com

Donald Moine 18, 49, 189
Association for Human Achievement, Inc.
Rolling Hills Estate, California
http://www.DrMoine.com
ImptReading@aol.com